About Island Press

Island Press is the only nonprofit organization in the United States whose principal purpose is the publication of books on environmental issues and natural resource management. We provide solutions-oriented information to professionals, public officials, business and community leaders, and concerned citizens who are shaping responses to environmental problems.

In 1998, Island Press celebrates its fourteenth anniversary as the leading provider of timely and practical books that take a multidisciplinary approach to critical environmental concerns. Our growing list of titles reflects our commitment to bringing the best of an expanding body of literature to the environmental community throughout North America and the world.

Support for Island Press is provided by The Jenifer Altman Foundation, The Bullitt Foundation, The Mary Flagler Cary Charitable Trust, The Nathan Cummings Foundation, The Geraldine R. Dodge Foundation, The Charles Engelhard Foundation, The Ford Foundation, The Vira I. Heinz Endowment, The W. Alton Jones Foundation, The John D. and Catherine T. MacArthur Foundation, The Andrew W. Mellon Foundation, The Charles Stewart Mott Foundation, The Curtis and Edith Munson Foundation, The National Fish and Wildlife Foundation, The National Science Foundation, The New-Land Foundation, The David and Lucile Packard Foundation, The Surdna Foundation, The Winslow Foundation, The Pew Charitable Trusts, and individual donors.

About the Greening of Industry Network

The Greening of Industry Network is an international partnership, a research and policy institute without walls, focusing on issues of industry, environment, and society and dedicated to building a sustainable future. Three offices coordinate Network activities: Clark University, USA; Chulalongkorn University, Thailand; and the University of Twente in the Netherlands. The Network's mission is to stimulate, coordinate, and promote dialogue and research of high quality and relevance to ensure that the activities of industry—including business, labor, consumers, government, and others—are consistent with building a sustainable future.

Since 1991 the Greening of Industry Network has engaged participants from more than 50 countries to respond to the challenge of sustainable development. Through linked conferences, publications, and communications, the Network seeks to create new relationships, visions, and practices for sustainability.

The Network coordinators may be contacted using the information provided in the back of this book.

Sustainability Strategies for Industry

Titles published by Island Press in the GREENING OF INDUSTRY NETWORK SERIES include:

Kurt Fischer and Johan Schot (editors), *Environmental Strategies for Industry: International Perspectives on Research Needs and Policy Implications*, 1993.

Peter Groenewegen, Kurt Fischer, Edith G. Jenkins, and Johan Schot (editors), *The Greening of Industry Resource Guide and Bibliography*, 1995.

Nigel J. Roome (editor), *Sustainability Strategies for Industry: The Future of Corporate Practice*, 1998.

Series Editors

Berit Aasen
Norwegian Institute for Urban
    and Regional Research
Oslo, Norway

Kurt Fischer
The George Perkins Marsh
    Institute
Clark University
Worcester, Massachusetts

Nigel Roome
Chair in Environmental
    Management
Faculty of Economics
    and Business Administration
Tilburg University
Tilburg, The Netherlands

Johan Schot
Centre for Studies of Science
    Technology and Society
University of Twente
Enschede, The Netherlands

This book series embodies and strengthens the mission of the Greening of Industry Network. It includes works that will be appreciated by people working in business, government, nongovernmental organizations, and academia—cross-cutting books covering concepts, theory, analysis, and actionable ideas. The books in the series are interdisciplinary, drawing mainly on three areas of strategic management and organizational studies, innovation studies, and environmental studies, but also extending to such areas as urban studies, philosophy, political studies, and ecology. Working with Island Press, the Network develops book concepts that are aimed toward an international readership. The series helps to build and strengthen the emergent field of greening of industry studies by including resource guides, textbooks, and trade books that make the various issues and themes accessible to a wide, general audience.

SUSTAINABILITY
STRATEGIES FOR INDUSTRY

The Future of Corporate Practice

Edited by Nigel J. Roome

Published as part of

THE GREENING OF INDUSTRY NETWORK SERIES

ISLAND PRESS

Washington, D.C. • Covelo, California

ISLAND PRESS is a trademark of The Center for Resource Economics.

LIBRARY OF CONGRESS CATALOGING-IN-PUBLICATION DATA
Sustainability strategies for industry : the future of corporate
   practice / edited by Nigel J. Roome.
      p.   cm.
   A collection of essays by various authors.
   Includes bibliographical references and index.
   ISBN 1–55963–598–3. — ISBN 1–55963–599–1 (paper)
   1. Industrial management—Environmental aspects. 2. Social
responsibility of business.   I. Roome, Nigel J., 1953–
HD30.255.S87   1998   98–22500
658.4'08—dc21   CIP

Printed on recycled, acid-free paper

Manufactured in the United States of America
10 9 8 7 6 5 4 3 2 1

Contents

Foreword

Five years ago we compiled *Environmental Strategies for Industry* (Island Press, 1993) as the first volume in the book series of the Greening of Industry Network. At that time we found that work on emerging questions of industry, environment, and society was scattered across disciplines and countries and thus in need of a platform for study and exchange of ideas. That book was very timely and moved the discussion forward. In the meantime, many new studies and books have appeared—and new developments, practices, and concepts have emerged. *Sustainability Strategies for Industry* captures these developments and pushes the frontiers ahead again. It is a timely book, and Professor Nigel Roome has captured one very important strand of thinking within the Greening of Industry Network. Distinguishing between environmental management and managing for sustainability, this book tries to capture the idea of broad system change in response to the sustainability challenge, and ways of getting there. These have evolved as being among the most important issues for the active participants in the Network, whether they are researchers seeking challenges in the creation of knowledge; policy makers advancing the optimization of social, environmental, and economic goals; or business people looking for new strategies and practices to survive and to create value.

The sustainability challenge is different from environmental management, and we struggle to find new ways of expressing our new understanding. One businessman, Tom Fehsenfeld, put it this way in describing his experience at a recent Network conference: "The benefit for me is that I can immerse myself for four days in a different world view. Like an immersion course for a foreign language, it results in a rapid acquisition of a new vocabulary, grammar, and perspective. Having this new 'language' at my command gives a greater depth to my strategic thinking and improves my ability to bridge the gap when dealing with the members of both the environmental and regulatory communities in my business." *Sustainability Strategies for Industry* grew out of the fourth international conference of the Greening of Industry Network, "Building Sustainable Industries for Sustainable Societies," organized in 1995 in Toronto by

Professor Roome. Selecting top conference papers for rewriting and updating for this volume, Professor Roome as editor has also invited several new contributions to round out the book concept. Another business participant in the Network, Harry Fatkin of Polaroid Corporation, told us that "in a global sense the Network contains ingredients (challenge, tension, energy) and actors (government, industry, NGO, academic) needed for positive and pragmatic change toward sustainability." We expect that this third volume in the Greening of Industry Network Series with Island Press has the ingredients to continue to educate and to stimulate new strategies for sustainability.

Kurt Fischer and Johan Schot
Co-founders, The Greening of Industry Network

Introduction: Sustainable Development and the Industrial Firm

Nigel J. Roome

We confront a crucial time in human history. As we approach the end of the millennium the choices we face are stark. We can continue to accept the traditional principles of the market and the direction of economic and social change that has been hewn over the last two hundred years, seeking out economic opportunities without concern for their broader consequences. Or we can confront the environmental and social consequences of industrial activity as a major challenge for the modernization of industrial organizations and their management for the new millennium.

Currently, some businesses are considering these issues through questions such as: What is the difference between environmental management and sustainable development and what position should our company adopt? How are social and environmental expectations changing and how do we fashion a response? What do these changes mean for the governance and management of the organization? How should we manage our technology and our relationships with others in society over the next 10 to 20 years? What skills and understanding will we need to manage the process of change that we anticipate? How do these changes impact the identity of organizations?

These questions are profoundly difficult because they raise new visions of the contribution of industry to modern society. And they need to be resolved so that appropriate responses can be put in place.

A key issue here is that the current pattern of production and consumption which conditions our material lives and shapes the resource endowments available from the planet cannot be sustained in the face of anticipated levels of population. All the actors—individuals, organizations, institutions—and technologies that contribute to this pattern,

1

including industry, will be affected by our failure to confront this basic fact; they must therefore be involved in the changes necessary to avoid that failure. The intent of this book is to examine these changes and to consider the role of the industrial organization in bringing them about. The book addresses the challenge to industrial organizations arising from the concept of sustainable development. In particular, it focuses on the contribution that managers of industrial organizations can make in fashioning a more sustainable society over the next 10 to 20 years.

The book is designed as much for the curious as for those with an interest in, or commitment to, sustainable development. The book seeks to provide an image of how industrial thinking and practice will need to change if industrial organizations are to make substantive contributions to sustainable development and a more sustainable society. That image may be viewed as radical by some, but it is considered consistent with the challenge of sustainable development. To claim that industry can not bring about this change is to accept that industry can not assume responsibility for sustainable development.

Perspectives on Sustainable Development and the Industrial Firm

Sustainable development is a social and institutional response to the environmental (or ecological) dimension of global change. The pressure for sustainable development has been brought about by two distinct problems. First is the resource and energy demands of industrial activity in developed and rapidly industrializing economies. This problem is evident in a range of global problems such as climate change, the depletion of the ozone layer, the loss of biological diversity, and growing levels of resource use. It is also the basis for regional and local problems connected with air and water quality, land contamination, waste accumulation, and the accumulation of toxic materials in the environment.

The second problem is the cycle of poverty, mainly experienced in developing countries, which results from population pressures and the division of resources, so that sectors of the global population are deprived of basic human needs and security with respect to food, shelter, health, education, and family planning. This has forced the most needy to survive, either by exceeding the carrying capacity of their environment or by choosing pathways for development that fail to respect environmental constraints.

These environmental and social changes have been with us for much of this century, but society now faces additional environmental and social stresses stemming from the rapid move toward a more open, global economy and the more open exchange of peoples, cultures, and lifestyles. As a result, sustainable development needs constantly to be redefined in the light of our successes and failures and as new issues add to the problems that have to be addressed.

The agenda for sustainable development set out in Agenda 21 at the Earth Summit in Rio de Janeiro, in 1992, was designed to bring the satisfaction of human needs, now and in the future, into line with environmental constraints. While this agenda is provoked by concerns about change in environmental systems, the key pressure points for change are at the center of human systems: These originate from our shared definition and experience of development, our lifestyles and quality of life. In this sense, sustainable development is more than an extended form of environmental protection. Sustainable development is a continuously unfolding pathway for change centered on bringing environmental, economic, and social considerations to the core of our understanding of social and personal development. Potentially, this involves the reconfiguration of industrial activity. It also suggests the need for a reworking of social and institutional structures based around altered lifestyles and experiences of development.

At the very least, the concept of sustainable development requires us to question our assumptions about development, especially the way that development generates economic, social, and environmental change. But as Gladwin (Gladwin et al., 1995) argues, sustainable development demands more than this. His work places sustainable development in the continuum between technocentric and ecocentric world views, arguing that it is a distinctive paradigm. Drawing on Kuhn's (1962) ideas of paradigmatic change in science, we can argue that the changes in the institutions and practice of science that accompanied the transitions from Newtonian to Einsteinian physics, or the advent of the "new science" of chaos, are orders of magnitude less profound for society than the changes in social institutions and the practice of industry that will accompany acceptance of sustainable development as the dominant social paradigm. Sustainable development therefore provides the framework to integrate the environmental, social, and economic dimensions of human activity at every level and scale from local to global.

But the main concern of this book is with the role of industrial organizations and their contribution to change. Over the past 10 years some parts of industry have undergone a fundamental reorientation in their attitudes toward environmental issues and the relationship between environmental management and traditional organizational activities. An increasing number of companies have moved from the view that environmental management requires compliance with current laws and regulations, to positions based on an understanding that environmental management is a legitimate business function driven by, among other things, legislation, markets, relationships in the supply chain, investors, local communities, and activist groups. The first volume in the Greening of Industry Series, *Environmental Strategies for Industry* (Fischer and Schot, 1993), says much about this shift from reactive to more open, innovative approaches to environmental management by industry.

Environmental concerns, and the concepts these concerns generate, have given rise to different types of organizational change. These changes range from the strategic reorientation of companies such as Monsanto (Magretta, 1997),[1] the implementation of environmental management approaches that are better integrated with company systems, and the modification of existing business processes to accommodate environmental issues (Ditz et al., 1995).

Many of the recent changes in industrial production and management to bring about environmental improvement are related to a wider acceptance of the concept of product stewardship. Product stewardship recognizes that organizations involved in the production of a product share a responsibility for the product's environmental effects with other organizations in the supply chain and with consumers of the product. Product stewardship is increasingly replacing the traditional perception among industrial managers that the environment is an "economic externality" and that environmental issues are the organizational domain of the company's Health, Safety, and Environment group. In particular, the shift to product stewardship places on companies a need to develop more strategic perspectives on environmental concerns. It supports the development of routines to gather and use environmental information in decisions and activities. In addition, other concepts are now gaining ground that support the principle of product stewardship. These include the drive to reduce the material inputs to products, and to move industrial thinking away from products to the provision of services. Product stewardship, dematerialization, and products to services are part of a continuing process of environmental or ecological modernization of industry.

Companies have developed their environmental management responses using a variety of organizing concepts, often based on ideas drawn from systems thinking. These include environmental management systems, total quality environmental management, industrial ecology, and ecoefficiency (Hall and Roome, 1996). Some companies, in the environmentally vulnerable sectors, such as chemicals production and the oil and gas industry, are driven by concerns about their overall "license to operate." Others have linked their environmental practices to leadership positions in their industry.

Implementing these concepts has been profoundly difficult, as it requires new understanding of the relationship between the business organization and the environment. It also requires the application of systems approaches to capture the environmental changes brought about by industrial activity. This has not been easy to develop within the formal structure of industrial organizations. The organizational culture and practices of leading companies in the field of environmental management have enabled them to accommodate these new concepts within their organizational structure. However, these approaches to environmental management are often subordinated to the existing organizational culture, with the result that established systems of managerial sense making are used to rationalize environmental activities. Managers consequently seek to justify environmental management activities through appeals to traditional business arguments. Few companies have seen environmental issues, alone or in concert with other systems issues, as the motivation for wholesale, strategically led organizational change. Moreover, some commentators have argued that all of these approaches to environmental management fall short of the changes demanded for a meaningful contribution by industry to sustainable development (Gladwin et al., 1995).

In the absence of any significant empirical experience of the meaning of sustainable development for industry, this book sets out to answer two key questions: How might sustainable development influence the thinking and practice of industrial organizations during the next 10 to 20 years? And what does this mean for management practice, management education, and research?

These are timely questions. The recent Special Session of the United Nations held in New York in June 1997 reviewed progress and setbacks in the five years since the Earth Summit and the 10 years since the Brundtland Report (Brundtland, 1987). The special session looked at how the agenda for sustainable development would unfold to the new millennium and beyond. Major problems were identified in shaping national and international responses to sustainable development. Despite earlier commitments by governments, both as signatories to Agenda 21 and as advocates of national sustainable development strategies, the overall assessment of progress since the Earth Summit is overshadowed by failures on the part of governments of developed economies to meet targets for development assistance, to reform the policies that currently encourage the unsustainable use of energy and resources, and to devise new tax structures that discourage continued unsustainable use of resources. Part of the problem here rests on the way governments have consigned sustainable development to the agency of Environment Ministries, rather than to see it as a guiding approach in Ministries for Development and Economic Affairs. A few governments have begun to pursue more innovative approaches to development aid and domestic environmental protection based on policy frameworks and instruments that encourage others to more sustainable practices (Earth Council, 1997).

In contrast to the palpable lack of political leadership at the national level, significant progress is found at the more local level. Many municipalities have developed policies around local agenda 21; improved participation in decisions is steadily gaining ground in many democracies; and there are an increasing number of campaigns to encourage more sustainable lifestyles and to develop education for sustainability.

From an industrial and managerial perspective it is recognized that some companies have made strides to develop environmental management approaches. This commitment must continue and develop, by virtue of the scale of the energy and resources consumed by industry, its capacity to apply capital and to harness technological and social innovation, and its role in transforming materials into products and services. But industry must also address the broader challenge of sustainable development. Industry must do this, despite the lack of political leadership, the continuing difficulties over the definition and operationalization of sustainable development, and the patchy translation of commitments into action. Industry has the potential either to drive or to subvert progress toward sustainable development. In either event sustainable development cannot be brought about without the involvement of business and industrial organizations in the changes that are required.

Key Frames of Reference

Four key themes underscore these introductory comments and shape the responsibility of industry toward sustainable development over the next 10 to 20 years.

Sustainable Development as Reforming Paradigm

In practical terms it is important to unpack the implications of the sustainable development paradigm as a way to help assess the type of reform it demands. Although many accept that development and industrial activity leads to change in three domains—social, economic, and environmental—there is often uncertainty about why change is taking place, how changes interrelate, what changes can be anticipated, and what actions or instruments might reduce or ameliorate change. In addition to these risk and information problems, the socially contested nature of change leads to disagreement. Groups evaluate change in different ways and ascribe different degrees of significance to those changes. These evaluation problems mean that trade-offs between changes in different domains, the allocation of responsibilities for change, and the negotiation and implementation of responses is fraught with administrative and political difficulties. These negotiation problems are complicated by distributive issues, with some groups in society benefiting from change while others lose out through the redefinition of rights and responsibilities.

These effects are evident in most visible sustainable development issues—for example, the debate in the United States leading up to the Kyoto Summit on Global Warming. Energy industries and energy-intensive small businesses, in general, oppose attempts to rein back CO_2 emissions. They argue that reducing emissions by the United States would not necessarily reduce global warming and would impose an unfair economic burden on their sector. Moreover, there are claims that this is not an appropriate "sacrifice" for the United States to make, given what other countries are doing in terms of their CO_2 emissions.

Finally, sustainable development obliges shifts in technology and the institutional arrangements that enable success in technological innovation. Consequently, issues of social and institutional inertia need to be overcome in the move to more sustainable lifestyles.

These problems have led some to argue that sustainable development is an appeal for a new social order involving new and restructured institutional and organizational relationships based on mechanisms that make explicit and transparent the changes taking place in economic, social, and environmental domains. In this sense sustainable development is a social process that resolves disagreements through the application of approaches that are informed by principles of inclusiveness, precaution, and justice (Carley and Christie, 1992). These authors recognize that they are advocating characteristics for decision making that are not widely practiced in most sectors of many societies.

Sustainable development also begs questions about whether industrial organizations as "pure economic agents" can embrace sustainability or whether this requires new social and environmental considerations to be placed in their framework of choice. Adopting principles of justice, precaution, and inclusiveness limits the options for action available to the firm and affects the speed of choice, as more actors are engaged in the decision processes. Constraining choice in this way will inevitably limit the overall value that can accrue to the owners and shareholders of a business, although not all businesses will be equally hampered in the value they can develop for their shareholders.

For business in general, and industrial organizations in particular, the concept of sustainable development implies that many of the rules and conventions that have guided actions in the past are no longer appropriate. A critical concern, then, is whether industrial organizations can contribute effectively to sustainable development within existing perceptions of their role in society, as pure economic agents, or whether sustainable development, as a definition of development, calls for change in the common view of the role and purpose of business (Roome, 1997a).

Systems, Systems Relationships, and Systems Change

Underlying this concept of a sustainable industrial organization is the view that industry is part of an indivisible, open system in connection with other systems. Sustainability is concerned with the nature of industry's embeddedness in social and environmental systems as well as its economic relationships. While industry can be separated from this complex web of relationships, sustainable industry cannot.

Sustainable development does not just affect industrial organizations. Industry, alone, cannot create the changes needed for a more sustainable future. Industry must act in concert with other actors and institutions in society. However, the systems perspective implies that industrial organizations are critical agents of system change as a result of their capacity to generate intended and unintended effects (O'Connor et al., 1996; Roome, 1997b).

In their analysis of sustainable organizations, Starik and Rands (1995) discuss the web of relationships within which organizations are embedded. They identify the elements, or properties, that flow along these relationships. They suggest that sustainability induces organizations into particular kinds of relationships, at many levels. They identify and characterize the relationships that operate at the individual, organizational, political-economic, sociocultural, and ecological (environmental) levels.

For example, at the ecological level, sustainability implies that industry will use natural resource inputs at sustainable rates. Among the requirements at the organizational level, industry is expected to engage in environmental partnerships. Starik and Rands argue that each of these relationships, as well as the totality of relationships, are important in the achievement of sustainable development.

This multiparty, multilevel conceptualization of the web of industrial relationships simplifies reality. Relationships operate at different scales not just different levels. For example, relationships arise at scales from local through to global. Scale is critical to all organizations, not just those industries with a global span of production and/or sales. For example, using Starik and Rand's levels, at the ecological (environmental) level, multinational corporations (MNCs) should operate within sustainable rates of natural resource utilization at the global as well as at multiple local scales. At the organizational level, there are important environmental partnerships at the global, regional, national, and local scales. Furthermore, these partnerships need to operate in consistent ways.

Scale issues also arise for industries operating at a single site due to the interconnections between environmental and human systems. An automobile paint shop should be concerned about the local impact of volatile organic solvents in paints on the environment as well as the contribution of those solvents to global warming. Scale and level issues arise in the social as well as the environmental dimension of sustainable development. These effects are captured by the observation in the Brundtland Report (1987) that "no single blueprint of sustainability will be found, as economic and social systems and ecological conditions vary widely. . . ." This means that industrial organizations committed to sustainable development must have information that enables them to judge the extent to which they satisfy the conditions for sustainability through their relationships at each and every level and scale.

Sustainable development then is concerned with the satisfaction of social needs through concerted change in organizations and the institutional and social systems within which they are embedded. These complex relationships provide opportunities for organizational learning. Hart (1997) suggests that sustainable companies will have clear visions of the future and will serve as educators for their stakeholders. In contrast, the emphasis here is on the industrial organization learning together with its stakeholders. Industrial organizations embarking on the course of sustainable development must engage a broad set of social actors, listen carefully to their interests and needs, and through that learn to act in concert with a wide set of stakeholders to achieve the changes that are necessary to accomplish sustainability. This approach extends the longer standing trend in industry away from its focus on products and production, through the concern for the best fit between production, organizational capabilities, and consumers' interests, to the broader management of supply chain interdependencies as a means to satisfy consumers' requirements while maintaining the legitimacy or license of the organization to operate in society.

In particular, sustainable industry argues the need to manage technologies and devise products and services that meet economic, social, and environmental requirements—requirements that are not just those set by consumers but by a wide set of social actors, including future generations.

The Future

Sustainable development places a particular emphasis on the needs of the future as well as those of the present. But coping with the future is highly problematic for industrial organizations and their managers. With the rapid pace of change in technology reshaping our understanding of the world, with the effects of test discount rates of 7 percent halving the present value of future cost every 10 years, with the long-term investment decisions measured on a time scale of 5 years, and with new product development cycles of 3 to 15 years, the capacity of organizations to project their markets, products, and impacts beyond 10 years is problematic. Yet, the minimum time scale for sustainable development is one generation, 25 years, and it is more appropriate to thinking of planning horizons that extend over seven generations, or 200 years.

This is all the more important when it is considered that technologies get embedded in trajectories because of institutional structures. For example, since the 1950s, the notion of personalized rapid transport provided by automobiles has underscored most town planning in developed economies. The planning process has now locked the residents of these towns into the use of this mode of transport long beyond the environmental prognosis of the internal combustion engine. In the same way, the environmental consequences of industrial activities can easily exceed the longevity of most business organizations, remembering that one of the oldest North American businesses, the Hudson Bay Company, was founded only just over 350 years ago.

Corporate environmental management may be focused on choices among investments in site cleanup, new plant, or the design of new products and processes that are more environmentally benign. However, the issues for sustainable development concern the transformation of technology, institutional structures, and the responsibilities and relationships of organizations over coming generations. Sustainable industry is therefore concerned about these extended time horizons as well as the scale and level of its interrelationships. How to chart a pathway for these relationships, which begin with the organizational culture, structures, systems, and practices of the present in their institutional and social context, and move to a more sustainable future, is a particular concern for industry committed to sustainable development.

Building the Future through Scenarios

One tangible outcome of sustainable thinking is a concern to envision and learn from the future. The construction of scenarios is an important managerial and organizational tool for sustainability. It provides perspectives that enable future conditions and systems to be envisioned and related to the changes that organizations might undertake. Scenarios can be used to test whether organizational strategies are robust in relation to alternative futures. Idealized futures can be projected and used to identify the types of organizational change that are necessary to bring them about. The use of scenarios is briefly discussed in the *Greening of Industry Resource Guide and Bibliography* (Groenewegen et al., 1996). Moreover, other groups have been working on the development of scenarios of sustainable society and sustainable business to take us into the new millennium (for example, European Partners for the Environment [1994] and the World Business Council for Sustainable Development).[2]

In a narrower sense, *The Greening of Industry Case Book* (forthcoming) identifies how the environmental management practices of a company in the year 2005 were used to help shape the change contemplated in 1996. Futuring and scenarios are powerful tools to develop images of the overall context within which future industrial (or any other) organizations might be embedded.

Global Economy, Society, and Environment— Two Alternate Scenarios

The discussion so far has introduced the background and key themes for sustainable industry. Here, the prospects for sustainable development to shape the industrial organization of the future are considered through the device of two alternate scenarios. These consider how global changes might influence the position of industrial organizations in society during the next 10 to 20 years. These scenarios develop the idea that sustainable development represents a first wave of institutional response to global change, and that successive waves of change are now beginning to overlap the agenda for sustainable development established in the early 1990s.

New changes are being provoked by more open economies and the increasing freedom of movement of capital and trade, spurred in part by advances in information technology and communications infrastructure. Moreover, the cultural axis of global change involves the exchange of images and icons that symbolize lifestyles and the patterns of consumption associated with those lifestyles.

The main vehicles for these icons is the marketplace itself, the communications superhighway, and the visual media. All are currently dominated by the economies of the developed world, notably the United States. In addition, images of lifestyles are portrayed through the mingling of peoples and cultures that follows economic exchange, tourism, and the migration provoked by economic, environmental, or political flight. The point here is that the agenda for sustainable development, which was set in the late 1980s and early 1990s, is progressively being overtaken by unanticipated waves of change.

With this background two scenarios can be constructed. The first scenario anticipates an era of unbridled capitalism, as the world community adjusts to economic liberalization and open markets. In this case national governments surrender their control over economic enterprises in the wake of the momentum for economic expansion and growth pursued by multinational enterprises and the larger domestic firms. Corporate development through global economic expansion dominates the international economic order as well as the internal agenda of major firms. Corporate strategies are built around growth through strategic alliances, global production, and global sales. The legitimacy for corporate action stems from appeals to narrow economic definitions of the role of industry in society as a generator of wealth and, more contentiously, as the provider of jobs. The mantra is global "competition and efficiency, efficiency and competition." The role of the state in controlling economic activities continues to diminish as the responsibility for the regulation of world trade and economic activity moves to the World Trade Organization and other supranational agencies with limited, or at least extended lines of, democratic control exercised by nation states or civil society.

Under this scenario, the pressure on business to assume a position of global leadership in economic, social, and environmental domains is overwhelmed by the pressure for a narrow capitalist view of the firm that is reinforced by the global economic order. Success here derives from the capacity to develop superiority through technological innovation, to create the strategic alliances that drive competitiveness in international markets, and to communicate product offerings to many people around the globe. The successful manager is able to translate technology into desired products and services, can broker alliances with partners around the globe, and is an adept communicator.

The alternative scenario also acknowledges the inexorable move toward global economic exchange but suggests that this will be accompanied by countervailing social trends. These will be expressed around the idea of distinctive cultural, social, and environmental identities.

In this scenario there is still a significant redistribution of the power of the nation state: Economic liberalization draws national power to the global scale, while the rise of new, nongovernmental organizations and forces in local civil society pulls the identity of many individuals more deeply into their local communities. In short, the global economic system is not seen by the majority of peoples as the foundation of a "global village." The global economy does not provide individuals with the sense of identity and sense of place they need to feel bonded to a context. Consequently, broad-based statements of social needs and interests are expressed, and actions in line with those interests are taken, locally. These expressions in local civil society act as a foil to the forces of global economic growth.

Nongovernmental organizations, and other groups in civil society, more and more assume custodianship of social and environmental values—with the result that these groups emerge and proliferate locally and nationally. Civil organizations assume a role in society hitherto the province of local and regional governments. While the values they espouse, which were previously rooted in the power structures of ministries and departments of government, remain fragmented, these organizations provide the ground for new social pressures that serve as counterweights to narrow economic concerns and industrial interests.

With the transition of responsibilities for societies' values from governments to other groups in civil society, the orderly arrangement of power over those values, which has endured for much of the last 50 years of this century, is lost or dissipated. Under these conditions, those responsible for the governance of industries and the maintenance of corporate legitimacy can no longer appeal to their established relationship with the powerful ministries and departments of government. Rather, senior managers increasingly have to contend with a broader range of social values, represented by a more amorphous set of actors in society and expressed at many different scales of organization. This will provoke a far more complex mosaic of domestic markets and cultural and environmental patterns with which industry must cope.

In this view of the world, business will divide sharply between global companies that, despite their global span, will increasingly see sales and production as more and more local and an ever expanding population of smaller local companies that appeal to local markets. Consequently, the global marketplace will become a complex of individualized, cultural markets where the challenge for companies will be to understand and align their products and services with the elements of local distinctiveness.

The challenge to managers in global companies will center on the balance between the demands of corporate identity and the need for local flexibility and responsiveness. The example here is not that found in the "model" industrial communities of Victorian Britain—New Earswick, Saltaire, or Port Sunlight—or the early Japanese industrial towns—where employment, housing, recreational opportunities, education, and the health needs of employees and their families were provided for by benign industrial capitalists. The inflexibilities and conformity of these models do not conform to the "knowledge democracies" of the new millennium. Rather the global business will engage many local sectors—business, local government, nongovernmental organizations, and local groups—to create time-limited industrial partnerships. What the new multilocal company will bring to these partnerships will be its know-how in technological applications, its ability to access capital, company image, and the capacity to build successful partnerships.

The successful company will be the one that most potential partners want to work with. What the successful company will look like will be determined by its identity shaped through the set of time-limited partnerships. Its small corporate core, its track record of success, the values its stands for, and its ability to interpret and meet local needs will be its hallmarks. It will only be as successful as its reputation for success. The successful manager will be the one most able to facilitate the partnerships with many sectors that enable local needs to be matched by appropriate technologies.

It is possible that neither of these scenarios will emerge over the next 10 to 20 years. However, the scenarios illustrate three simple yet important points. First, the way the future unfolds is a key variable in determining the limits of the role and responsibility of industry in relation to sustainable development.

Second, what shapes the future is less to do with the adoption of a concept such as sustainable development and more the outcome of a complex, unpredictable mesh of social, economic, and environmental forces within which future states are negotiated and shaped. In this case the second of our scenarios is more likely to give rise to conditions in which progress toward a more sustainable society is possible, given its emphasis on the importance of the local scale, the implicit notion of organizational isomorphism with local conditions, the consequent diversity of industrial practice, and sensitivity to local social and environmental circumstances. The industrial organization in this scenario has dual properties—as a holistic and as a holographic[3] organization. It is holistic through its need to draw in and reflect the multiple tensions of economic, social, and environmental reality; to satisfy the demands of level and scale; and to contribute to the needs of the present and the future. But the organization is also holographic because, like the hologram, when it is broken into many parts each part reflects back the same image as the whole. Like the hologram, the holographic company will have a distinctive image and a virtual character. The capacity of the organization to simultaneously be holistic and holographic means that it will reflect consistent values that demarcate its relationships with others, while the activities it undertakes will be informed by the local circumstances that it encounters. This implies that managers in the holistic/holographic organization will have much greater autonomy to make decisions and much greater responsibility to reflect the values of the organization in the actions that they take.

The third point is that notions of sustainable development, or sustainable industry, contribute to both scenarios. However, the sustainable global business of the first scenario is more likely to be an extension of the thinking and practices of today's leading industrial exponents of environmental management. A model for this practice can be constructed by combining the elements of current best practice in the various areas of industrial activity—corporate social responsibility and community liaison; stakeholder participation and environmental reporting; facilities management and environmental auditing; new product development and design for the environment; and environmental policy making and performance measurement. However, the holistic/holographic organization of the second scenario is seen as a far greater departure from current orga-

nizational thinking and practice and is considered more likely to contribute to a sustainable future society.

For industry to assume a positive role in the attainment of a more sustainable society it must, therefore, be prepared to address the need for
change—change that impacts all aspects of the industrial organization,
from the way its managers make sense of the organization's activities, to
the way they define the organization's purpose, organize and plan its
activities, develop its technology and products, and cooperate with other
organizations to add value through the network of relationships, or
respond to current and future consumers and other social interests. This
book seeks to address those changes.

Content of the Book

Many aspects of the themes and issues set out above are developed in
the chapters of this book. They provide insight into the nature of the
challenge of sustainable development for industrial organizations.
However, the book is not structured according to these themes. For
convenience it is divided into four parts. Each part offers a different perspective or level of analysis on the emerging character of the sustainable
enterprise. Part I provides the contextual and conceptual perspective
to the book. It examines the nature of global change and its effects on
industry, discusses the issue of sustainable development as a new paradigm, and explores a framework for the firm committed to sustainable
development.

Gladwin's introductory chapter provides context by addressing the role
of economic globalization in shaping the future prospects for an ecologically sustainable world. He sets out a critique of the conventional arguments that are mobilized to support the current move toward economic
liberalization and open global markets. He contends that economic globalization, of itself, will move society away from a more sustainable state
unless the processes of global trade are reoriented, reframed, and condi-
tioned by new thinking and practice consistent with principles of sustainable development—economic justice, cultural diversity, people's sover-
eignty, responsibility, and common heritage.

Hoffman and Ehrenfeld (Chapter 2) examine the notion of environmental management and sustainability as paradigms, using an historical
review of thinking and practice. They argue that sustainable development
is a new paradigm that demands a reorientation of current notions of capitalism. They address what this means for the field of management stud-

ies as an envelope for research and thinking about organizational practice and the basis for the education of managers of the future.

Welford, Young, and Ytterhus (Chapter 3) develop a framework to guide the firm toward more sustainable forms of development. Their proposal builds on, and extends, the main frameworks advocated for improved environmental performance in business. The chapter offers a normative framework or charter for the sustainable firm, which consists of three main elements. A vision of sustainable development for the firm is developed around seven E's—Environment, Employment, Economics, Empowerment, Ethics, Equity, and Education. These seven areas for sustainability are related to the position of the company in terms of the overall pattern of production and consumption. The second element is a measurement framework, built around performance in the seven areas of sustainability. The final element involves a process based on sustainable development dialogues between the company and its stakeholders through which the company's vision and performance are held up for scrutiny and debate.

Part II considers the trends and emerging concepts that are shaping the character of the sustainable enterprise. The focus of analysis for the chapters in this part is the industrial organization. Following Hoffman and Ehrenfeld's argument that sustainable development provides the basis for paradigmatic reform and transformative change, these chapters examine different aspects of the emerging character of the paradigm, even though it is not yet evident in any coherent way within current industry behavior. Consequently, this part of the book draws on conceptualized models of sustainability, supported by evidence from trends in industrial practice, rather than presenting evidence from empirical inquiry.

Spencer-Cooke (Chapter 4) begins with a systems view of industry, seeing internal organizational practices as intrinsically connected to the institutional and social context. Her discussion of the implications of sustainability is set against the current interest in environmental management systems, particularly the European Eco-Management and Audit Scheme or the international standard ISO 14001. She sees sustainability as performance in the economic, environmental, and social domains rather than the more singular pursuit of economic and environmental win-win positions offered through environmental management systems and standards for disclosure. Sustainability is presented as a socially constructed practice that emerges from the interaction of the activities of all actors in society.

Spencer-Cooke offers three scenarios for a sustainable society drawing on work undertaken with the European Partners for the Environment. The chapter takes these scenarios further by suggesting that what is required for sustainability is the acceptance of quantum leaps in managers' mental orientation about industrial organization and production.

Belz, Schneidewind, and Hummel (Chapter 5) set out a heuristic called COSY (Company Oriented SustainabilitY), which goes part way to address the dimensions of the agenda for sustainable development identified by Spencer-Cooke. Their chapter considers how the COSY approach supports a shift in industrial thinking and practice from processes to products, on to services and functions, and finally to individual and social needs. The COSY framework also encourages increasing attention to demand rather than the supply-side issues of industry. The chapter sets out the thinking behind the COSY concept and relates it to two industries, food and textiles, that are fundamental to all societies.

They argue that organizations need to consider the economic, social, and environmental issues related to their activities at four levels— processes, products, services, and functions provided by what the organization offers in the market—and finally, society's need for these services and functions. They suggest that recent experience of environmental management practice has focused almost exclusively on the first two of these levels—processes and products—rather than on the two higher levels— services and functions—and needs. The authors use the case of the food and textile industries to illustrate the practical aspects of their approach and briefly discuss their own role in bringing together stakeholders of these industries in workshops designed to identify visions for sustainable food and textiles industries.

Jones's work (Chapter 6) offers a perspective on what a cultural development strategy for sustainability might entail for an organization. His chapter reports on an empirical, qualitative, longitudinal case study of The Body Shop. It provides a critical assessment of the experiences of the company. He traces the way it has moved from the values espoused by its founder, Anita Roddick, to embrace a more open and pluralistic culture. The picture of The Body Shop presented here is of an organization that began with a strong culture, based on the values and organizational control of its charismatic leader. The espoused values include leadership in forging a more sustainable ethic in the wider business community, as well as a commitment to appeal to the passion of those who work for the company and those who buy its products.

The criticism of this strong unitarist culture is that it does not support those in the company who have more modest goals and values. Strong unitary values are seen as a force for encouragement but also part of a process that alienates people from the process of values setting. This creates the potential for gaps to develop between rhetoric and reality. Rhetoric follows the statements of those who set the values, whereas reality is shaped by the actions of those in the company with more narrowly constructed interests.

Clarke (Chapter 7) addresses the relationship between an industrial organization's approach to technology management and sustainable development. In particular, she tracks the progress of technology management in an acknowledged industrial leader in environmental management. From that, she draws conclusions about what the experience of the company, HiTec, says to the issue of sustainable technology management. Like many of the other authors in the book, Clarke references her approach to sustainability to the recent evolution of environmental management practice at HiTec.

Clarke places technology management for sustainable development firmly in the context of the management of relationships that enable technologies to find sustainable applications. She terms this approach Design for and with Society (DFS) and distinguishes it from the current notions of Design for Environment which have begun to affect the product design activities of some industrial organizations, including HiTec. These stages, from earliest to most recent, are described as housekeeping, pollution prevention, and then product stewardship.

The changing role and interrelationship of three main groups within HiTec—engineering, environmental, and strategic management—are described against the backdrop of the unfolding understanding of environmental management and sustainable development in this technology-driven company. One of the considerable contributions of Clarke's chapter is the insight it provides into the black box of technology management and the critical role that informal networks of learning play in shaping the response of organizations, such as HiTec, to the environment agenda and the agenda of sustainable development.

Part III develops the analysis of the industrial organization in the network of industrial and social relationships. The level of analysis in the chapters in this part of the book switches backward and forward from the organization to the organization's network and its institutional domain. In this way the authors draw inferences about how sustainability is influencing the relationships between the organization and its domain.

Vergragt and van der Wel (Chapter 8) describe an experimental process of technological and social scenario building and backcasting facilitated at Delft University, The Netherlands. The example discussed involves stakeholders with interests in sustainable washing. Backcasting is the term used to describe an active process in which stakeholders use scenarios to trace back the stages in transformation needed to move from current organizational structures and practices to the future states envisioned in scenarios. The chapter describes both the process and the outcomes that arose from developing these visions or scenarios and using the backcasting approach.

This experiment goes to the heart of the ambiguous position of technology in society as an agent of change that can become entrenched or institutionalized in social systems yet can be caused to shift direction given the appropriate circumstances.

Overall the program was informed by the need to create a basis for enduring change in the trajectory of washing technology through the participation of a wide group of actors with interests in washing. A need is shown for new ways to reduce the material and energy requirements of washing. Industry was involved in the program alongside a broad group of users and interests groups.

Vorley's analysis of sustainable agriculture (Chapter 9) takes a systemwide perspective of agriculture with an emphasis on the position of the agrochemicals industry. He argues cogently that the powerful agricultural chemicals businesses have failed to address the need to challenge their own technological entrenched position. Vorley contends that sustainable agriculture obliges the opening up of the prism of organizational conformity and the singular perspectives of chemical-rich agriculture of the past 50 years. He advocates the need to confront the conventional organizational wisdom of the agrifood business through a process of self-reflection and learning, where this is brought about by envisioning the future rather than projecting trends from past practice.

Östlund and Roome (Chapter 10) also take a systemwide view, considering the progress being made in forestry management practices drawing on experience in Scandinavia. Proponents of sustainable forestry standards argue that forests are defined on a bioregional scale and are ecologically unique, living resources. Moreover, forests support multiple interests and uses. When determining forest management practices there is a need for forest industries to take explicit account of the varied interests that the forest serves. The forestry management standards that have been developed acknowledge that forestry management plans have to be built around both the ecological needs of the forest, as a bioregion, as well as the range of social interests contained in the forest.

It is suggested that the approach to sustainable forestry management says more to industry about the future shape of sustainable industrial practice than do current environmental management systems standards, such as BS 7750 or ISO 14001. The particular issue here is how to adapt the principles of sustainable forestry management to industries that operate in the area of nonrenewable resources (for example oil, gas, and minerals) or manufacturing operations (for example, domestic goods, automobiles, and chemicals). These industries use resources in their operations, and their products consume further resources during their life cycle. All these demands impact nonrenewable as well as renewable resources, process, and endowments.

The generic principles of sustainable forestry are that a company responsible for converting resources to products should engage in a process aimed to establish the interests that other stakeholders have in the resources needed for its activities; should assess the ecological characteristics that limit the use of resources; and, with the input of stakeholders, should develop a resource management plan that sets out how the industry will use those resources within ecological limits and stakeholder interests. This process is far more complex for an automobile company than a forestry company (given the many different resource systems the automobile impacts); nevertheless the principles of sustainable management still apply.

Part IV broadens the focus of analysis further. It tackles issues of sustainable development as a global concern and, at the same time, addresses the responsibilities of industrial organizations that operate in a global economy. Diverse settings are considered—the developing economies, rapidly industrializing countries, and the developed economies of North America, Europe, and Japan. The chapters suggest that by using processes of mutual learning and technology transfer, a better appreciation can be developed of the opportunities for the diffusion of sustainable development ideas and practices.

Wallace (Chapter 11) considers the mechanisms available to support the move toward more sustainable industry in developing and industrializing nations. He contrasts the potential for government-to-government aid as opposed to the possibilities of harnessing foreign direct investment of multinational corporations (MNCs). He suggests that the nature of MNC investment in greenfield sites in industrializing countries often involves state of the art technology and, in relative terms, advanced environmental management practices. It is possible, then, to build bridgeheads of learning for sustainable development by drawing on the models provided by the foreign direct investment of the MNCs that are most advanced in their environmental management and sustainable development practices.

Angel (Chapter 12) takes up the issue of learning for sustainable development and improved environmental management through international technology transfer. He asks what management for sustainability implies in terms of shifts in the principles and character of international technology development and transfer. He contends that experience to date is strong on commitments but thin on ambition and short on new modes of implementation. Angel argues that innovation of international institutions is as important to the international transfer of knowledge and practices about sustainable development as it is to the development of sustainable technologies by individual firms. In contrast, policy has focused mainly on the accelerated diffusion of existing cleaner technologies and the promotion of improved systems for organizations to use in developing environmental management responses, such as ISO 14001. This is held to be insufficient and inadequate given the changes taking place in the global economy, as new markets and production locations emerge (such as China) and as the imperative for swift action on sustainable development gains momentum.

Angel draws on the case of recent experience in joint US/Japanese efforts to support green technology transfer to the rapidly industrializing Asian economies to identify the barriers to improved technology development and transfer. He suggests mechanisms to improve the potential for international sustainable technology development.

The Conclusion provides a synthesis of the contribution of the chapters of the book to the four key themes identified earlier in this Introduction: sustainable development as a reforming paradigm, the role of industry in systems change, the future, and the need to build for the future through scenarios. This synthesis is then used to address the challenge of sustainable development in terms of the barriers, opportunities, and potential for learning to build sustainable industries for sustainable societies. The book ends by translating these ideas into an action agenda for management practice and for management education and research.

ACKNOWLEDGMENTS

I would like to acknowledge the suggestions made on earlier manuscripts for this introductory chapter by Kurt Fischer, Johan Schot, Berit Aasen, Anja de Groene, and Todd Baldwin. I would also like to thank the members of the Greening of Industry Network, particularly the participants at the Fourth International Conference of the Greening of Industry Network held in Toronto in 1995 under the title "Research and Practice: Learning to Build Sustainable Industries for Sustainable Societies," for giving freely of their enthusiasm and ideas.

NOTES

1. Monsanto's CEO, Robert Shapiro, argues that the company's major strategic reorientation away from conventional chemicals production into bio-engineering is consistent with sustainable development. However, it is also possible to contend that this position is a response to past criticism of the company's environmental record, during its chemical production period. The argument developed in this chapter (and echoed in Chapter 9) suggests that a sustainable company would be more likely to develop technologies and the institutional arrangements needed to support those technologies through opportunities identified by engagement with stakeholders than it would be to drive forward with particular technological solutions, as Monsanto presently appears to be doing.

2. The World Business Council for Sustainable Development (WBCSD) has been involved in developing scenarios against which to consider the emergence of sustainable business. At the time of writing, the results of the scenario work were about to be made available to member companies of WBCSD. It has been decided to put this material in the public a further six months after its release to member companies. It will probably be published in mid-1998.

3. I owe my insight on the point of the holographic organization to conversations with my colleague at York University, Gareth Morgan.

Part I
CONTEXT AND CONCEPTS

Chapter 1

Economic Globalization and Ecological Sustainability: Searching for Truth and Reconciliation

Thomas N. Gladwin

In the debate about economic globalization and ecological sustainability what, and who, are we to believe?

Do we side with Jerry Mander, chair of the International Forum on Globalization, when he asserts that "economic globalization, the instrument of the world's largest corporations, is an assault on biological diversity, democracy, community, cultural diversity, and the natural world," *or* with international economist Jagdish Bhagwati, who admonishes that "the aversion to free trade and GATT that many environmentalists display is uninformed, and it is time for them to shed it"?

Do we agree with Renato Riggiero, director general of The World Trade Organization, accepting that "globalization represents a huge opportunity for countries at all levels of development (representing) one of the most important factors in the rise of living standards across the globe," *or* with ecological economist Herman E. Daly contending that "free trade sins against allocative efficiency . . . against distributive justice . . . against community . . . against macroeconomic stability . . . and against the criterion of sustainable scale"?

Do we accept, as international economist Jeffrey Sachs does, that "global capitalism is surely the most promising institutional arrangement for worldwide prosperity that history has ever seen," *or* with Pope John Paul II who in his 1998 New Year's Day Address warned that "the process of globalization underway in the world needs to be oriented in the direction of equity and solidarity to avoid the marginalization of people and groups"?

Do we lean toward the view of Stephen Viederman, president of the Jessie Smith Noyes Foundation, who argues that "corporations and sustainable development are incompatible (since these corporations) have no commitment to community or place . . . to future generations . . . to democracy . . . to equity . . . or to alleviating poverty;" *or* do we endorse the view of the Business Council on National Issues that "when it comes to encouraging sustainable development, the market is the most important instrument available"?

Do we accept that economic globalization is "irreversible" (US President Bill Clinton), "unavoidable" (The World Bank), and/or "cannot be stopped" (McKinsey Global Institute); *or* do we concur with David C. Korten, author of *When Corporations Rule the World,* that "the global economy has become like a malignant cancer" and is "neither inevitable nor desirable"?

A Dialogue of the Deaf

The debate over the environmental and social effects of economic globalization (typically framed as "trade versus the environment") has grown large and ever more strident in recent years. (For a sampling of published work see Barber, 1995; Costanza et al., 1995; Daly, 1996; Esty, 1994; French, 1993; Korten, 1995; Mander and Goldsmith, 1996; Nader et al., 1993; and Organization for Economic Cooperation and Development, 1997.) In this debate the pro-globalization and anti-globalization forces have argued past, rather than with, one another. The pros often exaggerate the benefits of economic globalization while minimizing its costs and risks. The cons have generally done just the opposite.

The debate is complicated by the distinct worldviews held by those who support and oppose globalization. Supporters have a tendency to manifest "technocratic" worldviews. The world is largely empty. Economic growth is the answer to most problems. Technology and human ingenuity are ultimate saviors. The future is cornucopian. All forms of capital are substitutable. Human nature is competitive, and human progress is consumption. Liberalism is the true philosophy, and ethics are utilitarian. Efficient allocation via free markets is the guiding mechanism (see Gladwin, Kennelly, and Krause, 1995). These supporters are generally not neutral observers, rather they are well connected to those interests that will gain from a more global capitalist system (multinational corporate CEOs, officials of The World Bank, IMF or WTO, investment bankers, business school professors, to name but a few).

On the other side stand a rainbow alliance of anxiety-stricken representatives of environmental organizations, consumer rights groups, family farmers, religious organizations, advocates of democracy, and working people. They are all much less connected to the power of internationally mobile capital. In contrast to the technocrats, the critics of economic globalization tend to be "sustaincentric" in their worldviews. The world is up against the limits set by its carrying capacity—further expansion of resource throughput will produce overshoot and collapse. Precaution is needed. Technology is a mixed blessing. The future is neo-Malthusian. Natural and human-made capital are fundamentally complements and only substitutes at the margin. Human survival demands cooperation, and human happiness is not just a function of consumption. Metaphysics are holistic. Time horizons are long. Communitarianism is better than liberalism. We must be equally concerned with social justice and sustainable scale as with allocative efficiency (see Gladwin, Kennelly, and Krause, 1995).

Add to this the substantive challenges of the real debate itself—with its extraordinary complexities, large and irreducible uncertainties, direct and indirect effects, static snapshots and dynamic processes, micro and macro levels of analysis, and highly varied disciplinary perspectives. Anyone trying to make sense of this "dialogue of the deaf" is typically left dazed and confused. What prospects, then, for those who must decide between the choices provided within this debate—those whose decisions shape the future—?

If economic globalization and environmental (un)sustainability are indeed the two most powerful megatrends shaping human destiny, it is vitally important to cut to the heart of this debate, by seeking to understand these two phenomena and their interconnections within the framework of a more encompassing perspective. The objective of this chapter is certainly not to resolve the debate. Its more limited aim is to propose a conceptual framework for use by scholars who are engaged in the search for "truth and reconciliation" about the relationships between economic globalization and ecological sustainability. It sets out to define the key terms and summarize empirical trends, offers a set of new hypotheses that need formal investigation, and concludes with a very tentative vision of "ecologically sustainable economic globalization."

The Meaning of Economic Globalization

The general concept of globalization is typically conceived in the fields of international economics and political science in terms of rising magnitudes, intensities, and densities of interdependence among nations (see

Clark [1997] for an extensive review of the literature). Mittelman defines globalization as a "coalescence of varied transnational processes and domestic structures, allowing the economy, politics, culture and ideology of one country to *penetrate* another" (1996:2). While it is difficult to pinpoint where economics begins or ends in this process, adding this prefix before globalization places the focus on exchanges and transfers, by individuals or corporations, across national boundaries in relation to production, distribution, and consumption of goods and services.

Economic globalization takes place as the extent and depth of cross-border interactions causes "events" in one country to produce "effects" in others. Systems theory predicts that globalization will be accompanied by heightened mutual causality among interconnected economies. As globalization increases, greater *homogeneity* (convergence, hybridization, universalization) is induced among the richly joined economies. This confronts firms that are spread out, through the web of economies, with indivisibilities that require *coordination* and incongruities that call for *centralization*. Firms operating throughout the system gain comprehensibility through *standardization* and scale opportunities through *rationalization* (see Gladwin and Wasilewski [1986] for an extended causal model). Globalization thus "compresses the time and space" dimensions of economic and social relations (Mittelman, 1996:3).

In addition to these institutional responses, distributional effects can be anticipated. A symmetrical distribution of costs and benefits across the enmeshed nations can be expected to lead to greater mutual sensitivity, tighter coupling, denser network properties, with more extensive feedback loops and more complete integration. If the effects are asymmetrically distributed among interacting countries, we are likely to witness unequal sensitivity and/or vulnerability, perceptions of inequity, unequal exchange, and dependency in relations.

Economic globalization is driven by a complex array of competitive, market, cost, governmental, and infrastructural (communications and transportation) factors. It feeds on, and feeds off, trends such as marketization, industrialization, deregulation, commodification, securitization, Westernization, urbanization, privatization, regionalization, and structural adjustment. The process of economic globalization can in this way be seen as a self-reinforcing or positive feedback loop. As Niels Meyer (1995) has modeled it, more globalization provides more power to transnational corporations (TNCs), which in turn allows them to monopolize mass media and exert power over popular values. More power to

TNCs makes them stronger lobbyists for their commercial interests with public officials. This leads to more efficient, centralized decisions, which furthers the role of privatization, the freer movement of capital and trade, catalyzing even more globalization and embedding political decision makers and others in a spiral that yields ever more power to successful TNCs.

The economic effects of freer (deregulated) international commerce (trade and capital) at the root of economic globalization are typically framed by economists in terms of allocation and growth. The "free trade proponent" Melvyn Krauss states the standard case as follows:

> Specialization and interdependence through international exchange increase the average productivity of the nation's productive resources by reallocating or transferring them from lower- to higher-productivity uses . . . it creates income for the community by reallocating jobs and capital from lower-productivity to higher-productivity sectors of the economy. The gains from trade are the gains from a more efficient allocation of the nation's productive resources.

> (Krauss, 1997:xii).

Enhanced economic efficiency, according to the OECD, allows "world output to expand, in the form of additional economic growth (scale effects). It will also generate shifts in the composition and location of production and consumption activities (structural effects). More specifically, different technology paths will be promoted (technology effects), and different product mixes will be produced and consumed (product effects)" (OECD, 1997:19). George Soros, the billionaire financier, can thus proclaim that global integration brings

> . . . tremendous benefits: the benefits of the international division of labor . . . dynamic benefits such as economies of scale and the rapid spread of innovations from one country to another . . . and equally important non-economic benefits such as the freedom of choice associated with the international movement of goods, capital and people.

> (Soros, 1998:20)

Krause, the OECD, and Soros are mute above on the issues of equitable distribution or sustainable scale aspects of economic globalization. As Herman Daly (1996) notes, mainstream theories of trade, capital movements, and economic growth are essentially divorced from concerns of intra- and inter-generational justice on the one hand and issues of optimal scale of resource throughput relative to ecological carrying capacity on the other. Theories of globalization in economics are essentially theories of *markets* in search for "pareto-optimal" resource allocation (in conformity with the preferences of those with the ability to pay for the products and services of the resource flows). Such markets "are meant to be efficient, not sufficient; greedy, not fair. Markets were never meant to achieve community or integrity, beauty or justice, sustainability or sacredness—and they don't" (Von Weizsacker, Lovins, and Lovins, 1997:299).

"Fundamentalist" free-marketeers liberated from concerns about social justice and the biophysical limits on the throughput of energy and matter can offer up rational but "wild" ideas. For example, in the notorious "toxic memo" authored by Lawrence H. Summers, then The World Bank's Chief Economist, Summers asked his colleagues:

> Just between you and me, shouldn't The World Bank be encouraging *more* migration of the dirty industries to the LDCs (Less Developed Countries)? . . . [one reason is that] The measurement of the costs of health-impairing pollution depends on the foregone earnings from increased morbidity and mortality. From this point of view a given amount of health-impairing pollution should be done in the country with the lowest cost, which will be the country with the lowest wages. I think the economic logic behind dumping a load of toxic waste in the lowest wage country is impeccable and we should face up to that.
>
> (Summers, in George and Sabelli, 1994:98,99)

The outrage to this view is exemplified in a response to Summers from the (then) Secretary for Environment in Brazil, José Lutzenberger: "Your reasoning is perfectly logical but totally insane. [It is] a concrete example of the unbelievable alienation, reductionist thinking, social ruthlessness and arrogant ignorance of many conventional 'economists' concerning the nature of the world we live in . . . [It] is an insult to thinking people . . ." (in George and Sabelli, 1994:101).

The Wave of Economic Globalization

What is the scale of economic globalization? Statistics gathered and integrated from a range of sources (UN; OECD; The World Bank; IMF;

French, 1997; Greider, 1997; Korten, 1995; and others) reveal a massive surge of economic globalization over the past few decades that greatly exceeds the growth of gross world product. This is evident in the growing dominance of TNCs and the rapid increases in foreign direct investment, world trade, and cross-border capital movements.

Transnational Corporations

Gross world product expanded about fivefold during the period 1950 to 1990; the aggregate sales of the largest 500 TNCs expanded in the same period by a factor of 7. The number of firms doing business (having foreign affiliates) outside their home country borders rose by about 40 percent from the late 1960s into the 1990s, so that by 1995 the UN classified 40,000 firms as transnational (34,353 of these home-based in highly industrialized nations). The estimated 250,000 foreign affiliates of these parent firms cranked out about $7 trillion in sales in 1995, a figure larger than total world exports in that year. (Sales by these foreign affiliates grew in the 1990s at a rate 20 to 30 percent faster than exports.)

Of the top 100 "economies" in the world, 51 are now TNCs. The 200 largest TNCs currently account for about 28 percent of global economic activity, as measured by the ratio of TNC sales to gross world product. This ratio is up from just 7 percent back in 1971. The top 300 TNCs now own an estimated one-quarter of the world's productive assets. The top 500 of them are estimated to account for 33 percent of all manufacturing exports, 75 percent of all commodity trade, and 80 percent of all trade in technology and services. About 75 percent of global research and development is done by TNCs, with 80 to 90 percent of it performed in their parent nations. Despite these dramatic figures, TNCs are estimated to directly employ just below 1 percent of the world's work force (a figure of about 26 million that has remained flat for two decades).

Foreign Direct Investment

Since 1983 global foreign direct investment (FDI—investments in plant, equipment, and property owned by firms outside their home countries) has grown, on average, at the phenomenal rate of 29 percent a year. This is 3 times faster than the growth of exports, 3 times faster than total investment, and 4 times faster than world output. From 1980 to 1994, FDI grew from 4.8 percent to 9.6 percent of world GDP. The total world stock of FDI at the end of 1996 stood at over $3 trillion, with about 75 percent of it located in industrial nations. Total flows of FDI were $349 billion during 1996, with 75 percent of it both flowing from, and flowing into, OECD nations. Currently, the United States is simultaneously the world's largest recipient and largest source of FDI. Of the flows of FDI going to developing nations ($97 billion in 1995), 80 percent of it went to 12 countries alone, mainly the Asian "tigers" (for example, China [accounting alone for 40 percent of the total], Singapore, Indonesia, Malaysia, Thailand) and emerging markets in Latin America (such as Brazil, Mexico, Argentina). FDI accounted for 40 percent of all private capital flows to developing nations, with the rest taking the form of bond investments (21 percent), stock investments (20 percent), bank lending (18 percent), and export credits (2 percent) (see French, 1997). FDI is currently 5 times larger than official development aid.

World Trade

The volume of world merchandise trade grew 16-fold between 1950 and 1994; world economic output over the same period grew only by a factor of five and a half (trade increased at an average annual rate of 6 percent compared to 4 percent for world output). During the 1990s the annual percentage change in world merchandise exports was four times the growth rate of world merchandise production. Back in 1950, world exports represented 8.6 percent of world gross product; by 1995 the figure was 20.8 percent. The role of the trade sector in developing nations has increased markedly. In 1986, exports and imports accounted for 33 percent of the developing countries GDP—by 1996 the figure was 43 percent.

The world's TNCs accounted for about two-thirds of the $5.2 trillion of world trade in 1996. About half of this share took the form of "intrafirm" trade (trade among the affiliates of the same firm), and the other half involved exchanges among the TNCs. Intrafirm trade transactions account for 50 percent of US imports and 40 percent of US exports. Trade is also highly concentrated: 100 US firms account for 50 percent of US exports, and the top 15 exporters in the United States alone account for 25 percent. Observers looking at this data suggest that the role of TNCs in world trade implies that it is now probably shaped more by proprietary strategies of oligopolistic TNCs in search of "absolute advantage" than by the classical rationale for trade of "comparative advantage" (see Adam Smith, David Ricardo, proponents of welfare gains from open arms-length transactions among purely national and perfectly competitive firms in a world where capital was assumed to be immobile).

Mobile Finance Capital

The most astonishing growth in economic globalization has involved "borderless finance," involving the trading of stocks, bonds, currencies, and other types of financial paper according to a "manic logic of global capitalism" (Greider, 1997). Since 1980, the total stock of financial assets from OECD nations has expanded in value by 6 percent a year, increasing two and a half times faster than the GDP of OECD nations. Cross-border transactions in bonds and equities, as a ratio to GDP, was under 5 percent in Japan, Germany, and the United States in 1970; by 1996 the percentages had variously increased to between 152 percent and 197 percent. From 1980 to 1994 the movement of American money into stocks across borders jumped 16-fold to $1.5 trillion. The total stock of financial assets from OECD nations totaled $35 trillion in 1992 (double the economic output of those countries) and was forecast to reach $53 trillion in real terms by 2000 (then equal to triple the economic output—see McKinsey, 1994).

This mobile finance capital is now 13 times the size of OECD-nation exports and will increase to 19 times by the year 2000. About $3 trillion is moved via electronic transfer systems every day around the world by a small community of banks and brokerages, via an estimated 150,000 international transactions. Approximately two-thirds of this is trading in foreign currencies, of which only 10 percent are estimated to finance real trade and long-term investment; the remainder, according to the OECD (1997), are purely for speculation. Commentators worry that money is increasingly divorcing from real wealth since there is now 90 times as much money circulating in the world as there are goods and services to buy.

According to Greider, the principles of mobile international finance capital are

> ... transparent and pure: maximizing the return on capital without regard to national identity or political and social consequences ... financial investors monitor and punish corporations or whole industrial sectors if their returns weaken. Finance disciplines governments or even entire regions of the globe if those places appear to be creating

impediments to profitable enterprise or unpleasant surprises
for capital. If this sounds dictational, the global financiers
also adhere to their own rough version of egalitarian values:
They will turn on anyone, even their own home country's
industry and government, if the defense of free capital seems
to require it.

(Greider, 1997:25)

In this context it comes as no surprise that after Malaysia's stocks and
currencies were ravaged by global traders during the late summer of 1997
that Malaysia's prime minister, Mahathir Mohamed, would publicly
denounce currency speculators as "morons" and label most forms of currency trading as "unnecessary, unproductive, and immoral."

The Meaning of Ecological Sustainability

Sustainable development is a very "big idea of general usefulness" that
has generated a large literature and debate. (For a survey see Gladwin,
Kennelly, and Krause, 1995.) The idea is infused with multiple objectives,
complex interdependencies, and considerable "moral thickness." This has
caused some observers to forecast that operationalizing the idea in a scientific manner will remain forever elusive (see Lélé and Norgaard, 1996).
At a high level of abstraction the literature suggests that sustainable
development is a process of achieving human development (widening or
enlarging the range of human choice) in an inclusive, connected, equitable, prudent, and secure manner. Inclusiveness implies human development over time and space. Connectivity entails an embrace of ecological,
social, and economic interdependence. Equity suggests intergenerational,
intragenerational, and interspecies fairness. Prudence connotes duties of
care and prevention—technologically, scientifically, and politically. Security demands safety from chronic threats and protection from harmful disruption.

The direct focus in this chapter is on ecological sustainability. However, it is vital to note that the overall notion of sustainable (human) development embraces socioeconomic sustainability (dealing with questions of
poverty, population, human rights, female empowerment, employment,
income distribution, social cohesion, and so on). The socioeconomic
dimension of sustainability is equally important, in great need of attention, and perhaps far more intractable (see Gladwin, Krause, and Kennelly, 1995). Moreover, many of the potential causal linkages between eco-

nomic globalization and ecological sustainability are mediated through social and economic processes. (For an extensive examination of how poverty affects the environment, see UNEP [1995].) It is also the case that connections between economic globalization and socioeconomic sustainability channel through processes of environmental degradation. In other words, reductions of human capital arise through threats to health from climate changes caused by fossil fuel use that is boosted by globalization (see Daily and Ehrlich, 1996). That said, a full scope model of globalization in relation to overall sustainable human development is beyond the reach of this chapter.

The question of what constitutes ecological sustainability is far from resolved. Current formulations entail a "veritable minefield of slippery terms and hidden value judgments" (Lélé and Norgaard, 1996:363). Authors suggest that ecological sustainability involves notions of ecosystem health (Costanza et al., 1992), ecological integrity (Woodley et al., 1993), natural capital maintenance (Daly, 1994), self-organizing capacity (Norton, 1991), carrying capacity (Daily and Ehrlich, 1992), ecological resilience (Holling, 1986), and ecosystem service maintenance (Daily, 1997).

A sustainable system survives or persists over some time period. But even this simple notion is difficult to operationalize due to the limits of our understanding of ecology. Traditional models of natural systems, that emphasize equilibrium, balance, constancy, closure, homeostasis, and predictability, have given way to more complex models based on dynamic, open systems involving chaos, complexity, pulsing, flux, and multiple or punctuated states (see Botkin, 1990; Holling, 1992). The study of ecological systems is in its infancy. Uncertainty about ecosystem processes is large and irreducible. In addition, analysts must contend with an extraordinary range of ecosystem functions and services that bear on the viability of (human and other) life systems.

Ecosystem services "are the conditions and processes through which natural ecosystems, and the species that make them up, sustain and fulfill ... life" (Daily, 1997:3). From a human standpoint these services include:

> ... purification of air and water; mitigation of floods and droughts; detoxification and decomposition of wastes; generation and renewal of soil and soil fertility; pollination of crops and natural vegetation; control of the vast majority of potential agricultural pests; dispersal of seeds and translocation of nutri-

ents; maintenance of biodiversity (from which humanity derives key elements of its agricultural, medicinal, and industrial enterprise); protection from the sun's harmful ultraviolet rays; partial stabilization of climate; moderation of temperature extremes and force of winds and waves; support of diverse human cultures; and providing aesthetic beauty and intellectual stimulation that lift the human spirit.

(Daily, 1997:3,4)

These services are interdependent. They are driven by solar energy, only marginally substitutable (at affordable cost) by technological fixes, generated by a complex of biological, physical, and chemical processes, and barely discernible since "the most important ecological processes are prominently manifest at the bottom of biological food chains and energy pyramids often associated with the activities of invertebrate and microbial organisms" (Kellert, 1993:47). Typically these services are not priced. However, the current annual economic value of 17 of these ecosystem services for 16 biomes has been estimated to fall in the range of US $16 trillion to US $54 trillion ($10^{12}$) per year, with an average value of US $33 trillion per year—a value larger than the global gross national product (Costanza et al., 1997).

From a selfish human standpoint, ecological sustainability implies meeting human needs without compromising the capability of nature to continue to provide ecosystem services (in sufficient quantity and quality). It means ensuring the ability of the "metasystem of nature" to maintain its *vigor* (function or primary productivity in terms of overall metabolism or energy flow—see Odum, 1971); *organization* (internal structure or diversity of components and connectivity among them—see Rapport, 1997); and *resilience* (durability or ability of the system to maintain structure and patterns of behavior in the face of stress or disturbance—see Holling, 1986). Consequently, when asking how economic globalization affects ecological sustainability, we ultimately require a "comprehensive, multiscale, dynamic and hierarchical measure" (Costanza et al., 1992:240) of how human-induced disturbances (via chemical, physical, or biological pathways) associated with globalization impact ecosystem vigor, organization, and resilience. Yet we obviously lack the measurable, objective models and value-neutral criteria and indicators of change to accomplish this task. In their absence we will have to rely on very broad and crude "working" principles and indicators.

Principles to guide and measure "ecologically sustainable behavior" on the part of economic actors have been proposed (see Costanza and Daly, 1992; Gladwin, 1992; Gladwin, Kennelly, and Krause, 1995; and Hawken, 1993). For example, "The Natural Step" suggests three "non-negotiable" conditions governing human interaction with natural systems (see Holmberg, Robert, and Eriksson, 1996): (1) Substances from the Earth's crust (lithosphere) must not systematically increase in ecosphere (metals, fossil fuels, and other minerals must not be extracted at a rate faster than they can be redeposited and reabsorbed by the lithosphere). (2) Substances produced by society must not systematically increase in the ecosphere (manufactured materials must not be produced at a faster pace than they can be broken down and integrated back into the cycles of nature or deposited into the Earth's crust). (3) The physical basis for the productivity and diversity of the ecosphere must not be systematically deteriorated (renewable harvest rates must be below natural regeneration rates; and human activities should result in no loss of genetic, species, or ecosystem diversity). These system conditions integrate societal metabolism into natural cycles, ensuring that human wastes become new resources for nature or society. It is probably safe to assert that all three conditions are violated by most households and firms in today's energy-intensive, high-throughput, linear consumer economies of the "Northern elite" (see Gladwin, Newburry, and Reiskin, 1997).

The new concern is with the ecological degradation and impacts on ecological sustainability arising from the developing pattern of the global industrial structure. The Worldwatch Institute concludes that eight nations (four industrial and four developing) "disproportionately shape global environmental trends . . . accounting for 56 percent of the world's population, 59 percent of its economic output, 58 percent of its carbon emissions, and 53 percent of its forests" (Flavin, 1997:7). These eight are the United States, Japan, Germany, Russia, China, India, Indonesia, and Brazil. The first three have dominated the process of global economic integration in the past, while the latter five "emerging" economies have recently been entering into the world economy at rapid rates.

The Wave of Global Environmental Degradation

Global environmental degradation is traced to a complex interaction of "driving forces"—principally population change, economic growth, technological change, political-economic institutions, and attitudes and beliefs (see Stern, Young, and Druckman, 1992). All of these forces are altered or magnified by economic globalization.

A review of recent global environmental trend data (see Brown, 1998; Daily and Ehrlich, 1996; Meyer, 1996; Postel, 1994; United Nations, 1997; United Nations Environment Programme, 1997; Vitousek, 1994; and Vitousek et al., 1997) reveals four systematic aspects of erosion in the Earth's ability to support life (forms of "biotic impoverishment" using the term of ecologist George Woodwell, 1990): (1) declining renewable resources, (2) altered biogeochemistry, (3) diminishing biological base, and (4) threatened security of human health. Some of the most important human-driven environmental trends, patterns, and statistics in each bundle are discussed here.

Renewable Resource Scarcity

Human activity has now transformed about 40 percent of the Earth's terrestrial vegetated surface (via pumping, draining, logging, clearing, mining, paving, building, plowing, grazing, chilling, and so on). Since 1945 about 40 percent of the vegetated land surface has been degraded by overgrazing, deforestation, pollution, and agricultural mismanagement. An estimated 300 million hectares of agricultural land have been severely degraded and local farming systems abandoned. A further 1.2 billion hectares of agricultural land (including grazing land) have been at least moderately degraded. Land degradation of all types is accelerating in Latin America/Caribbean, Africa, West Asia, and the Asia-Pacific regions. Soil erosion exceeds soil formation in many parts of the globe, lowering land productivity and leading to massive desertification, especially in Africa.

The marine fish catch rose nearly fivefold between 1950 and 1989, but has leveled off at about 100 million tons in the 1990s. As of 1995, some 22 percent of recognized marine fisheries were overexploited or already depleted and another 44 percent were at their limit of exploitation. Since 1940, global water withdrawals have risen by an average of 2.5 percent annually, a rate faster than the rate of population growth. Per capita availability of fresh water worldwide fell from 17,000 cubic meters in 1950 to 7300 cubic meters in 1995. Humanity is overpumping (at rates higher than recharge) trillions of gallons of groundwater stored during the last glacial period. Eighty nations already confront freshwater scarcities and UNEP estimates that the number of people who are likely to face severe water shortages will double from 1.5 billion in 1990 to 2.8 billion in 2050.

Alteration of Biogeochemical Cycles

Since the dawn of the industrial revolution, humans have raised the concentration of carbon dioxide in the atmosphere by nearly 30 percent,
potentially changing the composition of the atmosphere enough to induce
significant climate change. Global temperatures have increased nearly
half a degree Celsius since 1950, and the 1990s has been the warmest
decade on record. Emission of substances such as chlorofluorocarbons
has depleted the stratospheric ozone layer most significantly over the
poles, but also over populated and agriculturally abundant areas of the
Earth, causing an increase in UV-B radiation at the Earth's surface.
Despite the industrial national phaseout of CFCs, the ozone layer is
unlikely to fully recover until about 2050. In the meantime, experts predict a rising incidence of skin cancers, cataracts, and suppression of
immune functions.

Fertilization and fossil fuel combustion has doubled the total amount
of atmospheric nitrogen that is converted or fixed on land, resulting in
acidification of rivers and lakes, loss of soil nutrients, and rising atmospheric concentrations of nitrous oxide, a greenhouse gas. Regarding the
water cycle, humans globally are estimated to now use more than half of
the runoff water that is fresh and reasonably accessible, with 70 percent
of it being used in agriculture. About 1.5 billion people still live with dangerous air pollution. Toxic substances and waste volumes continue to rise
in industrial nations.

The world is now producing each year more than 100 million tons of
long-lived synthetic organic chemicals (70,000 different compounds),
which are transported globally, accumulated in organisms, and magnified
in concentrations through food chains. Recent research suggests that
chlorinated hydrocarbons such as DDT and PCBs, along with dioxins,
may be disrupting animal (including human) endocrine systems via hormone mimicking and blocking. Toxic heavy metals and persistent chemicals have been building up steadily in the Earth's topsoil, groundwater,
and in silt in lake bottoms, estuaries, and deltas.

Declining Biological Base

The world's forests—the major stores of biodiversity and providers of
ecosystem services—have shrunk by about a third (2 billion hectares)
since the agricultural revolution. From 1980 to 1995 the world lost an

average of 13 million hectares of forest per year. This loss is mainly tropical rainforests, which are being destroyed at an annual rate of about 4
percent of the current areas. Fifty percent of tropical deforestation in the
1990s has occurred in Bolivia, Brazil, Indonesia, Malaysia, Mexico,
Venezuela, and Zaire (with about one-third of the loss due to logging and
the remainder due to farmers clearing land for agriculture). About 50 percent of the Earth's mangrove and wetland ecosystems have been lost via
draining and filling in the past 200 years (Europe has lost two-thirds of its
inland and coastal wetlands, while the figure for the United States is 53
percent). Marine and coastal zone degradation is increasing in Latin
America/Caribbean, West Asia, the Asia-Pacific, and in Europe and the
former USSR. Coral reefs are dying off significantly from nutrient runoff,
siltation, and overexploitation. "Bio-invasions" (transport of nonnative
species into new ecosystems) are on the rise with devastating effects on
original species.

As a result of all of the above ecosystem conversions, human activities
today are driving species to extinction at a conservative estimate of one
extinction per hour, a rate at least 1000 times as fast as the rate of evolution of new species. If current rates of habitat alteration continue, the estimates of species loss over the next 30 years range as high as 20 percent.

Human Health Insecurity

The health dangers of stratospheric ozone depletion and global spread of
long-lived organochlorine compounds were noted above. Global climate
change is forecast to increase the abundance and range of organisms that
spread vectorborne infectious diseases such as malaria, dengue, and
schistosomiasis. During the past 20 years, at least 30 new diseases have
emerged for which there is currently no treatment or vaccine (new varieties of haemorrhagic fevers, such as Ebola, or the AIDS virus, which has
now infected an estimated 24 million adults worldwide). Old diseases
such as tuberculosis, bubonic plague, cholera, and malaria are resurgent.
Some 35,000 children die every day from preventable diseases. The
World Health Organization estimates that about 25 percent of the global
burden of disease and injury is linked to environmental decline. Much of
this is related to the lack of clean water for 1.3 billion people, and lack of
sanitation for nearly 3 billion people, mainly living in either chaotic shan-
ty towns on the edge of rapidly expanding cities or in remote rural areas
being heavily colonized.

While the incidence of poverty and deprivation has declined over time (especially in Asia), it has grown in absolute terms. The World Bank estimates that 1.4 billion people (attempt to) live on less than $1 a day (up from 1.23 billion in 1987); 70 percent of these people are female. An estimated 1 billion people lack adequate housing; nearly 840 million people in the world remain malnourished; 900 million adults are illiterate today, up from 760 million in 1970; 250 million children between the ages of 5 and 14 are working in developing countries, with 130 million of them not enrolled in schools; and 1 billion adults, 30 percent of the world's work force, are currently either unemployed or underemployed below a living wage—this number stood at 820 million in 1993. As we look to the future in regard to human health insecurity, we should note that 10 million people are net-added to the planet every six weeks, and that by 2050 the total world population is likely to hit 9 to 10 billion (with 95 percent of the addition happening in developing countries).

A Research Agenda—Waves That Become Tidal

Ecologist Jane Lubchenco noted recently that "we're changing the world in ways that it's never been changed before, at faster rates and over larger scales, and we don't know the consequences. It's a massive experiment, and we don't know the outcome" (in Brown, 1998:19). She was commenting as much on the process of economic globalization as on the nature of global ecological change. These two waves of change, in their combination, become a tidal wave of threatening scale and force.

To what extent and in what manner, then, does globalization of the human economy explain global biotic impoverishment? We do recognize that the causal pathways between globalization and impoverishment are very complex; and that globalization may have positive as well as negative effects. While the ultimate answer to this question would be revealed by running our longitudinal, experimental world two times—once with economic globalization and the other without—this is not a practical or experimental reality.

We might tease out some understandings by comparing biotic impoverishment in countries, or regions, at similar levels of economic development, but which vary substantially in their entanglement with the world economy. But we are unlikely to reveal anything substantive by focusing simply on the marginal contributions of globalization to ecological change. For example, the existing academic literature on globalization and the environment has focused disproportionately on the procedural greening of global trade institutions such as NAFTA, EU, GATT, and

WTO (for a survey see Esty, 1994), the invalidity of the assumptions of comparative advantage as a basis for free trade (see, for example, Costanza et al., 1995), and the long-standing debate over multinationals and the "pollution haven hypothesis" (for a recent integration see Eskeland and Harrison, 1997). This work is important, but it diverts attention to matters of pollution and location while ignoring a vast range of ecological sustainability related to the scarcity of renewable resources and biological functioning reviewed earlier. It channels attention to matters of trade and direct investment, abstracting from the hypercompetitive conditions imposed on both by the power of global and myopic financial markets. It focuses the search for interaction onto direct and simple connections between global business and the natural environment, rather than confronting the reality of growing "dynamic complexity" in our world (the increasing separation of cause and effect in space and time).

The intellectual journey of discovery that lies ahead is thus bound to be linked to our capacity to envision whole systems and the many pathways of interaction as well as the many small yet important dimensions of those interactions. To borrow from Gregory Bateson, our search is for an "epistemology with a future" asking "what is the pattern which connects all living creatures? . . . the pattern of patterns? . . . the metapattern?" (1978). To begin this search for a systemic analytical framework, 10 interrelated propositions are offered in the spirit of theoretical and empirical research informed by genuinely transdisciplinary understanding of the ecological effects of economic globalization (other things being equal).

Economic globalization boosts the generation and displacement of environmental costs. The physical separation between production and consumption arising from economic globalization engenders time-space "distanciation." This confuses the relationship between intentions, actions, and outcomes (see Redclift, 1996). This further exacerbates the human tendency to discount environmental costs by making them seem even more remote in space or time. As distance increases, responsibility and accountability for environmental costs and risks are diffused. Yet the transaction costs involved in getting the information required to monitor, enforce, and negotiate the internalization of these costs also rises with distance. Thomas Princen contends that

> As distance increases along dimensions of geography, culture, bargaining power, or agency, negative feedback loops are severed, stakeholders expand while decision making contracts, environmental problems are displaced, and shading and cost externalization increase. The likelihood of sustainable re-

source use increases as distance is lowered, as institutions locate decision authority in those who receive negative eco-logical feedback and who have the capacity and incentives to act on that feedback, and as the burden of proof for economic interventions shifts to the intervenors.

(Princen, 1997:235)

Economic globalization targets and overexploits the global commons. Wackernagel and Rees argue that "global markets give rampant global demand access to the world's last remaining pockets of unexploited or 'under-utilized' natural capital, inevitably accelerating their depletion. Malaysia's forests disappear to satisfy the Japanese hunger for timber; Russia 'develops' by opening its forest and fossil fuel stocks to Western exploitation; Canada's fisheries collapse from over-exploitation to satisfy global demand; the Southern hemisphere suffers an ozone hole caused mostly by Northern technologies" (1996:155).

Economic globalization encourages the most globally powerful to gain the greatest and fastest access to both "source" and "sink" functions of the biosphere at the lowest possible cost. Their global reach and mobility enables these actors to target open-access or common property resource pools such as fisheries, forests, underground aquifers, and the global atmosphere where property rights are ill-defined or nonexistent, where regulatory regimes are weak, and where there is little incentive to exercise any personal restraint. Chichilnisky concludes that "the international market transmits and enlarges the externalities of the global commons" (1994:865), as export patterns fail to reflect the social costs of open-access resource exploitation, leading the North to overconsume, and the South to overproduce, resource-intensive products. Appropriation of the commonly held life-support functions of the Earth shifts the character of environmental problems from local to global.

Economic globalization elevates transport externalities. It is estimated that international trade of goods and people accounts for one-eighth of world oil consumption. Economic globalization in separating production and consumption lengthens the distances between suppliers and con-sumers. It raises the volume, speed, energy consumption, and pollution generated by global freight traffic. The environmental consequences include noise, air pollution, congestion, acid deposition, cropland loss, habitat fragmentation, and global climate change. Globalization, in pur-suit of speedy and flexible "anywhere, anytime" deliveries, promotes rates of increase in traffic above rates of increase in economic output.

The OECD (1996) predicts that the Uruguay round of the GATT will result in a 71 percent increase in transport between 1992 and the year 2004. This is approximately 15 times the growth expected to result from the trade liberalization. The European Union estimates that international truck transportation within the EU will increase by 42 percent by 2010 as a result of the economic integration through the common market. The North American Free Trade Agreement is expected to increase truck transportation sevenfold during the next decade (French, 1993). The Federal Express Company expects that the percentage of products shipped on a just-in-time basis will grow from about 17 percent in 1994 to 47 percent by the end of this decade; the express side of the international cargo market is expected to increase nearly eightfold by the year 2016 (see Barth, 1998). Boeing projects that for the period 1997 to 2006, worldwide economic growth will average 3.2 percent per year; air passenger traffic growth will average 5.5 percent per year; and air cargo traffic growth will average 6.6 percent per year (Boeing, 1997).

Economic globalization promotes resource-intensive lifestyles.

> Since 1950, the richest fifth of humankind has doubled its per capita consumption of energy, meat, timber, steel, and copper and quadrupled its car ownership, greatly increasing global emissions of CFCs, greenhouse gases, accelerating tropical deforestation and intensifying other environmental impacts.
>
> (Ehrlich et al., 1997:104)

Despite this doubling of consumption, the percentage of these people describing themselves as "very happy" has remained constant over the period. Economic globalization ". . . mesmerizes peoples everywhere with fast music, fast computers and fast food—MTV, Macintosh, and McDonalds" (Barber, 1995:4). Visual messages through television and advertising are primary stimulants of consumerism. TV ownership has risen by an average 8 percent annually since 1955—there are now TV sets in 1 billion households, comprising almost half of humankind. Total global advertising expenditures correspondingly multiplied nearly sevenfold from 1950 to 1990, growing one-third faster than the world economy and three times faster than world population. In 1950 advertisers spent $15 for each person on the planet; by 1990 the figure was $48. Bombarded with the message that psychological health depends on material wealth, an estimated 750 million additional people are consuming their way into the high consumption classes. We can safely predict both massive environmental degradation and a rising epidemic of "affluenza" (an unhappy condition of overload, debt, anxiety, and waste resulting from the dogged pursuit of more).

Economic globalization foments regulatory standards—lowering competition. A recent *Financial Times* special series on "Mastering Global Business" noted that

> As competition intensifies, it fuels the race among competitors to serve globalizing customers, to capture economies of scale, to exploit the cost-reducing or quality-enhancing potential of optimal locations, and to tap technological advancements where they may occur. The result is that globalization has now become a self-accelerating frenzy.

(Govindarajan and Gupta, 1998)

Local administrations are ever more pressed into competing for mobile industries, both through direct incentives and reduction of institutional barriers to the entry of FDI. Moreover the institutional structures regulating globalization seek to restrict the range of regulatory options available to national governments. Herman Daly predicts a resulting "race to the bottom" for "free trade among differing regimes of cost internalization will result in a standards-lowering competition, leading to a situation in which more and more of total world production is produced in countries that do a less and less complete job of counting costs" (1996:18).

Economic globalization materially intensifies agricultural production. The intensification of agriculture by use of high-yielding crop varieties, chemical fertilizers and pesticides, irrigation systems, fossil fuel-intensive mechanization, and long-distance food transportation supports the quest for scale economies by the global agribusiness industry. The "industrialization" of agricultural systems provides a source for export earnings for debt-service by the governments of developing nations. These conditions in global agricultural markets shift the composition of agricultural production from "nontradables" (food crops) to "cross-border tradables" (cash crops). Small, labor-intensive, low (energy, water, chemical) throughput farms are progressively replaced by large-scale, capital-intensive, high (energy, water, chemical) throughput systems. The intensification of agricultural systems "can have negative local consequences, such as increased erosion, lower soil fertility, and reduced biodiversity; negative regional consequences, such as pollution of ground water and eutrophication of rivers and lakes; and negative global consequences, including impacts on atmospheric constituents and climates. Concerns about the ability to maintain long-term intensive agriculture are also growing" (Matson et al., 1997:504). Intensification, in the absence of equitable land distribution, can occasion massive rural-to-urban exodus, slum proliferation, and income concentration, exacerbating poverty-related resource degradation.

Economic globalization homogenizes and simplifies natural systems. Along with the material intensification of agriculture, food and other commodity production linked to the "global exchange economy" is increasingly specialized, "resulting in reduction in the number of crop or livestock species, or both, that are maintained, often leading to monoculture" (Matson et al., 1997:504). This "global conversion process" homogenizes species and ecosystems. It constitutes a fundamental force underlying the reduction in global biological diversity (see Norgaard, 1988; Swanson, 1992).

The trends toward large-scale monocultures is evident in much of the export-driven biotech farming and food processing, as well as in forestry for pulp and lumber. Genetic erosion is fast gathering pace, with growing uniformity threatening "plagues of sameness" given the high vulnerability of monocultures to diseases and pests (see Fowler and Mooney, 1990). With the loss of biological diversity comes the loss of ecological knowledge and vice versa: "As traditional people are integrated into the global economy, they lose their attachment to their own restricted resource catchments. This could lead to a loss of motivation to observe social restraints toward the sustainable use of diversity of resources, along with the pertinent indigenous knowledge that goes with it" (Berkes, Folke, and Gadgil, 1994:269).

Economic globalization accelerates biological invasions. Invasion of ecosystems by exotic or alien species is estimated to be the second most important cause of biodiversity loss, just behind habitat destruction. Biologist E.O. Wilson calls it one of the most significant "mindless horsemen of the environmental apocalypse" (1992:253). Although biological invasions occur naturally, global economic commerce is "a primary cause of the breakdown of biogeographic barriers; trade in live organisms is massive and global, and many other organisms are inadvertently taken along for the ride" (Vitousek et al., 1997:498). Global commerce provides myriad "pathways of invasion," including stowaways in container cargo traffic, biotic mixing in ballast water operations, pathogen and virus transfer in air traffic, and pests riding along with exported food and lumber. Outside of the environments where they evolved, such invaders can be very destructive via direct predation, outcompeting and displacement of native species, altering of fire regimes, transmission of diseases, and disruption of ecosystem processes. Biological invasions are estimated to have caused billions of dollars of ecological and economic damage (see Bright, 1996).

Economic globalization perpetuates poverty-induced resource degradation. As Alan Durning has noted:

> . . . poverty drives ecological deterioration when desperate people overexploit their resource base, sacrificing the future to salvage the present. The cruel logic of short-term needs forces landless families to raze plots in the rainforest, plow steep slopes, and shorten fallow periods. Ecological decline, in turn, perpetuates poverty, as degraded ecosystems offer diminishing yields to their poor inhabitants. A self-feeding downward spiral of economic deprivation and ecological degradation take hold.

> (Durning, 1990:144).

Processes of economic globalization induce or compound this vicious cycle in a variety of ways. Expulsion of sharecroppers, squatters, and small holders from land by commercial interests to make way for intensified export agriculture, dam construction, logging, oil drilling, and mining constitutes a direct link. Indirectly, the poor tend to pay a disproportionate share of the cost of global environmental degradation caused primarily by the Northern rich (greater exposure to hazardous wastes, loss of primary protein base from decline of world fish stocks, sea level rise from climate change, and so on).

Poor nations are also affected by patterns of "unequal exchange" whereby the prices of their exports of natural resources or primary commodities fall systematically over time relative to imported manufactures—in other words, "deteriorating terms of trade" (see UNEP, 1995). The poor are often hurt by their nation's debt-service obligations and structural adjustment efforts when social welfare spending is slashed and export-led growth policies speed the depletion of natural capital. Boyce argues that "greater inequalities of power and wealth lead, all else equal, to more environmental degradation" (1994:169). It is instructive to note that in 1960 the ratio of the income of the richest 20 percent of humanity to that of the poorest 20 percent was 30 to 1; by 1997, according to the UNDP, the ratio had climbed to 85 to 1. Does economic globalization systematically make the rich richer and the poor poorer?

Economic globalization accelerates throughput growth beyond carrying capacity. The OECD predicted that the Uruguay round of the GATT would reduce tariffs and other barriers to trade enough to provide projected gains in economic output of $270 billion by 2002. Recent research by the WTO of a sample of 117 countries found that those with more open economies grew at an annual rate of 4.5 percent between 1970 and 1989, while those with relatively closed economies grew at only 0.7 percent (Ruggiero, 1997). Economic globalization accelerates the throughput of energy and materials from nature into the economy and back out—it speeds up, in other words, the Earth's metabolism and entropic decay. Trade makes it possible for some countries to live beyond their own regenerative and absorptive capacities by importing from other countries. Most industrial countries run significant "ecological deficits." Germany relies on imports for 35 percent of its material flows, Japan for about 50 percent, and The Netherlands for more than 70 percent (see Adriaanse et al., 1997). In terms of "ecological footprint," the Dutch "consume" a productive land area 15 times larger than their own country (Wackernagel and Rees, 1996). As Sandra Postel notes:

> In principle, there is nothing inherently unsustainable about one nation relying on another's ecological surplus. The problem, however, is the widespread perception that all countries can exceed their carrying capacities and grow economically by expanding manufactured and industrial goods at the expense of natural capital—paving over agricultural land to build factories, for example, or clear-cutting forest to build new homes. But all countries cannot continue to do this indefinitely.

(Postel, 1994:16,17)

Trade thus promotes the "Hong Kong or Netherlands Fallacy." It reduces the perceived risks attached to the depletion of local natural capital through the "illusion" of infinite supplies flowing in from elsewhere. And the resource imports may, in fact, not represent true "ecological surpluses," but instead the net depletion or liquidation ("ecological deficits") of natural capital stocks in the exporting countries. This tendency to live beyond geographic carrying capacity by importing natural capital will push the world economy as a whole to grow beyond its optimal scale relative to the containing global ecosystem (see Daly, 1996).

Envisioning Ecologically Sustainable Economic Globalization

The dean of the Yale School of Management, Jeffrey E. Garten, recently noted in *Business Week* that "in the twilight of the 20th century, making globalization work humanely is quickly becoming the dominant issue of our time." He evidently had only *Homo sapiens* in mind—his observation would be even more powerful if it also implied compassion for the other 30 to 100 million species living on this planet. Making economic globalization work for the full house of life is the next century's biggest challenge. This is assuming that many or all of the 10 propositions above are proven to be true. The reader has no doubt noted that all of them were framed in terms of negative impact. We owe it to the future to also explore a range of potential positive impacts of globalization (speeding the transfer of ecoefficient technologies, substituting information for energy, stimulating a transnational civil society concerned with sustainability, inspiring a global consciousness, and so on), but that was not the intent of this provocation.

We find ourselves in the late 1990s in a strange place in history, somewhat reminiscent of the time in the early part of this century when Antonio Gramsci remarked that "the old is dying, the new is being born, and in the *interregnum* there are many morbid symptoms." Tidal forces are simultaneously pulling the people of this world closer together and farther apart. The elite of the world know that the Horsemen of the Apocalypse are stalking a good part of the planet, but puzzlingly they show little sense of urgency or moral conviction to do anything about it. They instead seem to be retreating even more deeply into the psychodynamics of denial, evidenced in the narcissistic materialism that bedecks their guarded urban towers or suburban compounds.

The anxious lower and middle classes, meanwhile, are so caught up in making it from day to day that the wider and longer-term challenge of sustainable development is of little matter. The majority at all levels seem indifferent or apathetic to the fate of the planet, seemingly accepting that there is no alternative to the dominance of neoliberal, globalizing forces. As Eric Hobsbawm would observe, we are in a state of social breakdown rather than revolutionary crisis (1994). There is a large "ideological vacuum" in which the verbal extremism of progressives (such as myself) is not matched by their capacity to reach out to, touch, and galvanize the masses. The vision now offered thus is utopian. It is currently politically and socially unrealistic, and economically impractical. But here it is anyway.

Assuming that most of our hypotheses above were confirmed, what would have to change to assure that economic globalization in the future is ecologically sustainable? The short answer is immense economic, social, and political change, amounting to a thorough re-creation of the system of global capitalism. The *objectives* of the entire system would have to shift from increasing economic growth to maximizing the quality of life. Growth in terms of physical expansion would need to give way to development measured as qualitative improvement. The obsession with allocative efficiency would expand to encompass just distribution and ecologically sustainable scale of the aggregate economy. Time and space horizons would need to lengthen, shifting the calculus from short-term maximization to long-term optimization. All of this pursuit would be guided by the "precautionary principle," calling for decision makers to err on the side of precaution given extraordinary uncertainty (see Costanza et al., 1995).

Continuing with our utopian vision, system *incentives* would be altered to achieve the objectives above by shifting the tax base from labor and income to throughput and resource depletion. The local rootedness of capital would be rewarded by selectively regulating or taxing the movement of speculative "hot money" flows. Tax havens and offshore banking centers would be eliminated. Corporate, banker, and broker decisions would be made accountable and transparent to all stakeholders. The capture and corruption of politicians and regulators would also be ended, making way for genuine democracy and radical decentralization. In sum, both economics and politics would be delivered back to a globe of villages instead of to a centralized global village.

If the above could be achieved we would be encouraging patterns of *production* that were labor and skill intensive, rather than energy and capital intensive. People would be put back to the center of the economic system—valued for their skills rather than their demands to consume. The scale of operations would favor smaller and decentralized configurations. Economies would organize on the logic of local for local, rather than global for local, inspiring greater regional autonomy and self-sufficiency. Local and regional economies would be more diversified and attuned to meeting basic needs rather than luxury wants.

If the above could be accomplished, international *trade regimes* would shift dramatically. Trade would be determined by true ecological surpluses rather than by global market demand. Prices would more fully internalize environmental costs. Accounting for cross-border transfers would be gauged in terms of ecological flows rather than money flows. Trade and capital flows among nations would be balanced or "fair" rather than inequitable. The logic of global integration would give way to regional/local integration. All of this would be enforced by compensatory export taxes and import tariffs to ensure that prices reflect their true ecological and social costs.

All of this is obviously quixotic. The central question, as Wackernagel and Rees (1996:102) have captured it, is: ". . . does the human family have the moral and political will to negotiate a global social contract governing more equitable access to ecological goods and services for all the world's people?" If the answer is no, then we had better prepare for Armageddon.

Chapter 2

Corporate Environmentalism, Sustainability, and Management Studies

Andrew J. Hoffman and John R. Ehrenfeld

Environmental management has become an increasingly significant aspect of corporate practice in the past decade. Universities are assuming an important role in the evolution of environmentalism in general and the integration of environmental management into corporate practice in particular. Academic research on the environment is encouraged through the support of new research networks (such as the Greening of Industry Network, the Organizations and the Natural Environment interest group of the Academy of Management, and the Business Environment Learning and Leadership program). New environment-related journals include *Organization and Environment, Business, Strategy and the Environment, Total Quality Environmental Management; Pollution Prevention Review,* and *Tomorrow).* This research informs the teaching of environmental management in business schools (Makower, 1993; Mangan, 1994; Pham, 1994) and engineering schools (Dembner, 1994; Wagner, 1994) in the United States and in Europe (Roome, 1994).

What exactly is the focus of this research? More fundamentally, what exactly is environmentalism? What is its connection to sustainable development? And, what is the proper role of the modern corporation in dealing with it? To many, the intersection of environmentalism and the firm means very different things. A new and ever-expanding jargon accentuates the multitude of perspectives over what is being studied—"greening," "life cycle analysis," "waste minimization," "pollution prevention," "environmental justice," and "sustainability," just to name a few. Does the emergence of these and other environmental philosophies represent a transformative shift in the basic notions and values that drive corporate behavior? Or has it been an evolutionary process? If it is the latter, we can continue to study and teach about corporate environmentalism as an adduct to existing knowledge and normative models. If it is the former, we need to examine these channels and disciplines to consider how they must be altered or reinvented. We must first define the topic of study before substantive academic work in environmental management can itself be considered "sustainable" for the long term.

As a step toward that end, this chapter considers two issues. First, *What is environmentalism?* How has the emerging literature on environmentalism modeled and framed its evolving conceptions? Moving from this model, a second issue is addressed: *What is corporate environmentalism?* And what are its implications for management research and education? It is not likely that the whole of this task can be accomplished within the limits of this one chapter, but the issues we raise will be taken up elsewhere in this book. This chapter is an effort to promote debate and bring some convergence on the very topics that many within the environmental field assume to be inherently obvious, and many outside the field outrightly reject. Resolution of these questions is a necessity for explaining what it is we are talking about and establishing its legitimacy as a research agenda.

We will argue that the present state of environmental management has been evolutionary in nature. Companies are doing things differently in response to a world that is rapidly changing. Environmentalism has begun to diffuse throughout the corporate organization so as to redefine its role and objectives in response to social, political, and economic demands for new action. However, evolutionary changes in thought and practice may not be enough to reverse present-day trends in environmental degradation. Philosophies such as environmental protection and (present-day interpretations of) sustainable development highlight the contradictions between the dominant social paradigm and the damage it wreaks on our natural, social, and political environments, but they do little to challenge the underlying causes of these contradictions. Without such a challenge, environmental problems will continue. To alter this trajectory, a revolutionary paradigm shift will be necessary, one that envisions new practices and strategies both inside and outside the firm and is based on new forms of theories and disciplines. Resolution of the opposing evolutionary and revolutionary views of the future of environmental management will have significant ramifications for the way environmentalism will be integrated into the business school curriculum.

An Evolutionary Model of Environmentalism

A Consensus of the Literature

Are you an *environmentalist?* In an April 1995 CNN/*USA Today* survey, 63 percent of Americans identified themselves as such. What does such a statistic mean? In point of fact, very little. The term, and therefore the question, is so broad as to be meaningless. An environmentalist could be anyone from a hunter concerned with maintaining the natural environment for sporting benefits, to a feminist who sees the struggle to form an environmentally sound future as inextricable from the struggle for gender equity, to a consumer who donates money to a favorite environmental charity.

To consider the bounds of the term *environmentalism* one must acknowledge, first, that it represents a broad social movement that is neither monolithic nor static. In 1989, some 5817 organizations filed 501(c)(3) forms with the US Internal Revenue Service (IRS) calling themselves environmental groups (Hodgkinson et al., 1993). Some are staffed with lawyers and scientists and work within existing institutions to bring about corporate and social change (such as the Natural Resources Defense Council and the Environmental Defense Fund). Others remain outside those institutions, relying on less professionally oriented staffs and working in a more confrontational style (such as the Public Interest Research Groups and Greenpeace). And still others pursue a means and an end that differs significantly from the rest of the field. For example, Earth First!, with its goal of promoting zero economic and population growth through ecosabotage, differs dramatically from The Nature Conservancy, which seeks to protect the environment through an integration of environmental and economic concerns. Furthermore, the attention of these groups has evolved through various temporal cycles (Downs, 1972), reaching a peak in 1970, declining in the 1980s, and growing again in the 1990s (Dunlap, 1991). And finally, the meaning and values of this environmental movement have evolved in substance.

In reviewing the work of several prominent researchers (Colby, 1989; Dowie, 1995; Egri and Pinfield, 1994; Gladwin et al., 1995), this chapter presents a model for illuminating the historical substantive progression of environmentalism, its present configuration, and future trajectory. To begin, Colby presents an initial template of five fundamental (what he calls) "paradigms" of environmental management—frontier economics, deep ecology, environmental protection, resource management, and ecodevelopment. His categorization overlaps in large part with the three

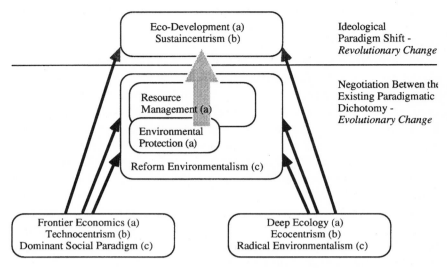

FIGURE 2.1. EVOLUTIONARY PARADIGMS.
Terminology utilized by (a) Colby (1989); (b) Gladwin et al. (1995);
and (c) Egri and Pinfield (1994).

ideologies provided by Egri and Pinfield (1994)—dominant social paradigm, radical environmentalism, and reform environmentalism—and the
three ideologies provided by Gladwin et al. (1995)—technocentrism, eco-
centrism, and sustaincentrism. The resulting combinant model, shown in
Figure 2.1, depicts schematically the nonlinearity of ideological evolution. The progression in time from one ideology to the next is depicted
vertically, with the horizontal scale indicating the upper ideologies' positions on a spectrum between the two "diametrically opposed" paradigms
(Colby, 1989:6). Movement through the components of reform environmentalism represents the evolutionary change that results from the political compromise of social movement dynamics. The lines represent existing evolutionary ties and the hypothesized future of revolutionary change
to a new paradigm that eases the tension between the contemporary ideological dichotomy.

Contemporary Paradigm Dichotomy

Frontier Economics

The initial paradigm of the model "frontier economics" is a term developed by economist Kenneth Boulding (1966) to describe the prevailing
beliefs within industrialized countries from the time of the scientific rev-

olution until the late 1960s. This is not an "environmentalist" paradigm per se but rather the "dominant social paradigm" (Catton and Dunlap, 1978; Daly, 1991) of industrialized society—the status quo against which environmental perspectives are compared (Egri and Pinfield, 1994). Fundamentally, it is a "technocentric" view that nature is both an infinite supply of physical resources (raw materials, energy, water, soil, and air) to be used for human benefit, and an infinite sink for the by-products of the development and consumption of these benefits, in the form of pollution and ecological degradation (Gladwin et al., 1995).

Frontier economics has as one of its fundamental assumptions the anthropocentric view that unlimited progress is possible through the exploitation of nature's infinite resources. Consistent with the frameworks developed by the philosophers of the scientific and industrial revolutions (such as Bacon, Descartes, Newton, and Hobbes), humans are considered separate from and superior to nature, which is itself viewed as an inert machine, infinitely divisible and moved by external rather than internal forces (Gladwin et al., 1995). Going further, Ellul (1964) argues that in this dominant social paradigm we ourselves have become mechanized "technicists," thinking only in an analytic, efficiency-oriented fashion and bound by systematic, instrumental rules.

Deep Ecology

Diametrically opposed to frontier economics is the "deep ecology," "radical environmentalism" (Egri and Pinfield, 1994), or "ecocentric" (Gladwin et al., 1995) paradigm. This paradigm draws from many schools that comprise a common ideology that nonhuman nature has intrinsic value and that economic advancement should be foregone for harmony with nature (Devall and Sessions, 1985). Each of the various environmental philosophies that make up this paradigm—such as spiritual ecology (Fox, 1990), social ecology (Bookchin, 1990), ecofeminism (Merchant, 1980), and bioregionalism (Dassman, 1976; Leopold, 1949)—advocates social and biological arrangements in which there is a balance between the interests of humanity and the interests of nature (Egri and Pinfield, 1994:4). A fundamental assumption of this worldview is that humans are not separate or superior to nature but rather occupy an equal place within the entire natural system.

Paradigmatic Conflict

The struggle between these dichotomous paradigms leads to profound questions. We view ourselves as wrapped by the environment or somehow above it? Is it "man [sic] *and* nature or man *in* nature" (Dowie, 1995:224).

Is the ecosystem to be protected from destruction for its own sake or to enhance the welfare of the human beings who depend on it (Commoner, 1990)? Are we capable of understanding the full complexities of the natural ecosystem so as to manage it to our own purposes? Or is it so complex as to be forever beyond human comprehension? Issues such as these form the basic ideological conflict that establishes the roots of the environmental movement.

Reform Environmentalism: Evolutionary Change

As a response to this ideologic conflict, evolving philosophies have emerged at the intersection of the two opposing philosophies. Egri and Pinfield (1994) lump them together as "reform environmentalism" while Colby (1989) differentiates them into "environmental protection" and "resource management." Contrary to the clarity of the initial two paradigms, these intermediate philosophies are more obscure conceptually because they represent the current state of flux and change in human society regarding the natural environment (Egri and Pinfield, 1994). They are not completely distinct "species" but rather have significant overlap in their basic assumptions about the relationship between man and nature (Colby, 1989).

Environmental Protection

The first reform philosophy, environmental protection, emerged in the early 1960s with the publication of *Silent Spring* (Carson, 1962). During the successive three decades, it has evolved through increasingly prescriptive levels of focus, although the fundamental approach remains fixed on the idea of repairing or setting limits on harmful industrial activity. It has not focused on planning development activities in ways that do not pollute or impair necessary ecological functions, or that facilitate ecological functions while simultaneously taking advantage of them (Colby, 1989). Instead, the philosophy of environmental protection has been a modest variation on the frontier economics paradigm. Impacts of excess environmental depletion (resource exploitation) or insertions (pollution) are treated as externalities to the economy (Colby, 1989). Models such as total quality environmental management, industrial ecology, and environmental economics are attempts to solve traditional environmental management issues by bringing the constraints of the physical environment into the dynamics of the business environment.

But this makes the assumption that there is a fit between the two. Some argue that there is not (Schnaiberg, 1980; Gladwin, Freeman, and Kennelly, 1994), that these models do not fundamentally change the social rules that are causing the environmental problem and therefore will not affect their ultimate result. The environment remains external to the economy. It is internalized through the application of norms and rules based principally on human utility as defined by a discrete set of social actors. As a result, nonhuman entities and the natural environment are excluded from the decision-making rubric, while social interests such as government, environmentalists, corporations, and the general public are included in organizational decision making (Egri and Pinfield, 1994). In this way, the dynamics of environmental protection become largely that of a political power struggle among competing interests.

Resource Management

The philosophy of resource management is both a substantial change from and natural extension of the environmental protection paradigm, but it remains a variation on the frontier economics paradigm. In this next progression, all types of capital and resources—biophysical, human, infrastructural, and monetary—are included in national accounts, productivity, and development planning (Colby, 1989). This approach counters frontier economics' rejection of the idea that natural resource exhaustion is a matter of concern. Pollution is now considered a "negative resource" rather than an externality. Long-term sustainability of resource use and development activities is emphasized, based on an appreciation of the interdependence of human activity and the environment.

In its present manifestation as sustainable development (Brundtland, 1987), this paradigm has developed, in theory, both a social (socioeconomic) component and a technical (ecoresource) component (Gladwin, 1995). In terms of the former, social sustainability requires the severing of links between environmental degradation and economic activity in the developing world (Hart, 1995). In terms of the latter, technology becomes the key to accomplish its goal. Social and environmental sustainability are inseparable. "What we call man's power over nature turns out to be power exercised by some men over other men with nature as its instrument" (Lewis, 1953:35). "The question must always be asked, for whom and from whom is it being protected" (Schnaiberg, 1980:5).

This social component of sustainability creates challenging complexities. In terms of application, most industrial actors will offer substantial resistance to policies that promote genuine sustainable development. In its present form, the concept of sustainable development allows governments and industry to "embrace environmentalism without commitment" (Jacobs, 1993:59). The ideology of the technocentric paradigm remains intact in the pursuit of scientific and economic progress. Its present manifestations are the result of an extension of the political power struggle over environmental protection. The approach remains anthropocentric at its core. It involves no paradigm shift but rather continues the evolutionary process, promoting variants on the dominant social paradigm.

As presently defined, sustainable development has become not an ideology but rather a tool or mechanism. It is treated as merely a set of actions, a selective set of strategies driven by the standard social, economic, and institutional mechanisms. All concern for nature is based on the fact that hurting nature is beginning to hurt economic man (Colby, 1989). The widespread perception is still one of trade-offs between environment and development. In effect, it has become "green" technocentrism (Gladwin et al., 1995:17). As presently emerging, "concern for the environment no longer implies that one is antidevelopment; in fact sustainable development depends on it. The neoclassical imperative of economic growth is still the primary goal of development planning, but criteria of sustainability are viewed as necessary constraints" (Colby, 1989:19).

Sustaincentrism/Ecodevelopment: Revolutionary Change

Permanently resolving the tension between the frontier economics and deep ecology paradigms will require revolutionary change. This will push norms and beliefs toward a new and as yet unrealized paradigm, what Colby (1989) refers to as "ecodevelopment" and Gladwin et al. (1995) refer to as "sustaincentrism." It will involve a discontinuous shift in thinking and practice geared toward restructuring the relationship between human society and nature.

> The earth is to be seen neither as an ecosystem to be preserved unchanged nor as a quarry for selfish and short-range economic reasons, but as a garden to be cultivated for the development of its own potentialities of the human adventure. The goal of the relationship is not the status quo, but the emergence of a new phenomena and new values.
>
> (Dubos, 1976:462).

Such a paradigm would be based on restructuring the economy to accommodate ecological principles, a shift from "economizing ecology to ecologizing the economy" (Colby, 1989:23). Economic growth would be redefined to include concerns for information intensiveness, community consciousness, and the experiential quality of economic activity rather than merely its material-energy intensiveness (Daly, 1991). Human societies would be conceived neither as totally desegregated from nor totally immersed in nature (Gladwin et al., 1995). They become both part of the biosphere in organic and ecological terms and above the biosphere in intellectual terms.

Out of this shift emerges both a societal respect for the objective value of nature and an acceptance of the role of steward of nature. Is there a conflict in this duality? Can we become stewards of the environment while lacking the knowledge necessary to understand the system as a whole? Without such knowledge, can we maintain the environment for its own sake, or will we continue to employ our own value system in evaluating its worth? The answer may lie in what Leopold (1949) refers to as the "intellectual humility" necessary for appreciating the complexity of nature. Humans "have become, by the power of a glorious evolutionary accident called intelligence, the stewards of life's continuity on earth. We did not ask for this role, but we cannot abjure it. We may not be suited for it, but here we are" (Stephen Jay Gould, as cited in Calvin, 1994:107).

Should the movement evolve to the ecodevelopment or sustaincentric paradigms, it would likely occur through a fundamental paradigm shift in which earlier dichotomous paradigms and their fundamental tensions would be eliminated. In such a transformation, the environmental movement would no longer have meaning or relevance as it is presently conceived. No interest group has meaning except with reference to other interest groups (Olson, 1965). Their identities are defined by their preferences for changing some elements of the existing structure of a society (Zald and McCarthy, 1987). It is founded on the differentiation between the social movement and the society in which that movement exists (Zald and Garner, 1987). Originally, the group identity for environmentalism was founded in terms of its rejection of the institutional mismanagement of resources by the modern state and economy (Buttel, 1992). In a shift to ecodevelopment that distinction is reconfigured. Instead of a struggle between a social movement and society, the struggle becomes one between society and itself, between the established system of how society is structured and the unintended environmental results which that system creates.

The social constituency behind environmentalism will become increasingly indeterminate and abstract. For one, the natural environment will become part of the negotiation process through an appreciation of the bounds created by its social and technical complexity. For another, the human constituency will transcend traditional alliances and include broad blocks of society. With labor groups, community groups, and even stockholders pressing for environmental change, the issue can no longer be divided into the traditional "pro" and "con" camps of a social movement.

Such is the natural outcome of the environmental movement. Unlike the ideologies of civil rights, the women's movement, or the labor movement, environmentalism has never had a natural constituency or bearers. "Opposition to environmentalism on the grounds of threatened material interests or aversion to state intervention would be easier to explain than environmental advocacy" (Buttel, 1992:14). These surrogates do not seek individual gain but gain that is shared among all, including those who oppose it.

This indeterminism represents society's shift from "wealth-distributing" to "risk-distributing" (Beck, 1992). The effects of a degraded environment, diminished resources, and a depreciated future are decreasingly based on conventional social strata, but instead transcend wealth and class structures. As a result, the social positions and conflicts of class stratification are joined by those of risk stratification (Beck, 1992). However, this new form of class structure remains unquantifiable. In Marxist writings, class identity was determined by how people stood in relation to the mode of production. Workers could see their collective class and identify their inequities by looking to their right or left in the assembly line.

A collective identity based on environmental risk will be increasingly difficult to identify. Environmental risks are nondiscrete, diffuse, and open to scientific and social interpretation. Therefore, those who are impacted by those risks will be equally nondiscrete, diffuse, and open to scientific and social interpretation. Although specific localized environmental issues such as abandoned hazardous waste sites or urban pollution can allow the loose affiliation of residents who perceive themselves to be at risk, broader environmental hazards such as food pesticide residues, acid rain, nuclear power, and ozone depletion defy such unification.

With the continued endangering of nature, health, nutrition, and so on, social differences will be increasingly spread across society. Over time, "risks display an equalizing effect within their scope and among those affected by them" (Beck, 1992:36). In "a social boomerang effect," the agents of modernization themselves are caught in the hazards that they "unleash and profit from" (Beck, 1992:36). In this circularity of social endangerment, the perpetrator and victim sooner or later become identical. Thus, contrary to the inherent structure of a social movement, there is no conflict between the "affected" and the "nonaffected" (Beck, 1992). Rather than creating new class divisions, ecodevelopment will foster a "one-class" or "classless" society, in which all are affected. This indeterminacy is important in that it represents broad social norms rather than individual blocs and so becomes a more pervasive legitimating force that will impact broadly on cultural structures and corporate strategy.

It is the transformation of these cultural structures that will form the foundation of a new paradigm. Evernden writes, "the crisis is not simply something we can examine and resolve. We *are* the environmental crisis. The crisis is a visible manifestation of our very being, like territory revealing the self at its center. The environmental crisis is inherent in everything we believe and do; it is inherent in the context of our lives" (Evernden, 1985:128). To come to terms with this realization, Leopold called for "an internal change in our intellectual emphasis, loyalties, affections, and convictions" (Leopold, 1949:210). Ecodevelopment will involve the social reconstruction of our fundamental values, effectively forcing an alteration of our basic social structures (Evernden, 1992), through both the adjustment or rediscovery of existing values, norms, and schema and the creation of new ones.

In regard to the former, finding inherent value in the environment and acknowledging a responsibility to future generations is not inconsistent with existing values of equity and justice. The fundamental values themselves remain unchanged. It is our consciousness of their full significance and applicability that changes, a cognizant realization of these existing values taken to new levels. Equity and justice now apply to actions the effects of which were previously believed to be isolated. The power plant emissions of one region serve an injustice to the forests and people of regions on which its acid rain falls. The extraction of oil, water, and other resources from the earth today serve an injustice to the perceived needs of future generations. In light of this new cognitive context, we are faced with a reaffirmation of existing values and beliefs through an adjustment in the conceptual framework of our value systems.

Beyond the adjustment of existing value systems, ecodevelopment also presents new beliefs, values, and norms. Our newfound ability to alter the global environment forces a reexamination of how we value the environment and what our role is in interacting with it. In evolving to the sustaincentric paradigm, we acknowledge that we are to become the stewards of the world ecosystem. Our social structures and technologies must be altered to ameliorate and avoid the environmental problems they create. Such a fundamental ideological shift is akin to, for example, the social construction of freedom in early Western culture (Patterson, 1991) or the emergence of self-interest as a guiding value for human behavior (versus obligation to the general welfare), forming a necessary foundation for modern capitalism (Hirschman, 1977; Buttel, 1992).

As in any value shift, the development of a new value system will conflict with the dominant structures in place. New paradigms are slow to emerge and, when first articulated, are usually fought by established interests (Kuhn, 1970). In this case, sustaincentrism becomes, at its core, a critique of modern capitalism. (Or, rather than capitalism alone as the sole destroyer of the environment, it represents a new value-set for which no broad social, political, or economic structure—such as socialism—has accounted.) Empowering the environment within our social and technical structures challenges the ability of capitalism, in its present form, to provide societal goals (such as prosperity, equity, leisure, satisfaction) for the long term. It does not question these social ends but rather the core assumptions believed to get us there: the social and physical autonomy of the firm, the profit motive as a singular objective of the firm, and the necessity of economic growth (Daly, 1991; Daly and Cobb, 1994; Gladwin et al., 1994). The emergence of an ethical (normative) sense that we must become stewards provides the impetus for action and change and requires a rethinking of the intellectual basis for action and education.

The needs of nonsocial actors (such as the environment and future generations) show up only in action through the interpretation and language of existing players. They will remain a social construct. So what is important is how the fundamental social cultural codes incorporate the world as meaningful and normative. This is the fundamental core of the transition from the current dichotomy to the new paradigm that will replace it. The outcome cannot be viewed in strictly environmental terms but rather in a systemswide viewpoint. The perspectives we employ to view our relationship with nature are central to our social conceptions of economic and material growth. To change the former must also change the latter. Rather than environmentalism being viewed as a basis for dismantling capitalism, it becomes a motivation for the search for altered forms of capitalism. Its effects are not so broad as to suggest a condemnation of all supporting values of capitalism but rather to selectively alter, augment, and restructure specific components.

The Contemporary Context

Where we are on this continuum and where we are going is open to considerable debate. Colby (1989) argues that three globally based conditions will provide the necessary force for a synthesis or convergence to the ecodevelopment paradigm: (1) an unprecedented degree of threat from global changes in the ozone layer and climate issues, (2) widespread problems of resource depletion/degradation, and (3) an easing of the military and ideological competition between the superpowers allowing for a redefinition of "security" and redeployment of resources for its achievement (Colby, 1989:31). Schnaiberg and Gould (1994) argue that we will forever lack the motivation or intellectual sophistication to evolve beyond our existing dichotomous social structure unless some cataclysmic event forces a significant adjustment.

Regardless of these necessary conditions, environmentalism has a present trajectory that is pointing toward some new reality. The assumptions of reform environmentalism are breaking down because of their ineffectiveness in dealing with the negative consequences of their foundation, the dominant social paradigm. Environmentalism continues to introduce completely new conceptions of technology and economic development to society. Fundamentally, these include a reexamination of the ethics employed for their assessment (Jonas, 1973).

Shifting the anthropocentric structure of our social systems challenges the preeminence of technological development (Piller, 1991), science, and economics (Capra, 1982). Even our religious conceptions, whose alteration Leopold (1949:210) saw as a necessity for changing society's "foundations of conduct," are undergoing change, driven initially by the 1986 Assisi Declarations, an agreement of the five world religions to begin to attend to environmental concerns (Rockefeller and Elder, 1992). More recently, the Presbyterian Church placed environmental concerns into the church canon in 1991, making it a sin to "threaten death to the planet entrusted to our care" (Associated Press, 1991), and the Catholic Church added environmental concerns to its new catechism in 1992 (Woodward and Nordland, 1992).

The present thrust of environmentalism challenges traditional ways of thinking about societal and industrial activities, including conceptual models of organizations that inform and direct those activities. Yet the emerging conceptions are in considerable flux (Colby, 1989). The lack of harmony and homogeneity among environmental organizations reflects a degree of social discord within the movement (Lowe and Goyder, 1983; Olson, 1965). The present state of environmentalism is open to wide interpretation. Such diversity in definitions is to be expected during the emergent phase of any potentially big idea of general usefulness (Gladwin et al., 1995). As Kuhn (1970) noted, new paradigms tend to emerge from entirely new fundamentals and, at first, without a full set of concrete rules or standards. Over time, as their rhetoric, norms, and objectives become more clear, the movement should solidify into a powerful whole and drive toward a common goal.

Evolving Conceptions of Corporate Environmentalism

While the impact of a new ecodevelopment paradigm will yield organizational forms not yet known, the transformational effects of reform environmentalism are becoming visible. The values it embodies have grown in directions completely tangential to traditional conceptions of the firm's objectives and practices. Companies and other institutions are doing strange things these days that cannot be explained on the basis of the standard models of behavior without some stretch. Reform environmentalism has incrementally challenged our technological, economic, and social conceptions of corporate behavior.

For example, the conservation movement of the early 1900s challenged the taken-for-granted assumption that the environment had no inherent value beyond human utility, while simultaneously threatening the absolute of property rights. No longer considered a private possession to be used in any fashion the developer saw fit, a country's natural resources now were coming under a primitive form of community control. Next, the ecology movement of the 1960s exposed scientific links between human activities and the stability of the ecosystem, challenging the firm's autonomy from nature. The imperfections of waste management in the 1970s began to cast doubt about the ability of business to properly manage the environment. Their taken-for-granted freedom of using the environment as a waste sink was challenged, thereby bringing the autonomy of corporate activities (in terms of pollutant effluents) under scrutiny. Pollution prevention and the right-to-know movements of the 1980s took this one step further by bringing industrial processes under the auspices of community oversight, thus challenging the goals of our production systems. And most recently, product stewardship of the 1990s challenges both production and consumption models, threatening the previously autonomous corporate decisions regarding raw material use, process design, and product considerations, not only of the producer but also of the supplier and the user.

Reform environmentalism also challenges our economic conceptions of the firm. It is altering the core objectives of the firm and the basic conceptions of production by which that objective is achieved. Other prominent social issues such as race, gender, or labor relations deal with equity and the fair distribution of opportunity and wealth. Although the resolution of these issues will create winners and losers, the total economic output should remain the same. These issues bear directly on the aggregate output of an economy.

Environmentalism produces a different outcome. Efficiency as measured by conventional indices will generally be adversely affected by the introduction of control measures. The net benefits will be positive, but since many benefits are not counted in the regular calculus, the individual bottom line may be negative (Ehrenfeld and Hoffman, 1993). But, as these indices are altered to incorporate proper consideration for the natural environment (such as green accounting and life cycle analysis), economic conceptions of the firm's objectives will alter.

The dynamics of such a fundamental shift in the objectives and economic measures of a firm's success ultimately must be accompanied by a shift in the social conceptions of the firm and its relationship to the environment (Hoffman, 1997). This has both an external and internal component. Externally, firms are finding themselves responsible to a widening group of influential stakeholders. Such complexity distinguishes environmentalism from other socially defined issues. In settling issues of labor relations, managers negotiate with workers and union officials; in settling issues of civil rights or gender equity, female or minority workers and national organizations are set up to represent them. But the emerging environmental constituency includes government, insurance companies, investors, activists, employee groups, community groups, the press, consumers, competitors, trade associations, and financial markets. Emerging conceptions of "enlightened self-interest" (Marsh, 1965) signal a change in the very notion of "self" to include the field of actors (Hoffman, 1997). Interacting with such a wide range of interests has necessitated new structures and internal conceptions of the firm's organization and purpose. The boundaries of the firm become blurred.

Some blurring of organizational interests is already becoming visible as companies are forging voluntary alliances with environmentalists and the government to identify new mechanisms for lessening their impact on the environment. For example, McDonalds entered into a partnership with the Environmental Defense Fund to research ways to reduce solid waste. The Dow Corporation is creating citizen advisory panels at all of its plants. Many companies voluntarily joined the US Environmental Protection Agency's (EPA) 33-50 Program, agreeing voluntarily to reduce the emission of specific chemical contaminants. And, in a more unusual event, environmental groups recently sided with the American Petroleum Institute and against the US EPA in a successful effort to overturn mandatory use of methanol in emission-reducing gasoline formulations. The distinction between *pro*-environmentalist and *anti*-environmentalist is muddled.

Internally, the effects can be seen both culturally and structurally. Firms are finding that as environmental values take hold at the deepest levels of societal structures, it becomes increasingly necessary to include those values in their corporate cultures or risk creating value systems that are dissonant with those of their employees (Hoffman, 1993). The resulting alteration in structure can be seen in basic changes within the organizational framework. CEOs today are espousing the benefits of proactive environmental management while instituting programs for community relations, product stewardship, pollution prevention, and environmental leadership as being consistent with the objectives of increasing shareholder equity (Smart, 1992). A 1991 report by the Conference Board showed that 77 percent of US companies now have a formal system in place for proactively identifying key environmental issues, noting that "social responsibility" ranked second out of five most important factors motivating environmental policy decisions (Morrison, 1991:18). More broadly, the evolution in organizational structure has been multifaceted to include (1) an evolution of the environmental management function from buffering the operating core to maintaining a boundary-spanning function, (2) an alteration of the overall structure of the firm whereby environmental responsibilities diffuse from the periphery to the internal core, and (3) an alteration of the corporate culture from one that views environmental management as an external threat to one that acknowledges its impact on all operations of the company as a defining factor in its ultimate success (Ehrenfeld and Hoffman, 1993; Hoffman, 1994).

The effects of these evolving conceptions are not universal across industries. Environmentalism tends to impact firms and groups of firms differently, further differentiating it from issues such as affirmative action and gender equity, which cut across industries with relative uniformity. Some industries, such as oil and chemicals, face greater challenges in both the measurement and the control of hazardous emissions and in the social validity of their choice of raw materials, products, and processes. In much the way that population ecologists (Hannan and Freeman, 1977) view organizational survival as resting on shifting social expectations, it may be that the technical challenges of environmentalism will decide which firms survive and which perish. Or, in terms of corporate strategy (Porter, 1980, 1985) or resource dependence (Pfeffer, 1982), it may be those firms that successfully adapt to the changing business environment that will survive.

Conclusion

Evolving conceptions of corporate environmentalism demand new conceptions of management education. The models on which this education is based provide perspectives on reality, both explicitly and implicitly. They help to understand accepted ends and goals and guide actions in achieving them. Without alteration, management education will continue to create environmental problems as they are now understood. Present management theory tends to promote the need for increased productivity and economic growth, the perception of nature as a limitless sink, and the superiority of technological solutions while excluding "nature, the poor, and the interests of future generations from any notions of community, blindly professing the separation of organizations from biophysical reality and support systems of logic (such as profit and growth imperatives) that lead inexorably toward ecological and social deterioration" (Gladwin et al., 1994:42). Transforming management theory and practice so that they positively contribute to an understanding of emerging environmental paradigms is a challenge academia must address if it is to remain relevant. If models of corporate behavior do not include serious concerns about environmental survival as more than simply another factor to be added to the economic calculus or the political environment, then it is likely that survival within the economy will depart quickly from survival within the ecosystem.

Existing models should not be viewed as obsolete, to be discarded and replaced by a new set of ideas and theories. They must instead be adapted, bringing them closer to a realistic understanding of the behavior of the firm. This adaptation will manifest itself in a holistic approach to understanding corporate behavior (Egri and Pinfield, 1994). Environmentalism lies at a unique juncture of the physical and the social sciences, incorporating components from a wide group of disciplines, such as sociology, organizational behavior, political science, economics, management, engineering, science, and ecology, as depicted in Figure 2.2. This positioning offers valuable opportunities to bridge gaps among differentiated fields. An encompassing understanding of corporate environmentalism requires an integration of the philosophies and theories of each of these disciplines. It is this integration that will exemplify the resulting theoretical base from which corporate environmentalism must, by necessity, be studied.

The efforts that management schools have made thus far to integrate environmental issues into their programs can be categorized into three groups that represent an evolutionary perspective: (1) the formation of joint degrees, termed the "extension" approach; (2) the integration into existing course curricula, or the "infusion" approach; and (3) the creation of environmental majors or electives, called the "depth" approach (Jubeir, 1995). However, to the extent that environmentalism becomes revolutionary in nature and impact, an overall restructuring of the educational curriculum will become a necessity. New cultural structures will require fundamentally new ways of approaching the firm, as has been the case with total quality management (TQM), lean production, information technology (IT), and other forces for change.

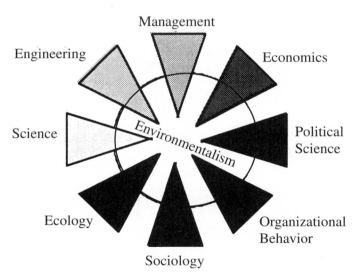

FIGURE 2.2. THE CROSS-DISCIPLINARY ASPECT OF ENVIRONMENTALISM.
Source: Hoffman (1997:184).

Environmentalism offers an opportunity to improve the academic theories by which we define the behavior of the firm, research its behavior empirically, and teach its behavior in the classroom. The role of management research and then education will be to explain both the impact of contemporary environmental manifestations and the future possibilities and consequences of a new environmental paradigm. Ultimately, as the ecodevelopment paradigm begins to materialize, environmentalism will merge into the cultural foundations of both the corporation and the fabric of the management school. It will be implicit in the theories and structures of the organization. No longer will dedicated departments or dedicated classes be necessary. Environmental concerns will become ingrained in every discipline so as to disappear from the conscious and become part of the unconscious (Hoffman, 1996).

In short, a fundamental generational shift is underway. Just as we may view the environmental norms and practices of yesterday's generation as primitive and naive, future generations will look in wonder at the wasteful environmental practices we maintain today. Where we view such practices as disconnected from other aspects of organizational life, they will view them as inseparable.

Chapter 3

Toward Sustainable Production and Consumption: A Conceptual Framework

Richard Welford, William Young, and Bjarne Ytterhus

Appropriate tools for the improvement of the environmental performance of companies is the subject of much debate. We have seen the introduction of environmental management systems and their associated standards, environmental auditing and reporting, and tools focusing on the environmental performance of products such as life cycle assessment. These have been most often applied to manufacturing industries and to tangible products. However, if our aim is sustainable development, there is now a need to go further than simply addressing the environmental performance of companies. This chapter addresses the issue of corporate responsibility in the context of sustainable development. It questions the appropriateness and efficacy of contemporary corporate environmental management tools alone and investigates ways in which all businesses can better respond to the demands of the sustainable development agenda.

This chapter contributes to the debate about useful frameworks and measurement systems that provide meaningful information to stakeholders. We do this by extensive reference to literature on environmental and sustainable development frameworks, recognized approaches to measurement and indicators of sustainable development, and some literature on social auditing. From this we derive a workable framework that can be used to track progress toward operations consistent with sustainable development and to engage in stakeholder dialogue.

The ideas presented here are equally applicable to product and to service provisions. We put particular emphasis on services, partly because service provision is an underdeveloped and under-researched area of the corporate environmental management and sustainable development debate. There is increased interest among firms in moving emphasis away from the supply of products toward the provision of services, of which the product may be a part. This shift of emphasis often assumes that service provision is likely to be less environmentally damaging. While this may be the case, we see little reason why it should necessarily be a better means to progress toward sustainable development.

Businesses find the concept of sustainable development hard to operationalize. A recent European survey of the world's more environmentally advanced companies' reactions to the emerging issue of sustainable development provides some conclusions (Bebbington and Gray, 1996):

1. Most companies have yet to fully examine the nature of sustainable development and its implications for current business practice. The vast majority of companies are treating sustainable development as an (implicit) extension of environmental management.

2. While companies do not appear to have fully embraced all the ecoefficiency implications of sustainable development, they do seem sensitive to and supportive of the ecojustice elements of the concept.

3. Much clearer guidelines must be given to businesses worldwide on the possible implications of sustainable development for business activities.

4. Conflicts arising from the constraints implied by sustainable development are more likely to occur in accounting/performance-centered and large organizations than value-centered and smaller or decentralized companies.

5. The use of life cycle assessment and/or the ecobalance approaches to analyzing the company's interaction with society and the environment seems to offer considerable, valuable promise.

6. The central message about the assistance that accounting systems and measurement frameworks can provide to companies addressing environmental issues has not yet been fully received.

Eden (1994) suggests that public trust in the environmental information provided by business is weak. This does not mean that the demand for environmentally marketed products and services will decline, but it does mean that businesses must do more to provide the information consumers and other stakeholders need for more informed judgments. This becomes more important with the move toward the provision of goods and services that have characteristics consistent with sustainable development. More significantly, public distrust may contribute to social and political pressure for more wide-ranging and strengthened social and environmental regulations and voluntary standards, as a means to ground legitimacy of business actions.

We take the view that it is important to give firms and their stakeholders an indication of how they can contribute to bringing about a society based on the principles of sustainable development. Our assertion is that it is possible to define a set of principles by which the firm can assess and track progress. This requires an examination of the activities of the firm that are consistent with moves toward sustainable development, in a wide sense, and the translation of those activities into a measurement and reporting framework. This approach emphasizes the connections between firms and implies the need to give attention to sustainable development in terms of sustainable production and consumption within a supply chain framework. Thus the chapter considers definitions of sustainable development at the firm level, measurement, reporting, and dialogue instruments, and then presents a framework that can be used by companies to monitor their performance and report to their stakeholders.

Sustainable Development, Sustainable Production, and Sustainable Consumption

The Importance of Both Production and Consumption

The aim of this chapter is to derive a conceptual framework capable of defining activities at the firm level that are consistent with a move toward sustainable development. We do that by considering both sustainable production (which we use as shorthand for production activities consistent with a move toward sustainable development) and sustainable consumption (similarly, shorthand for consumption activities consistent with a move toward sustainable development). In many parts of the service sector artifacts are often not produced; nevertheless, the term "production" is commonly understood to stand for the development, definition, and provision of a service or product.

Our approach also emphasizes the need for a two-way flow of information with stakeholders. Clearly, many different stakeholders are involved in a complex process to define these terms precisely. According to the World Business Council for Sustainable Development:

> Sustainable production and consumption involves business, government, communities, and households contributing to environmental quality through the efficient production and use of natural resources, the minimization of wastes, and the optimization of products and services.
>
> (WBCSD, 1996:10)

This is a narrow definition since it falls into the (common) trap of equating sustainable development only with environmental quality. We would argue that sustainable development (because it is a "development" concept) should focus on quality of life and that a better definition might be that sustainable production and consumption is:

> ... the use of goods and services that respond to basic needs and bring a better quality of life, while minimizing the use of natural resources, toxic materials, and emissions of waste and pollutants over the life cycle, so as not to jeopardize the needs of future generations.
>
> (Norwegian Ministry of the Environment, 1994)

Salim (1994) agrees with this approach because it emphasizes future generations as well as present ones and goes further in suggesting that:

> Sustainable consumption implies that the consumption of current generations as well as future generations improves in quality. Such a concept of consumption requires the optimization of consumption subject to maintaining services and quality of resources and the environment over time.
>
> (Salim, 1994)

As outlined above, a useful approach to operationalizing sustainable production and consumption is to consider it as a function of supply-side activities and demand-side activities:

> The emphasis of sustainable production is on the supply side of the equation, focusing on the improving environmental performance in key economic sectors, such as agriculture, energy,

industry, tourism, and transport. Sustainable consumption addresses the demand side, looking at how the goods and services required to meet basic needs and improve quality of life—such as food and health, shelter, clothing, leisure, and mobility—can be delivered in ways that reduce the burden on the Earth's carrying capacity.

(Robins and Roberts, 1997)

Sustainable production is viewed here as production that is economically, environmentally, and socially responsible. Moreover, "economically responsible" can be defined as both economic for the producer (i.e., profitable) and for those involved in the production process (i.e., in relation to fair wages, employment, and so on). Another useful definition of sustainable production is as follows:

To produce less of higher quality and durability with much lower environmental and social impacts at higher levels of employment, while making an acceptable profit or surplus.

(Welford, 1997)

The implication is that we should make fewer "throwaway" goods and more products and services of quality that will last longer and create less waste. In this way reduction, reuse, and recycling are less important than durability. But a fundamental part of sustainable production is to increase levels of employment. Here, the argument is simple. The search for ever increasing efficiency and lower costs has led companies to continue to substitute capital for labor. It is anticipated that this process is likely to generate social upheaval, led by those who are unemployed and disenfranchised from society, before it provokes an environmental crisis of similar proportions. We have already noted that labor is becoming less competitive as capital productivity increases. But this capital productivity is essentially being subsidized by the erosion of environmental capital, such as energy over consumption due to energy costs that do not reflect the true environmental costs of the resource. If energy (and therefore capital) costs accurately reflected these true costs, then a switch back to labor usage would occur, increasing employment and reducing environmental damage.

The word "production" can be quite misleading. When we talk of production we mean the creation of something new. Production is about changes in the state of things: One substance or form is converted into another. Thus production is really about conversion, and any creation that takes place must be associated with destruction. In this way production is viewed as a destructive process and takes on a much more negative connotation. This does not mean that all production should cease, but that production is only justified when the value of the things produced outweighs the value that is destroyed in the process. This links to the concept of product justifiability (Welford, 1996), where companies might be expected to consult with a wide range of stakeholders about the needs and costs of a product, using information from full life cycle assessments and supply chain initiatives.

Sustainable production needs to be matched with sustainable consumption, if the outcome is to be effective. More sustainable consumption requires individuals as well as businesses to accept responsibility for their lifestyles and consumption patterns. This implies a co-responsibility of producers and consumers for the social and environmental consequences of their collective behavior. There is nevertheless a role businesses can play through education. Perhaps more than any other institution in the world, business has direct communications with millions of people—its consumers. Linking marketing with education and campaigning is capable of influencing people in a more direct way than any educator or individual campaigner could hope for. We return to the issue of education, below.

Frameworks for Firm-Level Definitions of Sustainable Development, Production, and Consumption

Here we review a number of attempts to derive frameworks to guide business in adopting practices consistent with a move toward sustainable development. The intent of this review is to pull together common strands that define an overarching approach around which consensus can be developed. However, the frameworks themselves should provide the reader with ideas about the characteristics for choosing appropriate indicators of performance in specific sectors. Ten frameworks with prominence in the literature are reviewed. However, as the literature on the social aspects of sustainable development (as opposed to environmental ones) is relatively underdeveloped, some of the frameworks deal only with environmental issues.

The Norwegian Ministry of the Environment (1995) suggests that companies need to strengthen their environmental efforts by putting emphasis on supply chain initiatives, including procurement procedures and sales service provision. It also recognizes the issues associated with relationships between companies and developing countries as an important part of the sustainable development agenda. In terms of services, the ministry's work suggests that enterprises in the financial sector—banks and insurance companies—should incorporate environmental risk and ecoefficiency criteria and goals into assessments and management of their services. These should be conducted for personal and business consumers. Enterprises in the retail and distribution sectors should assist their customers through the provision of accurate information on the environmental impacts of goods and services and about the facilities available for materials recovery, recycling, and reuse. They should use their position in supply chains to influence the supply of environmentally sound goods and services.

Redirecting and reframing corporations for social sustainability, according to Gladwin et al. (1995), demands strong transformational leadership within both governments and corporations. Here the emphasis is on organizational change, empowerment, ethics, learning, and education. It is accepted that there is a need for clear measurement systems and performance frameworks. But there is also an interesting emphasis not only on reporting performance to stakeholders but also actively influencing them—making them more supportive of an organization's sustainable development behavior. This requires a commitment to two-way communications and the development of real dialogue.

Van Someren (1995) emphasizes forward planning in terms of time horizons and integrating issues such as the disposal, recycling, and reuse strategies for products. Although this approach is strongly oriented toward products, its emphasis on long-term planning horizons and supply chain management is equally applicable to the service sector.

According to Starik et al. (1996), research has shown that designing and skillfully acting on strategic plans are often keys to organizational effectiveness. "Seat of the pants" management has often been found to be a characteristic of mediocre or failed businesses, so the sensible strategic manager typically goes through a process, or set of steps, to construct and then carry out plans.

Shrivastava and Hart (1995) place great emphasis on the need for the firm to have a clear mission or vision. They see that the deep change toward sustainable development requires the firm to have sustainability as a corporate purpose. Such a strategy must go further than "Band-Aid" approaches, with their emphasis on end-of-pipe technology and pollution prevention. They also propose a framework that goes beyond more usual

approaches (termed "more serious"), which see environmental stewardship as a core value. They place emphasis on development in the South,
full cost accounting procedures, and stakeholder integration where sustainability is a key performance indicator.

Welford (1997), in discussing a number of frameworks, suggests a
three-dimensional approach to achieving sustainability in the business
organization by examining impacts on *people* (a broadly social dimension), the *planet* (broadly environmental), and *products* (taken to include
goods, services, and profits as useful outputs). It is possible to see the
whole purpose of the sustainable business revolving around these three
P's. The main objective of a business is to make a range of *products*
and/or provide services in a way that generates profits. But this is done in
the general context of having to work with a range of *people* through
employment, supply chain linkages, and as customers, using the basic
resources of the *planet* as the material foundation of these activities. The
aim, then, is to maximize the benefits within this sort of activity while
minimizing the negatives.

Rydberg (1995) takes a broad life cycle approach. He argues that the
company can more easily consider its social, environmental, and other
obligations. Thus life cycle assessment (LCA) covers long-term environmental needs. Life cycle cost (LCC) describes and assesses the economy
of the product using a life cycle perspective that covers the economy of
the product (the production phase or, in terms of services, the provision
stage) and the customer (use phase). Quality function development
(QFD) assesses the requirements of the user in relation to the extent that
the product fulfills functional (and other) needs, generally known as
"quality." These three methods are complementary in covering requirements of the customer, the producer, society, and the environment. This
framework can also be used in the service sector to address the service
needs for the customer, society, and the environment. Like previous models it goes beyond a simple analysis of the production stages (or service
provision stages). It requires the firm to think about, and assess, the full
life cycle of the product or service—demanding effective supply chain
management. It implicitly pulls together various stakeholders in some
degree of two-way communications.

Callens and Tyteca (1995) provide a framework made up of
performance indicators at various levels. Their approach considers four
categories of indicator. The first three are economic indicators, social
indicators, and environmental indicators. These are perhaps the most
commonly used in the literature on sustainable development. Welford

(1997) also talks of the need for measures in the area of environmental performance, social performance, and economic performance. Often these are integrated into an overall assessment of sustainable development. However, Callens and Tyteca (1995) argue that these only take into account particular aspects of sustainable development, which should incorporate all three kinds of considerations. A fourth category is also considered—overall sustainable development indicators. Until now, these have been developed mainly at a global level—the level of the state or country. There is clearly a need to consider what types of firm-level behavior are appropriate here in terms of records of sustainable development.

Stead and Stead (1992) argue that sustainable development should be a core value in any business organization, because it supports a strategic vision of firms surviving over the long term. Firms do this by integrating their need to earn a profit with their responsibility to protect the environment. This vision demonstrates the interconnectedness of economic success and the health of the ecosystem, with the organization seeing itself as part of a greater society and natural environment to which its survival is tied.

In another framework advocated by Welford (1997), he proposes a model that combines the work of a number of other authors, bringing together many of the issues discussed in the frameworks outlined above. This model has the advantage that it places more emphasis on social and ethical issues than many of the earlier approaches. This is consistent with the need to address the social dimensions of sustainable development as much as the environmental ones. It is based on six E's consisting of the environment, empowerment, economics, ethics, equity, and education. A firm contributing to sustainable production should have a position based on a clear policy and agenda for change that covers these six areas.

The model is essentially a "policy in, reporting out" approach, where the activities of the firm are transparent. In other words, business is expected to have a policy in each of these six areas, to operationalize that policy using the indicative tools that are suggested, and then to report on progress. Like all the models presented here, no firm will be able to produce a perfect profile in all six areas (even if that could be defined). Reports should detail progress in each element and demonstrate a degree of continuous improvement. They should also point to areas that still require attention and produce objectives and targets for the next reporting period.

Measurement and Reporting

Measurement Frameworks

All the frameworks discussed above need to be operationalized. It is not sufficient to present them to businesses without some idea of how they might be used. The frameworks lend themselves to the use of indicators so that progress toward sustainable development might be operationalized. In other words, the areas where the firm should be active need to be matched by measurement and reporting tools so that progress toward the firm's sustainable development policies is open, transparent, and capable of being assessed by various stakeholders.

James and Bennett (1994) discuss the measures of environment-related performance—why measure, what is measured—by current approaches, and finally they suggest how to measure. They recommend a continuous-loop model consisting of eight stages to define and measure environment-related performance (see Figure 3.1). This general approach can be extended to our framework of sustainable production and consumption.

The first stage defines the environmental context and objectives and states the organization's impact on the environment. Potential measures, including priority areas, are identified in the second stage. Step three selects the measures on the basis of their appropriateness to purpose, cost-effectiveness, comparability, and compatibility with other measures. Step four establishes the current position of the firm in relation to its environmental impacts so that targets can be set and the feasibility of achieving them assessed. The fifth stage involves the establishment of the system to measure, collect, and report the information against targets. It is important that the targets are communicated to the relevant staff and stakehold-

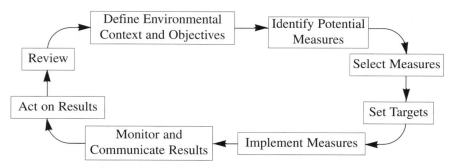

FIGURE 3.1. A CONTINUOUS LOOP OF STAGES OF ENVIRONMENT-RELATED PERFORMANCE MEASUREMENTS.
Source: James and Bennett (1994): 92, 93.

ers, and that staff are empowered and resourced to achieve the targets. The results are monitored and communicated in the sixth step. The results may have to be verified internally and externally if they are to have any credibility with stakeholders. The seventh stage acts on the results, including identifying what changes are needed to improve the measures and results. The final and eighth stage reviews the overall performance measurement system, establishing whether it works satisfactorily and whether there are new areas where measurement is necessary. The process continues through stage one and back to the review, advancing the measures of environmental performance. In effect this is an application of the usual continual improvement loop.

The current version of the ISO 14031 guidelines scheduled to be released in 1999 incorporates these stages and can be extended to include all sustainable development issues identified above. The definition currently being adopted by ISO for Environmental Performance Evaluation (EPE) is a:

> . . . process to select environmental indicators and to measure, analyze, assess, report, and communicate an organization's environmental performance against its environmental performance criteria.

> (ISO, 1997:5)

The scope of the EPE guidelines on the design and the use of EPE describes the process of EPE. It gives examples of environmental performance indicators for illustrative purposes only. The guidelines, however, do not establish environmental performance levels and are not intended for use as specification guidelines for certification/registration purposes. In the same way, it is not our intention to define precise sustainable development indicators; these are most appropriately done at the industry level. However, this general approach can be applied to some sort of sustainable development framework.

The ISO 14031 guidelines are aimed at all organizations regardless of type, size, location, or complexity. The process involves three stages—namely planning, evaluation, and review and improvement—emphasizing the importance of management commitment.

Performance Evaluation and Stakeholder Involvement

The purpose here is to outline the framework that companies might eventually use to provide a detailed and transparent policy and reporting system to demonstrate moves toward sustainable development, rather than to outline detailed performance indicators. At the industry level, however, there may be some useful benchmarks that firms and their stakeholders can agree on. While it is considered that the people working in a particular sector are best able to research and advocate the most appropriate measures for moves toward more sustainable forms of development, the literature we have reviewed places considerable emphasis on stakeholder involvement in this process. The process by which companies involve stakeholders in sustainable development performance evaluation is therefore important.

The approach proposed is consistent with the social audit outlined by Jones and Welford (in Welford, 1997). It is referred to here as a *sustainable development dialogue* since it focuses on firms' responses to sustainable development and engages stakeholders in that process. The rationale behind the approach acknowledges that a wide constituency of interests has a right to information. Firms engaging in a sustainable development dialogue are conceived as being at the center of a network of social relationships that are articulated in a manner akin to a stakeholder model. Put another way, social auditing recognizes the concepts of stewardship and accountability, and this in turn acknowledges that the whole of society has rights to information about actions taken on its behalf (for example, by businesses). The sustainable development dialogue process allows business to engage with its stakeholders (representing, in part, societal interests), listen to and respond to their views, and, where necessary, explain and justify its actions. But it is not only a one-way flow. Businesses are also able to influence their stakeholders so that the ultimate outcome is derived from consensus.

The important point to stress is the importance to a sustainable development dialogue of an over-arching and explicit values framework written in terms of corporate values, visions, aims, and objectives. This is important because it provides the basic parameters for the ongoing dialogue between the various stakeholders and management. A similar point about the connection between organizational values and a process of values referenced through alliances, collaborations, and networks of stakeholders is made by Roome (1997a). An explicit values framework avoids the anarchic flaws of this type of "accounting receptivity." In other words, it avoids a business degenerating into an unmanageable scramble of values, multiple aims, and multiple measures of performance (Roome, 1997b). In this way a firm can provide a sustainable development direction to its activities. To measure the organization's sustainable development performance, not only is stakeholder performance measured against core values but also company performance against stakeholder values. Figure 3.2 represents a stakeholder consultation model. It shows the two-way flow of learning and accountability necessary to fully realize the virtues of a pluralistic strategy: The company reports to, and learns from, its stakeholder, and stakeholders are invited to assess the organization's performance and aspirations. The company is also able to influence its stakeholders, particularly where its own aspirations may be higher than some of its stakeholders.

This sustainable development dialogue is operationalized through the three assessment loops depicted in Figure 3.2. At the center of the assessment process are the core values of the organization, made explicit in the organization's values framework, which is published and made widely available. The extent to which the organization is perceived to adhere to

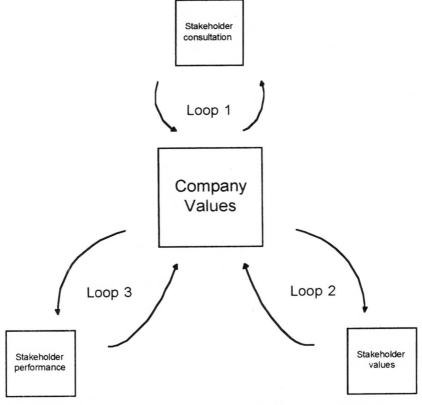

FIGURE 3.2. THE SUSTAINABLE DEVELOPMENT DIALOGUE PROCESS.

these core values is determined through consultation with a range of stakeholders and (often key) informants (expert opinion, publicly recognized figures). Where company performance is perceived to be poor, it will be either because that action really is poor or because the organization has not communicated its performance accurately or effectively. In both cases, action to improve performance (or its communication) is required. This may oblige some alteration of the organization's values framework. This process is represented by Loop 1.

At the same time, the organization can compare its own core values with those of its stakeholders (Loop 2). The process defines stakeholders' values (again through consultation) and then compares the organization's performance against these values. Where necessary (because gaps or deficiencies are identified), core values can be reassessed and the values framework rewritten.

The third loop involves action to influence stakeholders through the assessment of stakeholder performance against core values. Here, we may find the situation where the organization considers its values to be superior to those of its stakeholders. Through education and campaigning initiatives, the organization takes action to influence stakeholders. Stakeholders influence the organization through their perceptions of company performance based on its values (Loop 1) and through an assessment of performance based on stakeholders' own values (Loop 2). The organization, in turn, tries to influence stakeholders through an assessment of stakeholder performance against its own core values (Loop 3).

Supply Chain Management

A number of the models referred to earlier consider the need for life cycle assessment and supply chain management. We recognize the need to see sustainable production and sustainable consumption as embracing supply-side and demand-side issues. One of the most useful strategies to include in our analysis is supply chain management. Here, it is seen as the responsibility of the producer (service provider) to manage downstream activities, where the purchasing function may provide for significant power, and to influence upstream activities, where there may have less power but where, nevertheless, choices can be influenced through marketing, campaigning, and education initiatives.

The notion of "negotiated" social and environmental improvement along supply chains is very important and arises from the growth in inter-corporate dialogue on a range of different priorities. Reflections of well-documented cases of effective supply chain management can be found in studies of companies from a variety of industrial sectors. These ideas have been promoted in the UK by the Chartered Institute of Purchasing and Supply and Business in the Environment to encourage environmental awareness among corporate buyers and to assist with the complex issue of integrating environmental issues into purchasing (Morton et al., 1997).

Table 3.1 provides reasons for adopting supply chain management techniques and offers guidance for the introduction of environmental aspects into purchasing decisions. However, the move toward sustainable development will require these techniques to be extended to incorporate the social and ethical aspects of development, and to put more emphasis on the management and influence of demand for the product or service in question.

TABLE 3.1. PRINCIPLES OF BUYING INTO THE ENVIRONMENT

1. Understand the business reasons	Examine the implications of legislation, market opportunities and pressures, supply chain risk, community needs.
2. Know your environment	Understand environmental responsibilities, policies and issues, improvement targets and programs.
3. Understanding your supply chain	Rank key suppliers based on environmental issues and risks. Develop environmental purchasing policy and processes.
4. Adopt a partnership style	Communicate openly and clearly. Explore areas of cooperation for mutual benefits.
5. Collect only information needed	Identify key questions and define information needs. Select suitable collection methods.
6. Validate supplier's performance	Select, where necessary, a suitable method to validate information and management systems.
7. Set a timetable for improvement	Discuss and agree on improvement targets with environmental managers and suppliers.

Source: Green, Morton & New, 1996.

A Conceptual Framework for Sustainable Production and Sustainable Consumption

The basic framework we choose to adopt is based on the six E's approach advocated by Welford (1997). It encompasses many of the elements of the frameworks for environmental management and sustainable development at the firm level. However, the framework is extended in two ways. First, although Welford (1997) previously placed employment within the *economy* dimension of the framework, a number of commentators see this as so fundamental to any move toward sustainable development practices that it is added to the framework as a seventh "E." Second, and more fundamental, the framework developed by Welford (1997) is rather static. Many commentators make reference to the need for a more dynamic model consistent with product stewardship and life cycle assessment. Consequently the issue of supply chain management is introduced into the model.

Here the seven E's are described in more detail:

Environment

The environment is to be protected with minimum use of nonrenewable resources. Environmental performance will be monitored and measured using an environmental management system with a regular audit activity. Products will be assessed according to a life cycle assessment and redesigned where practicable to reduce environmental impact. Products will be subject to a functionality assessment to determine whether there is a better way of providing the benefits of the product. There will be strong connections along the supply chain to integrate all stages of the product's life. After production, firms will, as far as possible, manage the use and disposal of the product through product stewardship procedures. Much emphasis will be placed on local action, including close connections with local community initiatives and protection of the health and safety of all employees and neighbors.

Empowerment

Everybody must feel part of the process of improvement and must be empowered to recognize and act on their own obligations as well as working together closely with colleagues. There will be strong participation in the workforce with respect to decision making, profit sharing, and ownership structures. The organization will be open to new suggestions made by anyone in the workforce, and workers will be rewarded on the basis of contribution to this overall ethos as well as work done. Human capital will be valued, and workers will not be treated as simple factors of production. There will be enshrined rights within the organization relating to equal opportunities and individual freedoms. Diversity will be encouraged, not stifled.

Employment

It is impossible to imagine a sustainable society where there were not high levels of employment (and low levels of unemployment). It may be that working practices will change, but it is, in part, the responsibility of firms working within the capitalist system to provide people with the means to increase their quality of life. This can only be done by ensuring employment opportunities, at fair wages, in clean and healthy working environments. New technology needs to be designed to be job enhancing rather than job displacing. Nevertheless, as has already been noted, labor is uncompetitive compared with capital cost and productivity within the prevailing systems for taxation, and firms will need help from governments to implement high employment policies.

Economy

The economic performance of the firm will be sustainable in that it will provide the conditions for ongoing survival. Profits or surpluses are important as the payment of dividends to shareholders. However, financial audits will be extended to include a justification of profits made and a demonstration that they have been made through good business practices rather than cost-cutting exploitation. There will be periodic new investment both in physical capital and in human capital (through education and retraining). Business relationships should be mutually advantageous to all parties concerned, so that supply chain stability is possible. Jobs are a central part of sustainability, and the provision and growth of employment is to be encouraged. Products made will be of good quality, durable, and suitable for the purpose for which they were intended.

Ethics

Organizations will have a clear set of values which they will publish and periodically reassess through the social audit process. The firm will at all times be honest and will be open to questions about its ethical stance, providing evidence relating to any activities being challenged. Its activities will be transparent, and relations with subsidiaries, contractors, and agents will be clearly identified. Ethics are not something an organization simply declares. They must be translated into practice via codes of conduct, education, communication, and information. Businesses serve a variety of purposes for different stakeholders. Therefore, business activities are only justifiable insofar as they can be shown to meet the legitimate requirements of stakeholders.

Equity

Issues of equity exist both within and without the organization. Closely linked with empowerment issues, there must be clear statements of rights and equal opportunities within the firm. Trade along the supply chain must be equitable, particularly with regard to international trade. There must be assurances for workers in developing countries, for indigenous populations, and for human rights. End-price audits of goods, through which a product's final price is broken down into an analysis of who gets what share of that price, are immensely valuable. This information can be used to demonstrate, for example, that subsistence wages paid to the poor in Third World countries are not the whole basis for the product's provision. The distribution of the benefits of product (or service) provision must be seen as just. Where appropriate, the firm will be involved in wider development initiatives through technology and know-how transfer, sponsorship, charitable donations, and the provision of development aid to partners in developing countries.

Education

Education is at the root of the sustainable development process. We will make little progress unless we can communicate the challenge of sustainable development and educate people to live in a more sustainable manner. Every business has to accept that it can be an educator because of its close links with both employees and customers; it should be providing suitable information and education to anyone working for it or purchasing its products and services. The firm can also be involved in community initiatives, wider public campaigns, and part of the process to raise awareness, more generally. It can work closely with campaign groups and nongovernmental organizations through general cooperation, more specific sponsorship, and the support of staff. The firm is capable of bringing about much more sustainable consumption.

The seven E's approach therefore provides a set of ideals that a company can work toward. It contains a number of values and issues too commonly ignored in business; in many respects this approach challenges business to accept a much wider responsibility for its actions. The starting point is simply for management to think about these issues and, through interaction with the workforce, to produce policy statements in each of the seven areas. However, that must be followed by concerted action as the business seeks out the road toward sustainability.

Integrating the supply chain into the model is done by recognizing that sustainable production and consumption is made up of supply-side and demand-side issues. In managing sustainable production, therefore, we need to consider not only the practices of the firm but its relationships with other firms in the supply chain. We call this supplier pressure. Equally, it is important to promote sustainable consumption by influencing choice and managing the provision of services and products. It is important to be clear here. It is not possible to manage the services consumers demand; the best that a firm can do is to influence consumers' choices. However, in the case of service provision, the firm is more able to manage the process because ownership of a service is rarely transferred. This approach is summarized in Table 3.2.

As a starting point the company should be clear about its commitment to each of the 28 areas defined in the matrix in Table 3.2. In effect, what was referred to earlier as the vision of the company should be made explicit through its stated policy.

The operationalization of the framework should be based on three stages—planning, evaluation, and review. This is consistent with the approach taken by James and Bennett (1994).

Planning

- Define the environmental context in terms of the objectives consistent with moves toward sustainable development in the 28 areas identified in the matrix in Table 3.2.

TABLE 3.2. A FRAMEWORK FOR SUSTAINABLE PRODUCTION AND CONSUMPTION

Sustainable Production and Consumption			
Supply-side issues Managing sustainable production		Demand-side issues Influencing sustainable consumption	
Supplier pressure	Own practices	Influencing choice	Managing provision
Environment			
Employment			
Economics			
Empowerment			
Ethics			
Equity			
Education			

- Consider the appropriate potential measures, including priority areas, for the industry under consideration.

- Select the measures by their appropriateness to their purpose, cost-effectiveness, comparability, and compatibility with other measures.

Evaluation

- Evaluate the current position and set feasible targets.

- Implement the measures through systems that collect and report the required information and communicate this to the relevant staff and stakeholders.

- Monitor and verify results and communicate this in an appropriate way to ensure credibility with stakeholders.

- Act on the results, including identifying what changes are needed to improve the measures and results.

Review

- Review the overall performance measurement system, establishing whether it works satisfactorily and whether there are new areas where measurement is necessary.

- The process should then continue, starting again at stage one, with the aim of continual improvement.

At the same time, the measurement framework should be defined and reported on to allow for the sustainable development dialogue advocated above. This means seeing the policy as central to the vision of the company and using it, together with the results of the evaluation stage set out above, to create meaningful dialogue with stakeholders.

As Gray (1994) argues, the impact of this information on the stakeholder constituency and their response can be assumed to encourage the new practices necessary for sustainable development. If accountability and transparency are embraced, then the corporation will find itself more closely in tune with its wider constituents and the company will develop its culture on the basis of an awareness of different stakeholder expectations and needs. But this is by no means an easy process. Trade-offs will have to be made if sustainability is to be pursued.

Conclusions

Moving business practices so that they are consistent with the attainment of sustainable development is a huge challenge. In many ways it represents such a fundamental change in the values and visions of companies that it cannot be expected to occur quickly. Nevertheless as firms and their stakeholders see that the challenge of sustainable development is fundamental to the survival of the planet, so we will see more effort placed on procedures that can reflect the needs inherent in such a challenge.

As businesses accept the need to plan their operations in line with principles of sustainable development, they will look for useful frameworks they can adopt. This chapter proposes a framework to bring that transformation about. It is derived from the literature on corporate environmental performance and sustainable development strategies. It is based on three main elements: a framework for building a vision of sustainable development at the corporate level, which integrates supply chain management in ways that reflect the need for both sustainable production and sustainable consumption; a measurement framework based on the idea of continuous improvement; and a process of sustainable development dialogue that involves two-way communications between firms and their stakeholders.

It is acknowledged that much remains to be done. This framework needs to be tested by different firms in different sectors. This will almost certainly lead to further refinements to the approach. The framework also needs to be used to define benchmarks, or minimum standards, at the industry level. Last, but not least, the framework needs to be used in ways that create transparency and openness between a firm and its stakeholders so that real dialogue can map out a workable and effective transition toward business practices more consistent with sustainable development. We believe that this conceptual model is potentially able to deliver the promise of significant change toward sustainable development.

Part II

THE CHARACTER OF
THE EMERGING PARADIGM

Chapter 4

A Dinosaur's Survival Kit–
Tools and Strategies for Sustainability

Andrea Spencer-Cooke

In the history of the world, only two species have held dominion over the planet: dinosaurs and humans. One is now extinct and the other is fighting hard not to come to the same end. Several million years of evolution have equipped us with unlimited creativity and inventiveness. Yet looking at the way certain industry sectors are approaching sustainability, it is hard to believe anything has changed. As globalization gathers momentum and innovative companies reposition themselves, the challenge for industry is to devise a survival kit of tools and strategies for sustainability.

Beyond Environmental Management

Environmental management systems (EMS) are limited in what they can achieve. If every company in the world adopted the EU ecomanagement and audit scheme (EMAS) or ISO 14001 tomorrow, we might have a cleaner environment but we still would not be sustainable. Clearly, the quest for sustainability will require other tools. But what should these tools and strategies look like?

It will take well into the next millennium to get the majority of organizations to effectively manage their environmental performance. With environmental management only just beginning to find acceptance in the world of business, it may seem premature to be talking about sustainability—and ridiculous in the extreme to try to define a set of tools for managing something we have not even properly defined.

Sustainable development represents an entirely new paradigm for industry and will require profound changes in processes, outcomes, and perspectives. In particular it will call for new types of interaction and greater interdependence among actors at different levels. Looking beyond environmental management is not meant to detract from the importance of implementing and developing environmental management systems and strategies. This is a valuable step toward sustainability. But it is useful to start thinking about where we should be heading in charting the course from environmental management and reporting to sustainability management.

Managing sustainable development in an effective way is our long-term goal. In what will be a burgeoning world of 8 to 10 billion people, this may seem an impossible task. Most people have great difficulty envisioning the shifts that will be necessary to create such a sustainable world. Faced with the scale of the challenge, the pace of progress seems pitifully slow. We could draw a useful analogy with the medieval stonemason laying the foundations of a cathedral. He probably would have had no idea of what the final building would look like. It would be finished long after his death and the plans might change several times in the course of construction. Yet hundreds of years later, the stones he laid will support the finished structure.

Today, we cannot hope to know what the sustainable world of tomorrow will look like. Worse still, today's solutions may well become a part of tomorrow's problems. But within the limits of today's knowledge, we can lay the foundations for a sustainable world. A key place to start is in exploring the territory between environmental management and sustainability.

Sustainability Is More Than Environmental Performance

The first step toward managing sustainability is to recognize that it is more than environmental performance. Environmental performance is a critical part of what we could call *ecological* sustainability, but even this is only part of a more complex, interrelated system that includes socio-economic concerns. As with any system, there are limits, or thresholds. The sustainability challenge lies in striking a balance between these various parts of the whole, within the boundaries of the system. And striking a balance will inevitably mean some trade-offs between the various parts.

Confusing environmental improvement with sustainable development results in a very partial picture of the sustainability challenge. Throughout the United Nations Conference on Environment and Development (UNCED) and in the resulting *Rio Declaration* and *Agenda 21*, the international community emphasized that sustainable development is not about the environment alone but also about development, and that sustainable development requires the integration of environmental and social components into economic decision making.

Environmental performance is singlefold, sustainability is threefold. Put simply, it is helpful to think of environmental performance as part of a triangle made up of social, environmental, and economic considerations, or as the UK consultancy SustainAbility puts it, a "triple bottom line," on which sustainability depends. The aim is for organizations to "stay in the black" and add value in each of the three areas. If an organization were, over the medium to long term, "in the red" against any one of these three parameters, it could not claim to be sustainable.

Environmental management systems put strong emphasis on issues such as ecoefficiency and cleaner production but do not really deal with the question of social impacts, the third side of the triangle. Nor, for that matter, do they effectively deal with life cycle considerations and *indirect* socioeconomic and environmental effects. Moreover, as environmental managers know only too well, there are compromises to be made: What might be beneficial from an environmental point of view could be economically damaging—endangering the survival of the company. Arguably, then, any system or set of tools for dealing with sustainability needs to take into account not only *ecological* sustainability but also *economic* viability and *social* acceptability.

Sustainability is complex and systemic. While focusing on the site or organization may be important from a managerial perspective, it is secondary from an ecological and societal perspective—and can be misleading. The ecological "bottom line," when it comes to environmental quality and the sustainability of natural resources, is the ambient environmental quality standard (EQS), such as, for example, the pollution concentrations in a river. If several companies emit wastes into a shared environmental "sink" such as a river, the main issue from an ecological perspective is the total pollution resulting from the combined activities of those companies. If one company improves its environmental performance but that of the other companies deteriorates, environmental quality as a whole will still decrease. The individual company may be moving in the right direction for greater ecological sustainability, but this is collectively irrelevant if the resource ends up being destroyed by the combined actions of the companies sharing it.

The "sustainability" of a company can only be defined in the light of the behavior of the rest of the system. Sustainability management tools therefore need to take into account the behavior of the system, through use of EQS and indicators, and must catalyze cooperation between companies to protect shared resources. For example, this could involve an industrial park not only applying the concepts of industrial ecology but drawing up a "communal" environmental management strategy based on local EQS and incorporating global ecological priorities such as global warming, ozone depletion, and acidification.

Sustainability requires trade-offs. If you could have gotten close enough to ask the dinosaurs whether they were happy being wiped out so that mammals could thrive and replace them at the top of the animal hierarchy, I'm sure they wouldn't have seen it as a particularly attractive solution. Likewise, the extinction of certain industry sectors will herald the emergence of a new generation of more sustainable businesses—but it won't happen without a struggle.

What sort of tools would dinosaurs have dreamed up if they'd had an inkling of what lay in store for them? No doubt about it, their vision of sustainability—not unlike the behavior of many industry sectors today—would have been one in which dinosaurs, not mammals, continued to roam the earth, playing top dog—or dinosaur—with as little interference in their ways and habits as possible. But with inherently unsustainable industries such as those based on nonrenewable fossil fuels, fertilizer-intensive monocrop agriculture, or chlorine, a choice must be made: Evolve and adapt or become extinct.

From what little we know, dinosaurs became extinct—or unsustainable—not as a result of their own behavior but because of changes beyond their control in their surroundings, in their external environment. What humans face, however, is a situation where, in addition to any external changes that may take place, it is our own behavior that is making the external environment unsustainable. The primary cause of unsustainability is our actions, *within* our control.

The real issue here is that seriously addressing sustainability means empowering ourselves to change our behavior, making compromises, and accepting trade-offs. So a good set of sustainability tools will help people to weigh a situation, take different perspectives into account, and reach innovative decisions with some form of compensation for the inevitable trade-offs involved.

Last but not least, sustainability is global in space and time. Moreover, it is dynamic. Setting out to "achieve" sustainability is a bit like seeking the elusive state of economic "equilibrium," the nirvana of neoclassical economists: It rarely, if ever, exists—and when it does, only fleetingly. As modern physics shows, natural systems thrive in a state of chaos, only occasionally, by accident, slipping momentarily into what can be described as order or equilibrium. What these systems achieve is rather many different equilibriums—or "sustainabilities"—that vary over time and space and involve the various components of the system in differing ways. Sustainability management systems therefore have to be able to harness an organization's ability to learn, respond, adapt, and reinvent itself. And they need to be flexible, to cope with constantly changing variables in a dynamic environment.

We have seen that sustainability is more than environmental performance in a number of ways. Tools for managing it will need to reflect this broader agenda. Drawing on the discussion above, Table 4.1 presents

TABLE 4.1. CHARACTERISTICS OF A SUSTAINABILITY MANAGEMENT SYSTEM

Sustainability Challenge	Sustainability Management System Characteristics	Potential Models
More than environment	Integrated, threefold, triple bottom line approach	• Social/environmental accounting • Fair trade indicators and criteria • Valuation of intangible assets (e.g., intellectual capital) • UNDP Human Development Index
Systemic nature	Inter-firm cooperation and incorporation of indirect effects	• Indicators and environmental quality standards (EQS) • Industrial ecosystems • Just-in-time manufacturing (JIT) • Ecological footprints

(continues)

TABLE 4.1 (*Continued*)

Complexity	Flexible, open-ended problem definition, and systems inter-relationships	• Computer modeling • Biology and ecology • Physics • Life cycle assessment (LCA)
Trade-offs	Empowerment, enabling dialogue, facilitating compromise, and ensuring compensation	• Labor relations • Stakeholder partnerships • Game theory • Intellectual property rights
Multi-perspective	Inclusive approach, harnessing diversity, and engaging stakeholders	• Environmental and social reporting • Tomorrow's Company code of conduct • Shell consultation policy
Global and dynamic	Innovation, shared vision of the big picture, learning, relativity	• Sustainability scenarios • Learning organization theory • Total quality management (TQM) • Social anthropology
New attitudes	Value-based, long-term approach based on equity, governance, and minimizing dissonance	• Workers' rights • Abolition of slavery • Race relations • EU Social Chapter

some of the characteristics that will be required of a sustainability management system, along with potential models that we can draw on in designing a new generation of instruments.

Systemic thinking tells us that sustainability can only be defined for a complete socioeconomic–environmental system and not for its component parts. No person, company, or nation can *achieve* sustainable development alone, in isolation from others, since their actions can affect our sustainability just as we can affect theirs. However, it does make sense on a micro level to speak of individual *progress toward sustainabilities*. To measure progress, indicators are required and, critically, a vision of what is actually being sustained.

What Are We Sustaining?

Dinosaurs and mammals have different ideas of how a sustainable world should look. Any group's or individual's perspective on sustainability will vary according to their values and priorities. But it will always be built around their own survival—or the ascendancy of the cause or ideas they represent.

Widely accepted definitions of sustainability, such as that of the Brundtland Commission Report (1987), do not provide much *operational* guidance that can be used in developing policies or management systems to cope with the sustainability challenge. So although people may agree that strategies should aim to meet the needs of the present generation without compromising the ability of future generations to meet their own needs, they are unlikely to agree in detail on what these needs are, or on which are the highest priorities when it comes to the inevitable stage of making trade-offs. This does not mean that sustainability has no meaning but rather that it has many meanings. Different groups in different times and places will have different ideas about *what* needs to be sustained and *how* best to sustain it. Thus, for example, sustainability could be interpreted to mean the sustainability of a service, a company, an industry, or the biosphere and human community. The issue of what should be sustained and the strategies and actions needed to achieve this will vary widely according to the perspective adopted. Sustainability management tools therefore require a set of visions—or scenarios—to help visualize and articulate what should be sustained and how.

Sustainability Scenarios

In his bestseller *The Fifth Discipline*, Peter Senge (1990) describes the importance of shared vision as a driver of innovation and learning. The sustainability transition is a shift of paradigm that will require entire industries to be rethought and restructured—and some to be phased out altogether as new ones spring up in their place. The ability to learn and innovate is therefore a critical aspect of this transition. But how can we develop a shared vision of sustainability to drive this innovation?

The use of sustainability scenarios was pioneered by European Partners for the Environment (EPE), a nonprofit organization set up in 1994 at the joint initiative of the European Environmental Bureau (EEB), business, public authorities, and environmental nongovernmental organizations (NGOs). EPE's mission is to facilitate dialogue and stimulate cooperation between all sectors concerned with the EU Fifth Environmental Action Program by serving as a model for constructive dialogue and action in partnership for sustainable development. The wide range of interests and perspectives represented by EPE's membership made it critical to explore members' similarities and differences in trying to develop a shared vision of sustainability.

In two consecutive reports, EPE, alongside SustainAbility Ltd. and Environmental Strategies Ltd., drew on cultural theory to develop three sustainability scenarios, described below, presenting very different visions of a sustainable world (EPE/SustainAbility, 1994 and 1996). The purpose of these scenarios is not to predict the future but rather to prepare stakeholders for a range of possible futures and help them understand better the values and objectives of partners who hold different visions of sustainability.

Scenario 1: No Limits

This vision emphasizes sustainability at the level of individual needs, wants, and quality of life. Technological innovation and free markets play a crucial role in creating new opportunities and meeting needs more effectively, while at the same time reducing environmental and social impacts. Key terms include rapid change, technological innovation, adaptation, no limits.

In this scenario, sustainability management would:

- Help companies improve profitability by improving environmental and social performance

- Catalyze innovation and spur new ideas

- Make markets work more effectively

Scenario 2: Orderly Transition

The second scenario places less emphasis on the market as a mechanism for delivering sustainability, recognizing the need for government intervention and guidance. Problems are tackled by regulating production and consumption patterns. Sound science and careful assessment of costs and benefits are used to select priorities for policy intervention. Key terms are stewardship, managerialism, targets, steering, negotiation, optimization, carrying capacity.

In Scenario 2, sustainability management would:

- Test compliance through audited and comparable data

- Provide feedback for policy and control mechanisms

- Collect information for tackling emerging problems.

Scenario 3: Values Shift

This sustainability vision contains a sense of urgency and calls for a significant, immediate shift to sustainable lifestyles with much lower social and environmental impacts. Products are screened to see whether they meet real needs, and society plays an active role in defining visions and ensuring that behavior, values, and attitudes change. Key terms are prevention, urgency, participation, harmony with nature, decentralization, equity, community, caring, spirituality.

Sustainability management here serves to:

- Provide full transparency to monitor companies' use of social and environmental space

- Ensure acceptable social and ethical performance

- Enable trust-building, dialogue, and partnership with stakeholders

All of these scenarios are possible, yet the most likely outcome will be one that combines elements of all three scenarios. These visions are intended to help people picture what sort of future they identify with. Once that picture is clear, it is easier to "backcast" to the present to determine what sorts of strategies and systems need to be developed to foster such a future.

Strategies and Systems for a Sustainable Future

Based on the sustainability scenarios described above, a broadly shared vision of sustainability management tools is shown in Table 4.2.

Table 4.2 is intended merely to paint, in broad brushstrokes, some of the wider requirements of sustainability management, as seen from three different perspectives. At the level of the individual company, we have already seen that it only makes sense to talk in terms of progress toward sustainability rather than achieving sustainability itself. Drawing on Table 4.2, the core requirements of sustainability management tools are to:

- Improve corporate performance against the triple bottom line (sustainability)

- Test compliance and provide feedback for policy and decision making (accountability)

TABLE 4.2. SHARED VISION OF SUSTAINABLILITY OF MANAGEMENT TOOLS

	No Limits	Orderly Transition	Values Shift
Role of Sustainability Management System	• Improve profitability and environmental and social performance • Catalyze innovation and spur new ideas • Make markets work more effectively	• Test compliance • Provide feedback for policy and control mechanisms • Collect information for tackling emerging problems	• Provide transparency on use of social and environmental space • Ensure acceptable social and ethical performance • Enable trust-building, dialogue, and partnership with stakeholders

• Ensure legitimacy in the use of socioenvironmental space (stakeholder governance)

The aims of sustainability management tools should therefore be to chart progress toward sustainability, to achieve full accountability, and to promote stakeholder governance.

Sustainability instruments should help us address the really challenging questions, such as how to effect the multiple-level changes necessary in the way human needs are defined and satisfied—and products and production systems are designed and operated. Most of these changes involve spaciotemporal dimensions that the current industrial mind is not accustomed to thinking about. And given the size of the human brain, that may not be surprising.

Among the quantum shifts that will be a part of sustainability transition strategies:

Product to Function: A reorientation away from selling quantities of products to selling quality of services, whereby needs are met through the diminishing physical transfer of goods and increasing emphasis on function. Example: A floor surfacing company that leases recyclable floor coverings to customers. When the surface is worn, fashion changes, or the need alters, the floor covering is retrieved, the material recycled, and the flooring replaced in line with the new requirements.

Factor 0 to Factor 10: An exponential reduction in the energy and raw material intensity of products and services, with a strong shift in favor of renewables. Example: Prototypes pioneered by Amory Lovins at the Rocky Mountain Institute for a "Hypercar," slashing the amount of materials and fuel needed to meet the personal transport function.

Global to Local: A shift away from the unrestricted global production, trading, and transportation of "mono"-products that can be made to equivalent standards locally, eliminating significant environmental risks and impacts and stimulating diversity and local economies.

North to South: An equitable redistribution of the share of global resources currently consumed by the industrialized countries, brought about through technological transfer, capacity building, and fairer trading arrangements. Example: Joint implementation (JI) initiatives that offset negative environmental impact in the North and compensate countries in the South for preserving rainforest resources of global value.

Present to Future: An opening out of time horizons from focusing narrowly on today to considering the medium and long-term picture. Example: Would nuclear fission technologies be considered a viable energy option if the long-term risks and costs of waste disposal were factored in?

More to Enough: A recognition that the endless expansion of choice and the satisfaction of needs through increasing material consumption have limits that will have to be respected in an ecologically and socially sustainable world. Example: Do I *really* need that third car, that latest piece of software? Can something be fixed rather than thrown away?

Cost to Value: The shift from narrow assessment of costs and benefits in financial terms to the inclusion of externalities and intangibles in calculating the benefit to society of a product, a service, or a course of action. The issue at stake becomes not merely the price of something but its *value* to society. Example: What has been the societal value of the re-engineering trend in companies?

These trends will be a leading force behind the sustainability transition. Our tools for sustainability should at the very least reflect the ethos of these trends and facilitate, rather than impede, the necessary shifts.

At the micro level, a management system for a sustainable future would need to address the full cycle of organizational activities from concept and design to procurement and production, to transportation, through use, disposal, and recycling, and back to concept. It is unlikely that a single management instrument could achieve this. What is required is a framework or system that integrates the various tools, such as EMS or life cycle assessment (LCA), that are already available. Within the company, this management system would be designed to boost performance against the three bottom lines and spur innovation, so that the company becomes its own competitor, reinventing itself before it is threatened with extinction. Beyond the company boundary, it would be designed to deliver the information needed for sound policy making and facilitate stakeholder engagement in sustainability management.

To be meaningful, though, company management systems need to slot into a comparable macro level sustainability management system. The company is accountable to society through reporting on its progress toward sustainability and demonstrating that its governance is effective. Maximum transparency at the micro level should produce comparable, user-friendly information for monitoring performance of the system as a whole, checking compliance, giving feedback on policy, identifying emerging problems, and assessing social and environmental impacts.

A further, critical aspect of sustainability management—at both micro and macro levels—would be to ensure that dialogue and partnership occur with stakeholders on all core sustainability issues, the setting of priorities, the agreement of performance standards, and the monitoring of progress. This stakeholder governance will ensure the legitimacy of the "sustainable" corporation and help build critical social capital.

Sustainability management systems will clearly need to be better integrated and more sophisticated than our existing systems, but does this mean we have to start from scratch? The experience gained with our existing management tools can serve as guidance.

Is the EMS a Good Model?

We have seen in Table 4.1 that to meet the various challenges sustainable development presents, systems for managing sustainability can be inspired by a broad range of possible models. The EMS may seem a logical starting point, but it has a number of inherent limitations that need to be considered.

First, the EMS is site- or organization-based, whereas sustainability management must be life cycle and strategy-based, taking in the full range of organizational impacts. Whereas the EMS focuses strongly on the effective functioning of systems, sustainability will require far greater emphasis on impacts and indirect effects. Environmental management is voluntary and improvement targets are set solely by the company: Managing sustainability will require implementation by all companies and far greater stakeholder consensus on what is an acceptable rate of progress. Finally, the EMS is exactly what it says it is—an *environmental* management system. Sustainability, as we have seen, has further socioeconomic dimensions that must also be incorporated.

In the work by EPE and SustainAbility Ltd., a "strengths, weaknesses, opportunities, and threats" (SWOT) analysis of the EU EMAS regulation was carried out (EPE/SustainAbility, 1996). Among the key issues raised:

- Do the benefits of an EMS outweigh the costs, and how can bureaucracy and paperwork be kept to a minimum?

- How do you draw the boundaries of the organization, and how can we ensure EMS compatibility with other instruments?

- Is there a danger of free-riders, and how can we ensure clear definitions and consistent interpretation of standards?

- How adequate are targets set by companies under a voluntary system, and how can we measure overall progress?

- How meaningful to sustainability are tools that emphasize performance, not impact?

- Where do we start in defining the responsibilities of industry versus those of other actors (such as financial markets, consumers, governments)?

In addition, the report concludes, EMAS was designed to fulfill two functions: an internal management tool and an externally visible indication of performance. So far, it has only played the former role. The scheme is voluntary, so its impact is inevitably restricted. The few EMAS Environmental Statements that have emerged are of little use to stakeholders. The information presented is patchy, often full of hype, and can't be compared with data from other companies. Moreover, EMAS is site-based and many stakeholders, such as financial analysts or investors, are interested in corporate-level information. EMAS is therefore failing in what the EU Fifth Environmental Action Program describes as one of its primary objectives: to be a performance appraisal instrument "as important as traditional financial accounts" (CEC, 1992).

The picture that emerges is that the EMS still has a steep learning curve to climb before it begins to fulfill its primary functions, let alone attempts to address sustainability. Making these tools work properly at the basic level should be our first priority. The review of the EMAS Regulation scheduled for 1998 provides an opportunity to address some of its shortcomings.

The starting point is better application. We already have at our disposal many tools which, if properly applied, could deliver significant progress against the requirements of sustainability. To name but a few in the environmental domain: EMS, Environmental Impact Assessment (EIA), ecolabels, LCA, Global Information Systems (GIS), EQS, ecotaxes, and environmental laws (such as waste and recycling, liability, Right-to-Know). In the social arena, widespread application of international labor standards and human development indices—not to mention industry codes of conduct—would be a good starting point. If major efforts were invested in ensuring that these tools were working together effectively, by adapting them in the light of practical experience, by improving communication and education, and by emphasizing the monitoring and punitive aspects of these instruments, the situation would be dramatically improved almost overnight.

EMS-Plus

The core principle behind the EMS—monitoring continuous improvement—is sound. But in the light of some of the limitations viewed above, beyond proper implementation there is also a need for continuous improvement of environmental management instruments themselves—a shift from EMS to "EMS-Plus." As experience grows and hindsight builds, it will be possible to adapt these tools to meet emerging requirements. Potentially, then, the EMS can be a good model for designing sustainability management instruments, providing certain other conditions are met by the organization.

Into the VOID

The strength of the EMS is in its potential to integrate the functions of other environmental instruments, such as LCA, EIA, and EQS, and ensure that they work compatibly. As a tool for continuous improvement, the EMS can be extremely effective, but its effectiveness depends on the type of targets and priorities set by the organization: If the goals are too low, the policy poorly defined, or the demands conflicting, the ability of the EMS to deliver against the ecological bottom line—let alone sustainability—is undermined.

Values

This highlights the critical question of values. The best EMS and the most expensive auditors will make little fundamental difference in a company that does not embrace sustainability as a core value. Underlying the EMS, there must be real commitment to the principles of sustainability and to the quantum shifts this requires in production, function, and consumption. Sustainability must be integral to an organization's strategy.

Openness

Over and above values, another important factor is the degree of openness the company demonstrates toward stakeholders. Without quality information, actors like consumers and investors simply cannot play their part. Moreover, even where quality information does exist, it is often simply not believed: In the area of environmental reporting, studies confirm there is a "credibility gap" in the eyes of stakeholders (IRRC/GEMI, 1996; UNEP/SustainAbility, 1996). The key reason for this seems to be that companies themselves are setting the boundaries of what is and is not reported. Greater openness and collaboration with stakeholders on what is done and how it is reported would go a long way to close this credibility gap (Spencer-Cooke, 1997). Recent experience with social auditing can shed light on this process.

Innovation

The importance of innovation has already been stressed. Suffice to say that companies at the leading edge of the transition to sustainability will be those that reinvent themselves, their products and services, through a process of constant adaptation—epitomized in Intel CEO Andy Grove's mantra that "only the paranoid survive."

Dissonance

Possibly the hardest thing of all will be to ensure that dissonance—or conflict—is reduced to a minimum and that company policy is aligned with company actions. The gap between what companies say and what they do is often vast, resulting from a lack of shared values at the core of the organization and from poor management of the inevitable trade-offs between the economic, environmental, and social bottom lines. Dissonance can be reduced by making sure sustainability is integrated as a core value of the organization.

Taking these four qualities together, we get VOID (Values, Openness, Innovation, Dissonance). It is a daunting term, but companies wishing to lead the way in the sustainability transition will be doing just that—leaping into the void. The time and space dimensions and the complexity of sustainability mean that we are dealing with unprecedented degrees of uncertainty. The consequences of our actions will be experienced by others well into the future, and we don't have the means to predict what those consequences will be.

Does this mean that the Dinosaur's Survival Kit is empty? Not at all.

The Dinosaur's Survival Kit

As well as drawing on the ever-expanding environmental management toolkit, sustainability management will have as much to do with values as it does with science and technology. A growing number of companies from The Body Shop onward are embracing the concept of social accounting and auditing—as a way of gauging their social bottom lines through stakeholder dialogue. To survive, today's dinosaurs have a juggling act to play. Inside the survival kit is a range of tools, each useful, but they will not deliver unless their use is driven by values, supported by openness, sharpened through innovation, and smoothed by the absence of dissonance.

A senior manager in a large company once told me he really wanted to see his firm do something significant for sustainable development. I suggested that the single most important thing he could do was to educate and change the mind-sets of his colleagues. "Oh no!" he replied, "that would be much too difficult."

It won't be easy. And the sustainability toolkit will contain no panaceas. So, finally, I would recommend some plasters for small scuffles with stakeholders and a good bottle of brandy for reviving the faint-hearted.

Chapter 5

COSY (Company Oriented SustainabilitY)

Frank Belz, Uwe Schneidewind, and Johannes Hummel

In her speech at the Greening of Industry Network conference in Toronto, Ontario, in November 1995, Jacqueline Aloisi de Larderel, director of the United Nations Environment Program (UNEP) Industry and Environment Office in Paris, described the achievements and the bottlenecks of the greening of industry. She pointed out that great environmental improvements have been achieved so far, especially in large manufacturing companies in Western Europe and North America. However, to further improve ecoefficiency industry must shift its focus (a) from processes to products and (b) from the supply side to the demand side of consumption: "Very few companies have addressed the basic question of who (really) needs the product or service." The COSY concept addresses these issues. It is an integrated approach toward environmental management, which may help companies to make these shifts.

In the first part of this chapter we describe the basic idea and the four levels of COSY. In the second part we apply the COSY concept to the food industry and the textile industry. These industries fulfill basic needs such as eating/drinking and shelter. In the third part we describe the COSY Workshops of the Institute of Economy and the Environment at the University of St. Gallen (IEE-HSG) as a way to bring key players and stakeholders of an industry together to facilitate environmental and social change.

COSY Concept

COSY is an acronym for Company Oriented SustainabilitY (see Schneidewind, 1994). The basic idea of the concept is to support companies in stepping beyond environmental improvements in the production area. It is about the shift from processes to products, services, and functions and from the supply side to the demand side of consumption. Thus, COSY is about broadening environmental management. The conceptual framework may help companies take a different look at their industry and the products and services they produce. From the perspective of COSY, companies are not only defined by the goods and services they offer; they are also defined by the human needs they fulfill. Such a broad definition of companies and industries overcomes existing mental mind maps and may eventually lead to environmental and competitive innovations. The COSY concept comprises four different levels: processes, products, services and functions, and needs.

Processes

Since the beginning of the 1990s processes have been the focus of attention in management theory and practice (see Hammer and Champy, 1993). Business process (re-) engineering includes the alteration of existing processes and the design of new processes. "End of pipe" environmental technologies just alter existing production processes. Take, for example, air emission filters, which are installed by companies to comply with environmental regulations. "Integrated" or so-called "clean" technologies may lead to new production processes, which avoid pollution at its origin. The implementation of such environmental technologies is compliance-driven as well as cost-driven. An international comparative study in the area of environmental management shows that over two-thirds of companies in different countries of Western Europe have already undertaken environmental initiatives in the production area (see Belz and Strannegård, 1997:156,157). These initiatives help reduce the environmental impact of production processes and increase the ecoefficiency on this level (for example, energy efficiency and resource efficiency). Other processes that have to be environmentally optimized are transportation and administration processes. These also include business-related travel (see Neale, 1997:9–17).

Products

The second level of COSY focuses on the product itself. By taking the whole product life cycle "from cradle to grave" into account, companies can seek to optimize the product environmentally and thus reduce the environmental impacts caused. Life cycle analysis and assessment are tools to analyze the environmental problems of products (see Sustain-Ability [1993] and Berkhout [1995] for the application of LCAs in different industries; see Schaltegger [1997] for a critical point of view from the economic perspective). Life cycle management aims at reducing environmental problems of the product and integrates the pre- and the post-stages of the product into management thinking (see Linnanen et al., 1994). In Germany, the takeback regulations expand the product responsibility of the producer to the latter stages of the product and make companies "close the material loop" (see Kirchgeorg, 1995; Steger, 1996). Empirical results of the International Business Environmental Barometer show that only a small minority of companies follow such an integrated approach toward environmental management (see Belz and Strannegård, 1997:156–158).

Services and Functions

The third level of COSY focuses on the use and disposal of the product. In many cases the main environmental problems occur over these two product stages (as with automobiles, washing machines, refrigerators). By providing services such as maintenance and repair the product life can be expanded and the environmental impact can be reduced. Service concepts may eventually lead to a functional orientation—selling services or functions instead of products. From such a perspective the product itself is questioned. Producers may ask what business they are in: Is Siemens in the business of selling building-control equipment or in the business of providing shelter—a heated or air-conditioned building? Is General Motors in the business of selling cars or in the business of providing mobility? In the case of Siemens this question may lead to energy and performance contracting, and in the case of General Motors it may lead to offering car pools.

Needs

The environmental optimization of processes, products, services, and functions enhances the "ecoefficiency" as promoted by the World Business Council for Sustainable Development (see WBCSD, 1995), where needs are satisfied with less energy and material flows. The increase of ecoefficiency on these levels is absolutely necessary but may not necessarily deliver the ultimate goal of environmental sustainability. That is why the COSY concept combines ecoefficiency with sufficiency—the altered or restricted fulfillment of human needs. Here it is useful to differentiate between absolute and relative needs (see for such a differentiation Keynes, 1930). Absolute needs such as hunger, thirst, and shelter against the cold have to be fulfilled by material flows in order to keep the human organism alive. Absolute needs are limited. We can eat only a certain amount of calories per time period, sleep a certain amount of time, and wear a certain amount of clothes. The fulfillment of such basic needs is part of the human rights as declared by the United Nations. No one is likely to question these. Relative needs such as self-esteem and social recognition may be fulfilled materially or immaterially. Unlike absolute needs, relative needs seem to be unlimited (see Zinn, 1995:44).

From an environmental and social point of view it is important to ask to what extent and how we can fulfill basic and relative needs in the future and to what extent we can generalize about them. Do we need 20 pair of shoes? Does every single household need a washing machine? Is a journey to the other side of the world really more relaxing and interesting than hiking in the region? How much space do we need for living? And so on. These are critical questions we have to ask ourselves in the future. The answers to these questions may fundamentally change our way of life—our production and consumption patterns. Most people may view these questions as a danger to economic growth. However, the very need to improve ecoefficiency and ask questions of sufficiency are the key factors for growing markets in the future (see DOW Europe and SustainAbility, 1995).

These are the four levels of the COSY concept, which may help companies to extend their scope of environmental management and make the shift from processes to products, services and functions, and needs. The higher the COSY level the more fundamental is the change and the higher the necessary interaction of the company with its environment. In this context it is too limiting to regard the company as a sole operating or business unit. It might be more useful to view the company as a set of relationships, where the conventional organizational boundaries begin to blur and become more permeable (see Roome and Clarke, 1995:3). What are the shortcomings of the COSY concept? There are at least two limitations: (a) The evolution and the learning paths toward COSY are not known yet and probably will not follow a well-ordered pattern. Should companies start with environmental innovations on the process level and then go on with the product level? Or should they start with the fundamental question of what business they are in and which needs they fulfill? (b) The main focus of the COSY concept is on environmental issues of sustainability, whereas social issues such as unemployment, minority rights, and equal opportunity are widely neglected (see Welford, 1995).

The COSY Concept Applied to Two Industries

In this chapter we apply COSY to the food industry and the textile industry, which are defined in a rather broad sense. We discuss each level of COSY with regard to the two different industries and give illustrative case examples, simply to show the practical implications of the concept for companies.

Food Industry

If we take the whole ecological product life cycle into account, the food industry is defined as farmers, food processors, food retailers, caterers, and consumers (see for such a broad definition Belz, 1995:31–36). The main environmental problems along the food chain occur in the first and the last stage of the product life cycle: agriculture and consumption (see Belz, 1995:36–52). The environmental problems of packaging are widely recognized by the public and much has been done about it. Lately, farming has become the focus of attention in many countries. The environmental impact of buying, transporting, storing, and processing food is hardly discussed at all.

Processes

Environmental problems in the area of food processing are energy, water, and solid waste (see Belz, 1995:41–45). To meet legal compliance and to reduce production costs, the majority of food companies focus their environmental activities on energy savings, water savings, and sewage treatment. Typical environmental measures in these areas are optimization of production processes, installation of new energy-efficient production technologies, energy recuperation, water circulation, and installation of sewage plants. These measures help improve energy and water efficiency. Overall, they increase the ecoefficiency of food processing.

Products

Since the 1980s packaging has come under environmental scrutiny. This is particularly true of the food industry. Environmental packaging strategies are: reduce, reuse, and recycle. The introduction of environmental packaging systems is a first step to increase the ecoefficiency across the whole product life cycle. However, the main environmental problems occur in areas like farming, transportation, and consumption. Thus, the introduction of organically grown products and regional products are the next important steps in life cycle management.

Good examples for such an integrated approach toward environmental management are the Neumarkter Lammsbräu brewery in Germany and the Aargauer dairy in Switzerland: The Neumarkter Lammsbräu brewery purchases its raw materials like barley, wheat, and hops from organic farming and brews "eco-beer" of premium quality. To avoid unnecessary transportation they prefer regional suppliers, whenever possible. Traditional fermentation methods are used in the production process. Unnecessary pumping, filtration, centrifuging, and pressuring are avoided to ensure the premium quality of the product and to reduce the environmental impact. For packaging, the Neumarkter Lammsbräu exclusively uses glass bottles in returnable plastic crates (see Hopfenbeck, 1993:113).

The Aargauer dairy is a medium-sized company located in the middle of Switzerland. It produces a wide variety of dairy products such as milk, cream, butter, yogurts, and desserts. The environment is integrated into all functional areas such as procurement, production, recycling/disposal, logistics, and marketing/sales. In 1994 the dairy launched the "Aargauer dairy products" (milk, butter, and cream), which are locally produced and locally distributed. This "ethnofood" offers added value for the consumers by reducing environmental impact due to the short transportation distances and the environmental packaging. The superior environmental performance is communicated by means of "eco-numbers" on the packaging and in advertising. To coordinate, ordinate, and integrate the environmental activities the Aargauer dairy implemented an environmental management system, which was certified according to EMAS, ISO 14001, and BS7750 in the beginning of 1996 (see Belz, 1997:109).

Food companies are not alone in pursuing an integrated approach toward environmental management. Especially in the food industry, retailers are key players in the food chain. Due to their purchasing power they exert influence on suppliers, and due to their market dominance they have a great impact on consumers. Thus, retailers play the role of "ecological gatekeepers" in the food chain.

Take for example Migros and Coop, which are the two largest retail chains in Switzerland, representing over 40 percent of the market share in the food retailing business: Both pursue an active approach toward the environment with a special focus on packaging and products/assortments.

In the beginning of 1993 Coop introduced the "Coop Naturaplan," an environmental program for organically grown food products. Within a short period of time the revenue of the Coop Naturaplan quintupled from 30 million Swiss francs in 1993 to 150 million Swiss francs in 1996.

The success of Coop Naturaplan made Migros respond with "M-Bio" (organic farming), which is complementary to "M-Sano" (integrated production). In 1996 the revenue of the two environmental programs was over 450 million Swiss francs (M-Bio: 30 million Swiss francs, M-Sano: 430 million Swiss francs). Partly due to the environmental activities of the large food retailers, a development "from the eco-niche to the ecological mass market" is feasible in some food areas in Switzerland (see Belz et al., 1997). A similar development can be observed in other Western European countries such as Austria, Denmark, and Sweden.

Services and Functions

In general, storage, preparation, and consumption of food and drinks take place at home or out-of-home (such as restaurants, hotels). If we consider the functional level of food and drink, the food company may try to increase the ecoefficiency of storing, preparing, and consuming food and drinks. The producer of frozen food may cooperate with the producer of CFC-free freezers. The producer of coffee may cooperate with the producer of energy-efficient coffee makers. To go even further, food companies might advocate out-of-home consumption, since it may be assumed that restaurants and hotels are more ecoefficient than households (ecoefficiency measures the environmental impact of storage and preparation per meal). This is particularly true of single households.

Needs

No one is likely to question the basic need for eating and drinking, but there are already challenges in terms of what and how much we eat and drink: In its report on sustainable Netherlands the environmental organization "Friends of the Earth" argues that we must achieve a halving of meat consumption per capita by 2010 (see Friends of the Earth Netherlands, 1994:174). "Unappetizing for some, but the 21st century may need to ask the question: Who needs meat?" (DOW Europe and SustainAbility, 1995:32). What are the market implications of such thoughts? Food companies might want to move into meatless food products that support a healthy and balanced diet.

An illustrative example for such an environmental diversification strategy is Baer, the leading soft cheese company in Switzerland with a market share of 25 percent (see Belz, 1995:78–117). It is a medium-sized family-owned company with a revenue of approximately 100 million Swiss francs in 1995. To promote the idea of "sustainable eating" and to enhance substitution for meat, Baer introduced a vegetarian product line called "Yasoya." By now, the vegetarian products are responsible for 10 percent of total revenue. In the future, the CEO of the company expects a sharp rise in the revenue of vegetarian products (economic goals). The majority of the ingredients for the Yasoya products are organically grown and environmentally processed and packaged (environmental goals). The majority of people in developing countries do not have enough to eat or an adequate diet, especially young children. Baer contributes to UNICEF projects for children by donating 0.10 Swiss francs for every Yasoya product purchased (social goals). Here environmental issues are connected with social issues, similar to the "Max-Havelaar" goods such as coffee, tea, chocolate, honey, and bananas (see Max Havelaar, 1996).

Textile Industry

If we take the whole product life cycle into account, the textile industry comprises the following stages: primary production (natural and chemical fibers); production of fibers, yarns, and fleece; finishing (pretreatment, dying, printing, dressing); garment manufacturing; use; and disposal (see Enquete Commission, 1993 and 1994). The main environmental problems along the textile chain are the intensive pesticide use in cotton fields, the water emissions caused by the finishing processes, and the energy consumption for the washing and drying of textiles as well as the water pollution caused by detergents.

Processes

One of the main environmental problems in the finishing process is water. By cleaning and reusing water, the efficiency of water use can be increased. During the last decade many finishing companies have improved their water efficiency and the quality of their sewage. One illustrative example of these efforts is the Swiss "Glatt Commission." Textile finishing companies are highly concentrated in the east of Switzerland. For a long time these companies released their untreated sewage in the river Glatt. In spite of many sewage plants the water quality of the river reached an alarming level in the mid-1980s. This was the starting point of a broad cooperation between the affected companies, local authorities, and the producers of finishing auxiliaries to improve the water quality of the river. By implementing different production measures and using new auxiliaries, the biodegradability of the used chemicals was enhanced from 35 percent to 80 percent within six years. Ever since, the water quality of the river Glatt has improved significantly (for an illustrative example see Keller, 1991:185–198).

Products

If we take a look at the entire product life of textiles, several questions arise: How are the raw materials grown? What kind of color pigments are used? How can the clothes be washed? Are the clothes recyclable or biodegradable after use?

Environmental problems of textiles occur along the whole product life cycle. This is why many textile companies like Steilmann, Esprit, or Gore started implementing a comprehensive approach to life cycle management. They offer special "eco-collections." For these products they use only cotton from farming based on "integrated pest management" or organic cultivation. The finishing process is carried out by companies with high ecological production standards. Chemicals that are critical from a toxicological or environmental point of view are no longer used. GORE (Gore-Tex Products) started an initiative to take back and recycle their products ("Balance-Project").

Another example of a comprehensive life cycle management is "Coop Naturaline" of garments launched by Coop in 1993. The environmental textile collection is based on cotton from integrated pest management production, chlorine-free bleaching, environmental textile dyes, and natural materials for buttons. In 1995 Coop extended its efforts and changed nearly the whole underwear collection to cotton sourced from organic farming. The project was developed in cooperation with a yarn trading company and a textile manufacturer (see Hummel, 1997).

Services and Functions

Washing the clothes is one of the main environmental problems along the textile chain. A combined effort of textile, detergent, and washing companies would reduce the environmental impact on this stage and increase the ecoefficiency of washing. Service concepts like "textile care centers" are possible approaches to the environmental challenges in this field (see

Roome and Hinnells, 1993:22–23). They are an effort to combine the best environmental practice in textile types, detergents, washing machines, and washing habits of the consumer to an environmentally sound solution.

The promotion for Coop Natura Line incorporates comprehensive information about environmentally adequate care of the textiles and special recommendations for environmentally optimized detergents—also sold by Coop. By this kind of presentation Coop tries to support functionally oriented solutions within the textile care. A closer cooperation with the manufacturers of washing machines and textile care centers could be the next step of such a function-oriented strategy.

Needs

Finally, the textile company may question our washing habits and the recent trends in the fashion business: Do we really have to wash our shirt every second day? Do we need new clothes and shoes every six months? And so on. Ecological improvements in the textile chain do not only rely on efficiency measures at the production, product, and functional levels. These improvements can also be reached by sufficiency strategies. To avoid colored textiles, to wear durable textiles only, or to use secondhand textiles are possible ways to reduce the ecological problems caused by satisfying the need of clothing.

Some companies already try to support these sufficiency approaches. Two illustrative examples: Hess Naturtextilien, the largest supplier of natural textiles in Germany, promotes unbleached and uncolored textiles, whereas GORE focuses on the durability of its products as a contribution to reduce textile consumption.

COSY Workshops to Facilitate Environmental and Social Change

The COSY concept is an integrated approach toward environmental management. It is defined on four levels and may help companies to extend the scope of environmental management beyond processes and products. Empirical evidence indicates that most companies have already taken environmental measures regarding processes. The minority of companies pursue an integrated approach toward environmental management by taking the whole product cycle into account. Just a few companies sell services and functions instead of products in order to reduce their environmental impact. And even fewer companies think about needs in the environmental and social context.

That may not be surprising: The higher the COSY level, the more fundamental the change. Whereas environmental strategies on the levels of processes and products require incremental changes, environmental strategies on the functional and need levels often imply fundamental and radical change (a similar differentiation is offered by Hoffman and Ehrenfeld earlier in this book). The more fundamental and radical the change, the higher are the psychological, social, political, and economic barriers to overcome. However, the higher the COSY level, the greater are the potentials for reductions of environmental impacts. Environmental strategies, which question certain products, may be more effective and efficient than environmental strategies on the process level, which take existing products for granted. What can be done to overcome the existing problems? How can environmental and social change be facilitated?

One opportunity to facilitate change is the creation of communication platforms. In 1997 the Institute of Economy and the Environment at the University of St. Gallen organized the so-called COSY Workshops, bringing together key players and involving the main stakeholders of the food and textile industries (see Schneidewind, Hummel, and Belz, 1997). The 15 to 20 participants of the COSY Workshops were carefully selected and personally invited by the organizers. Invited participants ideally have (a) a great interest and knowledge in environmental and social issues, (b) the creativity to envision a sustainable future, and (c) the power to realize common visions. The aim of the first workshop during summer 1997 was to create sustainability visions for the food and textile industries in the year 2020. Here mainly environmental and social issues were discussed by the participants. The conceptual background of this workshop is the COSY concept; methodological backgrounds are "future workshops" to facilitate social change (see Jungk and Müller, 1991; Pichel, 1993). The aim of the second workshop during fall 1997 was to identify steps for the implementation of the common visions. Here the main economic and social barriers for the realization of the shared visions were to be identified and solutions reached to overcome them. Examples for possible outcomes of COSY workshops are a shared vision of sustainable food and textile industries, new innovative ways to realize the shared vision, new cooperations between companies and stakeholders, and the introduction of new sustainable products. Companies participating in the COSY Workshops may eventually take up the sustainability challenge and incorporate it into their management thinking. From this perspective companies are perceived as "change agents" toward sustainable development.

ACKNOWLEDGMENT

Acknowledgments for supporting the research on which this chapter draws are due to the Oikos Foundation for Economy and the Environment. Sponsor companies of this foundation include Baer, Gallus Ferd. Ruesch, Hilti, Mettler Toledo, and Unilever (Switzerland). Thanks to Susse Georg, Minna Halme, Ken Green, and Joseph Huber for their helpful comments.

Chapter 6

Cultural Development Strategies and Sustainability: A Case Study of the Body Shop

David Raymond Jones

This chapter focuses on a founder-driven company, The Body Shop. Anita Roddick founded The Body Shop in 1976. She opened a shop in Brighton, England, selling cosmetics based on natural ingredients. Having become a public limited company in 1984, by 1995 it had grown to 1210 shops in 45 countries, with a turnover of £219.7 million and a profit before tax of £33.5 million. Reflecting on its growth aspirations, recent 1996 figures (Hanson, 1996) showed that The Body Shop had almost 1400 shops.

The purpose of this case study is to identify and examine the rationale behind a cultural development strategy for firms wishing to move toward sustainability. Top management within The Body Shop are already committed to moving toward sustainability, defined in its most holistic sense—actively endeavoring to fulfill what they see as their long-term financial, environmental, and social responsibility. For The Body Shop there is a perception of an overriding moral obligation to drive toward sustainability in business (Roddick, 1991). Its commitment to the concept of sustainability was emphasized in 1993, through its second environmental report:

> Our mission is nothing less than to forge a new and more sustainable ethic for business.
>
> (The Body Shop, 1993)

In early 1996, The Body Shop published not only its fourth environmental report but also a separate social report. The Body Shop also commissioned a Social Evaluation (Hanson, 1996) that characterized The Body Shop as a company publicly committed to social values and to having a substantial and positive impact on society. The report identified the company founder, Anita Roddick, as an extraordinary advocate for corporate responsibility, with a vision of business as an agent of social betterment and change. Many of the company's activities and much of its communications are geared to encourage other companies to emulate this model. This institutional responsibility matches one of the measures of sustainability in business identified from a group of expert workshops conducted by Welford and Jones (1994). Organizations as "facilitators of change" implies a wider interpretation of the meaning of sustainability for business. The Body Shop is therefore moving toward sustainability by promoting societal systemic change.

Given the top management commitment to sustainability, the specific aim of this case study was to identify those elements of The Body Shop's cultural development strategy that maximize employee commitment toward both the company and its sustainability goals. This was achieved by exploring employee attitudes toward the different elements of The Body Shop's cultural development strategy. Attitudes were determined by extended interviews with eight key employees, primarily from The Body Shop's Ethical Audit Department. This department is part of a larger Values and Vision Center headed by Anita Roddick. The center incorporates The Body Shop's environmental, fair trade, animal protection, and human rights activities (The Body Shop, 1994a). The Ethical Audit Department provides advice, ensures policies and procedures are up to date, and creates awareness on ethical issues throughout the workforce.

To contextualize the different elements of The Body Shop's present cultural development strategy, the case study began by looking at The Body Shop's past cultural development strategy. This approach enables the development of an appreciation of the cultural learning process The Body Shop has moved through in its pursuit of sustainability. It must be pointed out that separating The Body Shop's past from its present strategy does not mean that at any particular point in time The Body Shop has suddenly and purposely changed its strategy. The change from its past to its present strategy has been evolutionary and incremental over time. This way of looking at strategy conforms to views advocated by Mintzberg (1987). He objected to the concept of strategy as a plan worked out in advance in the head of the strategist. Rather, he saw strategy as a pattern of activities over time, which includes observations of what occurs. For

Mintzberg, plans are not irrelevant, but strategy as action speaks louder than intentions. Mintzberg contends that strategy does not need to be deliberate but can emerge. In the same way, The Body Shop's past and present strategies can be seen as emergent strategies. For simplicity, The Body Shop's past and present strategies can be dealt with as two separate subcases. The following discussions represent a split between a description and a critique of The Body Shop's past and present cultural development strategy.

The Body Shop's Past Unitarist Strategy

Introducing The Body Shop's 1994 "Values and Vision" statement, Anita Roddick states:

> Values are a part of The Body Shop's genetic code. Nothing will ever change that. . . . Our values saturate every bit of the company, every department, every shop.

(The Body Shop, 1994b)

This statement characterizes the ideals and goals of a unitarist cultural development strategy. Invariably, a unitarist strategy is expressed in a call for a "strong culture." Organizational culture is said to be strong where there is consistency in the elements of culture and this consistency is powerful in determining individual behavior. Put another way, an effective organization in a unitary system is bound by common tasks and common values. The argument for strong culture is that it fosters good performance by engendering high levels of purpose among employees (Denison, 1990). Companies with a unitarist strategy of cultural development believe that they are more innovative and generally more effective when the cultures of its parts are integrated into a single, consistent, uniform whole.

Cultural development is a matter of integrating diverse orientations and interests to establish a common orientation toward the organization's affairs (Martin and Meyerson, 1988). Uniformity and standardization of culture is preferred to diversity and heterogeneity: Plurality is resisted. Consequently, maximizing employee commitment toward the company and its goals is inextricably linked with the development of a set of shared values. As Newton and Harte (1994) point out, the implicit, and quite often explicit, reference point for this approach rests on the importance of core values as identified by Peters and Waterman (1982) in their book *In*

Search of Excellence. In search of sustainability, however, rests on the importance of matching values for making your organization an economic success with those values needed to be environmentally and socially sound.

Mission Support

The type of unitarist strategy employed by The Body Shop can be placed into perspective using the work of Perrow (1972) and various political scientists and philosophers (see Feenberg, 1986). Perrow identifies three levels of organizational control, which could equally describe three different types of unitarist strategy:

1. Control expressed in direct orders

2. Control operating indirectly through programs and procedures

3. Control exerted by operating on the ideological premises of action

The Body Shop's unitarist cultural strategy belongs very much to level 3. Recalling Gramsci's classical theory of power (Hoare, 1977), level 3 represents a form of ideational control that works by controlling the way people think rather than their behavior. Harrison and Stokes (1992) refer to this type of strategy as an aligned strategy because it "lines people up" behind a common vision or purpose. The strategy relies on organizational values, which support an organizational mission that intrinsically motivates employees. The implicit notion is that the mission induces people to transcend personal advantage. Harrison and Stokes argue that this evokes altruism, which is satisfying to those involved. People feel that they are working for something bigger than themselves. Employees believe they are making a contribution to society, as well as gaining something for the company. In contrast, unitarist strategies from levels 1 and 2 seek to control employees through the use of external rewards and punishments.

The fundamental basis of the mission support strategy is that internalized meanings and values are more effective in achieving coordination than external control systems, which rely on explicit rules and regulations (Denison and Mishra, 1989:168). At a minimal level, a mission support strategy plugs a gap in the levers of managerial controls by providing an internal (and internalized, self-regulating) mode of control. As Inzerelli (1980:2) points out, no organization can rely entirely on external controls because human activities cannot all be controlled in this way and because external controls generate their own dysfunction. Organizations depend to a large extent on their members' voluntarism and identification as motivation to perform. Harrison and Stokes (1992) argue that without a mission support strategy, the organization has available to it only that fraction of each person's personal energy they are willing to commit in return for the extrinsic rewards the organization offers. One of the interviewees was well aware of this point when he said:

> "The Body Shop is a life path, a personal journey, fueling people's inner drive, their inner passion with something worthwhile to do; you never have to worry about productivity, absenteeism and all these other provincial, archaic methods of managing."

Bate (1994) argues that a wide range of positive feelings and thoughts are engendered by a mission support strategy toward the company and its leaders. These embrace loyalty, commitment, dedication, devotion, enthusiasm, even love and passion. As Anita Roddick stated:

> Most businesses focus all the time on profits, profits, profits . . . I have to say I think that is deeply boring. I want to create an electricity and passion that bonds people to the company. You can educate people by their passions, especially young people. You have to find ways to grab their imagination. You want them to feel that they are doing something important . . . I'd never get that kind of motivation if we were just selling shampoo and body lotion.
>
> (Burlingham, 1988)

She pointed out that if there is a single motivation for what we do, it is, in the words of Ralph Waldo Emerson, "to put love where labor is" (Roddick, 1991). All The Body Shop interviewees described an expectation on them to either love or possess a passion for working at The Body Shop:

> "You are expected to actually love working for The Body Shop."

> "There is a big expectation to be there [high level of passion]."

> "The Body Shop has a sort of zealot ambiance around it."

> "It is a very emotional place and passionate place."

Charismatic Leadership

The value of mission support is that people can be relied on to set their own standards and discipline themselves, within the bounds of the mission. Freedom is conditional on delivering that mission. Hence, the leader's role is not so much to give detailed instructions but to define and promote a broad mission for people to achieve as they think fit, as long as they achieve it. Peters and Waterman (1982:318) describe this kind of control system as "simultaneous loose-tight." It combines firm central direction with individual autonomy. It is a system that merges the two apparent opposites of freedom and constraint. On one hand, everyone can be a pioneer, an experimenter, an innovator, and a leader, while on the other hand the system exercises tight control over them and ensures "nothing gets far out of line."

Bate (1994) argues that unitarist or "strong culture" involves a pre-planned, top-down, nonemergent strategy that aims to assimilate and integrate the workforce, eliminate conflicting interests and perspectives, and create shared meanings and values. Klyn and Kearins (1995) argue that The Body Shop basically works through a process of top-down communication. Child (1984) sees a unitarist strategy as consciously designed to turn pragmatic acceptance into a much more enthusiastic support for management's purposes. Consequently, a key management task involves enhancing integration of different sets of norms, values, and beliefs (Green, 1988:123).

In the same way, Gladwin (1993) argues, "substantial cultural leadership, symbolic management, and even evangelism will be needed to inculcate such green value systems within large organizations." He also stresses, "the most important, and perhaps the most difficult, leadership task may be that of creating and maintaining green values within the organization." Schein (1983) sees the most important role for a leader in a unitarist strategy as reinforcing in word and deed the values of the organization. Mathews (1988:135) extends this by stressing the importance of senior managers as role models. The impact of role modeling is more potent if the organization has a charismatic or transformational leader(s) (Bennis and Nanus, 1985). Anita Roddick has provided such a role model for The Body Shop. Indeed, the importance of Anita Roddick's direction and passion as part of The Body Shop's unitarist strategy was recognized by all interviewees. The typical comment was:

> "It has a very bold image; it's a very didactic kind of company, and a lot of that is due to Anita. She keeps everybody moving both internally and externally."

To cope with the growth of the company, Anita Roddick's entrepreneurial spirit was developed by splitting the company into separate subsidiaries in 1992. Through this initiative, Ward (1994) has argued that The Body Shop maintained a small, entrepreneur-led management structure. It enabled the subsidiary companies to have clearer, more focused objectives (The Body Shop, 1994c), while being connected to the corporate headquarters through Anita Roddick's mission. Over the past two years, a process of centralization and corporate restructuring has established departments that provide a key link communicating The Body Shop's mission to all staff. This restructuring was described in *L.A. News* as follows:

> One of the most exciting things so far is an organizational structure that reflects our true values. Two divisions were created specifically to ensure both that we practice what we preach and engage all staff in making The Body Shop the most successful, values-led company around. Gordon heads "Company Culture" and Anita the "Values and Vision Centre."
>
> (The Body Shop, 1994c)

Anita Roddick concentrates on the style, image, and future direction of the company from within the Values and Vision Center. Corporate restructuring also meant that Anita Roddick moved from the position of Managing Director to Chief Executive—a move from an operational to a more strategic position (The Body Shop, 1994a). The Values and Vision Center has four departments: Anita Roddick's team, Fair Trade, Public Affairs, and Ethical Audit (comprising environment, animal protection, social—including health and safety—and information audits). Its purpose is to support and encourage the full involvement of staff, managers, franchisees, and suppliers in The Body Shop's values (The Body Shop, 1994c).

The Effectiveness of The Body Shop's Unitarist Strategy

In relation to the unitarist goal of shared values, all interviewees remarked that there were enduring differences in values and commitment up and down and across the workforce. Some typical comments illustrating the diversity of personal values and commitment are as follows:

> "You get a lot of ideologically driven people who want to be there. Now there are also people who come to The Body Shop

because they want to have a job and make money. And then there are those people who want to come and do a good job and they like to be associated with the company. So, there are different levels of commitment."

"The majority of people are here to make a living."

"People feel that their home life and their family life are far more important than their work."

"People coming in who are not of the same ethics—they are here because it is good on the CV to work at The Body Shop; so you get people like that who aren't pushing to make sure everything is squeaky clean."

The diversity of values can be understood by seeing employee's personal values as not being solely formed by top management (through a unitarist strategy) but more by a complex mix of experiences both external and internal to the organization. Depending on the personal priority placed on internal and external experiences, employees could be seen as being predominantly unitarist or pluralist in outlook. Researchers have increasingly focused on the degree of variance in values and ideologies between hierarchical and functional levels of the organization (Arogyaswamy and Byles, 1987). Research by Bate (1994) reveals that frames of reference are hierarchically and occupationally differentiated within the organization studied. For The Body Shop, the head office and senior management were the creators and custodians of all things "corporate." They held a strongly unitarist outlook. In contrast, The Body Shop's Supply Division, shop floor, and independent franchisees were judged in terms of what they did locally on their "patch" and whether they had achieved their "bottom line." To them, corporate goals were, as they say, "for the birds." Their own success was measured in terms of the achievement of local targets, and if this meant sacrificing the interests of other subsidiaries or the company overall, then so be it:

The nature of the work in Supply areas means that it is a regular houred, regular paid, regular shift type of job, and the type of people who take those jobs are people who generally just want to earn a living. The type of manager who works in such a practical, nontheoretical product-based target-based area by his or her very nature will be practical, product-based, nontheoretical, more action orientated to the immediate needs that they have got; they have got to produce x amount of product by x time. . . . There is a big difference in perspective and goals between somebody who say works in the warehouse and somebody who works in the corporate headquarters.

(Bate, 1994)

Results from the 1995 Social Statement (The Body Shop, 1996a), while not pinpointing particular departments, substantiated this opinion. While the majority of the workforce agreed that they and their departments felt part of The Body Shop community, approximately one in five respondents disagreed and more than one-third of the respondents did not feel able to express an opinion.

This suggests that important personal values were not being satisfied by The Body Shop's mission support strategy. The Social Statement identified that the highest levels of dissatisfaction were around the company's practices in job, career, and personal development. The need for more attention to these areas indicates that employees are motivated by much more than the company values. It would appear that to increase employee commitment levels at The Body Shop, a strategy was needed that was based not only on inspiring organizational values but also on personal values—a personal support strategy. As Harrison and Stokes (1992) point out, a personal support strategy values employees as human beings, not just contributors to a task. They suggest that a personal support strategy fosters employee commitment toward the company not through a common purpose or ideal (in contrast to the mission support strategy) but by offering employees satisfactions that come from relationships: mutuality, belonging, and connection. The emphasis is on human needs, which at its core respects and supports employees as individuals who have diverse opinions and values.

The experiences at The Body Shop support Gabriel's (1991:439) proposition that ideational control through a mission support strategy is not the simple affair that cultural engineers advocate. In an uncertain world employees may yearn for meaning, but it does not follow that any meaning will suffice. Corporate strategy literature substantiates the finding that a reliance on a mission support strategy defined through a management vision is flawed. It raises serious doubts about the ease with which management vision can be communicated to employees. For example, Coulson-Thomas (1992:81) draws on three sets of survey data to argue that "a wide gulf has emerged between rhetoric and reality" of attempts to "communicate visions and missions: Instead of inspiration and motivation there is disillusionment and distrust." Moreover, while corporate strategy writers stress that this is because of "mistakes" in communicating visions and missions, the literature remains strongly prescriptive and offers limited evidence of successful communication beyond brief descriptions of supposed "success stories" (Newton and Harte, 1994).

In addition to the expressed need for a more personal support strategy, employees expressed a desire for a more bottom-up participative strategy in contrast to a predominant leadership strategy. It was felt that greater participation could provide the means to identify which of the diverse personal values need to be engaged:

> "If they [top management] can pick up on the vibes of everybody in the organization, they won't get major antagonism in the staff."

> "It [The Body Shop] needs to stop or moderate the building and the creating and the moving on and attend to the human records that have occurred over the last couple of years."

> "We have lost that personal touch and the ability to make joint decisions."

> "There is a disaffection at the lower levels who have been left behind. The reason this has not been addressed is because the company is too busy going forward with commitment to values and to change and growing the business."

> "We really do have a vanguard of values and visions idea-based people. But they haven't looked behind them to see who they are bringing with them. It's fine for a few people who are enthusiastic, but not everybody is with them. The Values and Vision people are analogous to Napoleon going into Russia. Napoleon suddenly discovered that he has got no troops behind him because they had all died of frostbite. He then had to come all the way back."

However, contextualizing these findings, one employee contrasted The Body Shop's unitarist practices with other more mainstream companies:

> "There isn't a values fascism in The Body Shop. It is one of

the most vociferous environments I have been in, with arguments and debate."

It is important to recognize that The Body Shop employees were, in general, no more dissatisfied than those in comparable UK firms (Hanson, 1996). Furthermore, the majority of employees within The Body Shop thought top management was open to alternative opinions. In its Social Statement, 59 percent agreed with the view:

"The Body Shop has established a culture where staff can challenge traditional ways of doing things."

However, Hanson (1996) also argues that any company that makes socially responsible claims a key element in its marketing will be scrutinized to a greater extent and held to a higher standard than a company that does not. These high expectations are found internally as well as externally. In its 1995 Social Statement, one employee described the effect of these high expectations:

"On the whole I enjoy working for The Body Shop and am proud of what it stands for. Unfortunately, I think this means I have high expectations of the company and when sometimes it fails to live up to these I am very disappointed. However, in the main at least, we try."

To account for employees' and other stakeholders' high expectations, Hanson (1996) recommends that "the company must demonstrate extraordinary transparency and a willingness to hear and act on criticism of any dimension of its behavior."

The Body Shop's Present Unitarist-Pluralist Strategy

Reflecting on The Body Shop's past strategy, it appears that it would support Bate's (1994) argument that for practical employee-acceptance reasons, even the most committed "strong culture" companies need to attend to employee-based pluralism. Similarly, Reed and Anthony (1990:18) conclude: "To the extent that cultural management is to be successful, rather than cosmetic or deceptive, it will have to comprehend comparative values and belief systems." One interviewee described this need for pluralism in the context of sustainable development:

"Part of sustainability is to have a biodiverse sort of psychology in an organization, so it's not to become a cult and you can't

manage it that way either. Those who don't have the passion,
you have to allow room for them as well."

Meima (1994) and Roome and Clarke (1994) argue that people do not
understand or interpret environmental concepts with one voice. They hold
contrasting beliefs and value systems that are often in conflict with the
dominant interpretations of the firm. They point out that these differences
not only create barriers to change but also openings for change.

Similarly, Crane (1995) argues that cultural cohesion is not a prerequisite, nor might it be desirable, for business to be able to respond to the
environmental imperative in a cooperative and proactive manner. In short,
The Body Shop has realized that it needs to manage the inherent pluralism of the situation in respect to goals, values, and aspirations. Indeed the
company's own self-evaluation suggested it needed to provide a more
personally supportive working environment and to increase employee
participation in decision making. For example, in its 1995 Social Statement The Body Shop's commitment to a personal support strategy was
highlighted when it outlined its "Next Steps for Human Resources":

> . . . we cannot satisfy the aspirations of all of our employees,
> and we must look to other ways of keeping staff interested and
> motivated. . . . We need to make sure that the tremendous ded-
> ication and commitment of our staff does not manifest itself in
> over-long working hours, negative impacts on family life, or
> denial of opportunity to staff with caring responsibilities.

(The Body Shop, 1996a)

Furthermore, The Body Shop's commitment to increase employee participation in decision making was emphasized in its Social Statement:

> We also need to ensure that we provide opportunities to enable
> staff to speak up on issues that affect them, the business, and
> our values in the year ahead. Finally, as with our external audi-
> ences, we need to ensure that we provide the appropriate infor-
> mation to different groups of employees. Information needs to
> be targeted and tailored to these different groups.

(The Body Shop, 1996a)

Although The Body Shop is moving toward a more pluralist strategy,
it appears not to be abandoning its unitarist strategy. Instead, it appears to
prefer to combine its predominant unitary commitment to creating and

extending shared sustainable values and interests with its new pluralist commitment to providing mechanisms that will resolve, or at the very least contain, the disharmonies that exist between divergent systems of meaning within the organization. This strategy for cultural development is unusual as it moves away from conventional reactions to a simplistic unitarist strategy (Bate, 1994). The common reactions are to recognize the anarchistic tendencies of corporate pluralism—seek to hold them in check with a reinvigorated unifying strategy; or instead, as the pluralists suggest, devise more realistic mediating strategies for dealing with the perpetual conflicts that arise among different individuals and groups.

This stark dualism seems to leave little scope for a third option or anything in between. It is set up in such a discrete way as to oblige us to choose between one state or another. As Bate (1994) argues, despite their substantive differences we need to recognize that unitarism and pluralism are, in fact, identical in type, being the conventional products of "either-or" thinking. This mode of conceptualization loves to invent extreme polarities—simple dichotomies that carve up the world into two parts, the one part "good" and the other part "bad." Bate (1994) argues that the one-or-the-other strategy presented by the uniculturalists and the pluriculturalists are not representations of reality but idealizations of reality.

The unitarist and pluralist strategy represents a fundamentally different conceptual approach to a strategy of cultural order and development that begins with the question, What do organizations and cultures tend to be like in reality and practice (rather than how we would like them to be)? This moves away from Smircich's (1983) ideas, which distinguish between those who see culture as a managerial tool to bring about greater performance (unitarists) and those who see it as a way of understanding the social and moral terrain of the organization (pluralists). The beauty of a combined perspective is that it aims to bring about greater performance by a process of understanding the social and moral terrain of the organization. In contrast to "either-or" thinking, "both-and" thinking is an approach to cultural development that involves the simultaneous pursuit of unitarism and pluralism. This approach is intended to produce a hybrid culture capable of achieving an organization's sustainability goals by taking into account the increasingly diverse personal goals of its growing workforce. In the same way, Halme (1994), despite endorsing the virtues of the "bottom-up" approach, was careful to not conclude that this was evidence for a bottom-up model's superiority. One of the conclusions of the summary report from the 1994 Greening of Industry Conference (Clarke and Georg, 1995) was that change programs should be sensitive to the multidirectional nature of change: top-down, bottom-up, and side-to-side.

An example of this strategy in action at The Body Shop arose in May 1995 when its Human Resources Department launched a Bill of Rights and Responsibilities for staff that showed both unitarist and pluralist attributes. For instance, some of the more unitarist Rights and Responsibilities of the Company were an expectation that staff respect The Body Shop's values, to make final decisions with those values in mind, and to educate employees about the company's culture and values. However, it also emphasized the more pluralist Rights and Responsibilities of the Individual, such as to have a voice, to challenge, to be developed as an individual, and to treat others with trust and respect. Furthermore, as highlighted within its 1995 Social Statement (The Body Shop, 1996a), this Bill of Rights and Responsibilities was said to recognize and publish the special nature of The Body Shop's relationship with its employees, commenting that they are not just resources for the Company but are people whose own needs and aspirations are recognized and taken seriously.

A future initiative that further institutionalizes the unitarist-pluralist strategy is the establishment of a new department, to be given the general name of "The Development Group." As David Wheeler, head of Stakeholder Development at The Body Shop points out, the function of this department is to recognize and nurture behaviors that not only conform to business objectives but to personal objectives as well.

The elements of The Body Shop's future cultural development strategy are seen in the internal document *HR Vision 2000*. This document sets out how The Body Shop's Human Resource function sees the company by the year 2000, in terms of its relationship with its employees. The following extract represents a working practice vision for The Body Shop blending both unitarist and pluralist elements.

> To have a well run and successful company with maximum flexibility for producing a "win-win" situation for employees and the Company.
>
> (The Body Shop, 1996b)

Openness to pluralism while being committed to move toward The Body Shop's core sustainability values is summed up by a senior manager within The Body Shop:

> "To develop The Body Shop culture, you have to have a band

of some common themes and values, and admittedly people who are not within that band don't fit in, but that doesn't mean they are bad or evil but just different."

This should not be interpreted to imply a strategy based on "balance" between unitarism and pluralism. Bate (1994) sees no virtue in the notion of a balanced culture. He argues that different cultures must give different weight to pluralist and unitarist elements. It may be quite appropriate to be "unbalanced" in one direction or another, ranging from the uniculture of a hospital casualty department or a fighting regiment, to the pluriculture of a democratic parliament, debating society, or liberal arts college. The issue here is a culture that matches organizational intent with operational realities. As Clarke and Georg (1995) point out, "There is no one best way." However, as Bate (1994) argues, the main concern should be to studiously avoid the natural temptation to drift toward the extremes.

This chapter has shown that using the unitarist strategy alone is not totally effective, as seen by The Body Shop employees. On the other hand, the extreme of pluralism may enable creativity to flourish for a while, but the whole edifice is likely to collapse from lack of consistency, coordination, and direction (Murphy, 1989:89). For example, a recent case study on Traidcraft (Jones, 1996) found that its past pluralist strategy promoted a "free-rider culture," where many employees were seen to be taking advantage of the individual benefits a pluralist culture encourages. These apathetic employees did not work toward the betterment of Traidcraft and relied on the more values-driven employees to do the majority of the work.

As Harrison and Stokes (1992) point out, tough decisions about people's performance may be postponed out of kindness, which negatively impacts the organization's effectiveness. In turn, the reliance on a few more values-driven employees develops an atmosphere of mistrust and backbiting. Furthermore, the pluralist strategy extreme was seen as unjust, where differences in skill and ability were ignored in the interests of equal treatment (Harrison and Stokes, 1992). Difference, if valued for its own sake, is a recipe for organizational anarchy:

Accepting the legitimacy of differences in organizational culture cannot and should not lead to the kind of cultural relativism which presumes there is some justification for any and all cultural differences.

(Metcalfe and Richards, 1987:82)

It is important to note that The Body Shop, while moving away from unitarism, still appears to favor unitarism, with a continued explicit top-management commitment of moving toward sustainable development values. In other words, it still looks and feels much more like a fighting regiment than a debating society. This unitarist bias is due to the durability and legacy of its past unitarist culture and the leadership style it was built on. David Wheeler echoed this point when he stressed that:

> "Policy development [from top management] will always stay
> at the forefront of The Body Shop strategies."

The Body Shop's "both-and" strategy with a unitarist bias was described by all the interviewees. Some representative quotations are:

> "There is a movement to participative management but there
> still seems to be a lot of autocracy."

> "While we are giving a greater say to all employees, we have
> not lost our central direction."

Indeed, the Vision 2000 document implies that consultation remained top-down and directive. Leadership appears to be an important and positive factor within its cultural development strategy, as a means to maximize employee commitment toward sustainability. However, as Welford (1997) argues, leadership is only possible where there exists a followship. Thus, more cooperative, interactive, two-way processes are always likely to have a place in moving an organization forward. A previous expert workshop conducted by Welford and Jones (1994) offered the following wider recommendation:

> Open institutional structures are required in the firm so that
> any stakeholder has the ability to challenge and question the
> organization over any issue. Once again, we are looking for
> two-way process here with interaction and dialogue shifting
> the organization on to a more sustainable path.
>
> Welford and Jones (1994)

Conclusion

This case study of The Body Shop has shown that the popular extreme "strong culture" approach to cultural and sustainable development is impractical in an increasingly diverse and large organization. Unitarist strategies centered on imbuing shared organizational sustainability values through mission statements and charismatic leadership are not fully effective. The evidence from recent initiatives is that a more pluralist strategy, which more fully respects individuals' diverse goals, values, and aspirations, is being encouraged at The Body Shop. A pluralist strategy recognizes not only an increase in worker participation in decision making but also an increase in employee personal support (in contrast to an organization-oriented mission support strategy). This represents a gradual shift toward a strategy which realizes that an individual's motivation and commitment is not only a function of a company's sustainable set of values but of a wider set of personal and career support values. It also represents a realization that some individuals are motivated more (and not solely) by the company's goals and some individuals more (and not solely) by personal goals.

Although The Body Shop is moving to a more pluralist strategy, it is retaining its unitarist, leadership, and mission support elements. It is recognizing that extreme unitarist or pluralist strategies are simplistic products of "either-or" thinking. Each approach has its strengths and weaknesses. However, developing a unitarist-pluralist strategy does not mean aiming for a balance between them. As Bate (1994) argues, there is no virtue in the notion of a perfectly balanced culture. It is argued that a company needs to aim toward a contextually appropriate cultural combination. A unitarist-pluralist strategy is therefore an approach with the intention of producing a hybrid culture that is appropriate in balancing its sustainability goals with the increasingly diverse personal goals of its growing workforce. For The Body Shop, while unitarism is favored, pluralism is still encouraged.

This chapter leads to the hypothesis that companies wishing to move toward sustainability should consider employing a combination of both unitarism and pluralism in its cultural development strategy. For The Body Shop this strategy is defined as:

> A predominant unitary commitment to creating and extending sustainable shared values and interests, with a new pluralist commitment to providing mechanisms that will resolve or at least contain the disharmonies that exist between divergent systems of meaning.

Moreover, the chapter reveals two pairs of opposite but complementary principles, which form the basis of a unitarist-pluralist strategy (refer to

Unitary Principles	Pluralist Principles
1a. Mission Support	1b. Personal Support
2a. Charismatic Leadership	2b. Participation
Past Cultural Pressures	Personal Pressures

FIGURE 6.1. PRINCIPLES OF THE BODY SHOP'S UNITARIST-PLURALIST STRATEGY.

Figure 6.1). A unitarist principle of mission support is coupled with a pluralist principle of personal support, and a unitarist principle of charismatic leadership is coupled with a pluralist principle of participation.

At the bottom of Figure 6.1, pressures that have the potential of moving a company toward unitarism or pluralism are highlighted. For The Body Shop, the predominant pressure was unitarist, arising from the durability of its past culture. However, as The Body Shop has grown, pluralist personal value pressures have increased due to the increasing diversity of its workforce. In other words, as its workforce has grown, The Body Shop has learned that its cultural development strategy needs not only to create a predominant shared sustainable set of values but to simultaneously account for and respect alternative values.

Chapter 7

Sustainable Technology Management: The Role of Networks of Learning[1]

Sarah F. Clarke

Technology, from the "low-tech" spoon to the "hi-tech" satellite, is embedded in all societies. It has been since humans first used tools to hunt for food and to construct dwellings. Technology takes a variety of forms, such as a simple, communal water pump and latrine or a sophisticated water and sewerage system. It performs important roles in both developed and developing countries. Consequently, technology[2] holds a central position in debates about, and movement toward, more sustainable forms of societal behavior. Societies committed to sustainable development must therefore ask questions about what this commitment means for the processes through which technology is developed and finds application. Answering these questions is made problematic as sustainable development and technology arise in complex multilevel and multiparty systems. The purpose of this chapter is to address the issue of what is sustainable technology management from the perspective of one group of actors with a central role in technology management—the firm. However, while the chapter addresses sustainable technology management from the perspective of the firm, it continually seeks reference to the broader multiparty, multilevel system.

Technology and Society

It is important to set out some contextual remarks about the firm (and through that, technology) in society. Unfortunately, the role of technology in social development in general, and sustainable development in particular, is highly contested: For some, more and "better" technology provides solutions to society's most acute social and environmental problems and enables the equitable redistribution of wealth. For others, technology is the cause of social inequities, the deterioration of individual well-being, and the destruction of the natural environment (Cramer and Zegveld, 1991). Beyond this "paradox of technology," some propose a new technological landscape—a "green" techno-economic paradigm— one that requires a radical transformation of social behaviors, consumption patterns, and lifestyles (Foray and Grübler, 1996). While technology plays a key role in this transformation process, the paradox is broken by directing the debate toward a more holistic conceptualization of technology and its interfaces with society and the natural environment: The focus becomes the technical artifact and the social, political, economic, and environmental processes that surround and shape it.[3]

In contrast, the pursuit of clean(er), green(er), more environmentally friendly technological[4] solutions to social and environmental problems is dominated in both research and practice by the desire to perfect the artifact and minimize its impacts (see, for example, Burall, 1996; Roy, 1994). Here, technology is considered largely in isolation of the social, political, and economic processes that shape it—processes that are themselves shaped, altered, and adapted by technology. Instead, we see the predominance of ideas about "Design for the Environment" (DFE)—an approach that aims to minimize the environmental and social consequences of human activities through modification of technological artifacts. At the firm level, this translates into the application of environmental constraints to traditional business beliefs and behaviors. The goal is one of optimization of economic prosperity, environmental protection, and social innovation through the development of existing relationships and marginal modification of industrial systems.

Technology is the engine drawing on the fuel of resource endowments that drive this process. In this context, the management and development of appropriate technological solutions is given momentum by technological experts within the firm, guided by the strategic direction of corporate management and external regulatory and legislative frameworks. Technology is a driver of development, and innovation is an essential consequence of development. It exhibits "natural" trajectories governed by the cost, form, function, market, and performance demands of the firm's stakeholders (see, for example, Kemp, 1994).

Sustainable Technology and the Firm

A more holistic conceptualization of technology, however, directs attention away from the technological artifact toward the knowledge, relationships, values, and assumptions that underpin technological choices and social behaviors and to the moral and ethical validity of those choices. Green(er), clean(er), more environmentally friendly technology is no longer the means to the end of more sustainable forms of development. Rather the goal, described here as "Design for and within Society" (DFS), is to produce environmentally sound technology (Perrings, 1994) by reshaping the knowledge and relationships that comprise a particular technology into a more sustainable form (see, for example, Schot, Hoogma, and Elzen, 1994; Irwin, Georg, and Vergragt, 1994). Technology, from this perspective, is the product of a complex set of relationships internal and external to the firm, many beyond its direct control. It embodies social, political, psychological, economic, and professional commitments, skills, prejudices, possibilities, and constraints and does not have an internal momentum of its own that predisposes it to one path or another (Bijker and Law, 1992:7).

Designing for and within society extends the research and practice of technology management and development beyond the traditional frameworks of engineering and management decision making and asks fundamental questions about the nature and role of firms and technologies in their social and environmental contexts. The task for the firm is to understand these relationships and, where needed, to forge new relationships with individuals both within the firm and with actors in the external social, political, and economic environment.

These contrasting views of technology expose distinctions that are made increasingly between environmental management and management for sustainability (Clarke and Georg, 1995:37; Eden, 1996:158–162). Conventionally, environmental management appears to refer to all those policies and practices, largely within a utilitarian ethical frame of reference, that direct an organization's activities toward product stewardship, bring environmental values into economic analysis, and allow for the emergence of new relationships across the supply chain. Management for sustainability, however, reflects policies and practices, underpinned by principles of justice, respect, equity, stewardship, precaution, and futurity, which fundamentally question and reshape environmental, social, economic, and political relationships and which enable the equitable redistribution of wealth and opportunity within and among generations and societies.

This distinction is critical when addressing the issue of more sustainable forms of technology management and development. Management strategies and practices incorporated in the notion of DFE are more consistent with concepts of environmental management. Typically, they are blind to the complex relationships that shape the nature of technologies, and they emphasize a more deterministic model of technological innovation. However, concepts embodied in the philosophy of DFS are more closely associated with management for sustainability. In the DFS approach, there is an implicit recognition of the interconnected, and mutually shaping, relationships between firms, their technologies, and society and the need for just and equitable technological solutions.

Networks of Learning

This chapter adopts a design for and within society perspective of sustainable technology management and does this by exploring how actors in the networks of learning within and surrounding the firm contribute to technology management. The concept of the network of learning is used to describe the mechanisms, processes, and relationships that shape a particular technology. The analysis, therefore, takes as its point of departure relationships around technologies rather than a technological artifact. Here, technology management refers to the collection of decisions, actions, mechanisms, and processes, internal and external to the firm, that contribute to the form of a particular technology. This approach extends technology management beyond the conventional boundaries of the community of managers, engineers, technologist, and researchers making technological decisions to include broader social, political, and economic spheres. It includes both the purposeful management of technology and more ad-hoc, spontaneous, and intangible processes and behaviors that play a role in shaping technology.

Critically, in the context of more sustainable forms of technology management, it incorporates the network of relationships encompassed by those actors who influence environmental policies, practices, and thinking that lead to environmental management and management for sustainability. An aim of the chapter is to disentangle the relationships between more sustainable forms of management and more sustainable technology management which, at their most elementary, might be appropriately described as the relationships between the process(es) of environmental management and the system(s) of technology management. It has been argued earlier that these relationships have been neglected in previous research (Clarke and Roome, 1993).

The network of learning described in this chapter is taken from a larger qualitative, grounded theory study of technology management undertaken between Fall 1993 and Spring 1995 (Clarke, forthcoming). This chapter focuses on that part of the network of learning surrounding an electronics company, known here as "HiTec."

The chapter is divided into three sections. The first presents a case study of the sustainable technology management aspects of HiTec. It draws on interviews with over 30 members of HiTec's network of learning, which spans North America and Europe.[5] These included senior management, environmental specialists, and engineers within HiTec and members of nongovernmental organizations, environmentalists, and environmental and technical managers outside of HiTec. It also draws on documentary evidence from the public domain. The second section discusses the nature and characteristics of HiTec's network of learning. A particular focus is on the relationships between environmental management, technology management, and strategic management activities. These are explored using the concept of "islands of knowledge." The conclusion outlines the implications of the network of learning approach for research and practice in more sustainable technology management.

HiTec

A case study of more sustainable technology management at HiTec is presented in four sections. The first section establishes the business context within which HiTec's environmental and technical activities operate. The next section outlines HiTec's emerging response to, and interpretation of, the sustainable development agenda. The third section describes how HiTec approaches sustainability issues in its technology management. The last section then considers the avenues of learning between technical and environmental communities within HiTec that constitute its network of learning.

HiTec: Business Context and Strategic Orientation

HiTec is a multinational supplier of a wide range of electronics equipment. The technology it uses is found in products that range from relatively simple consumer items to highly complex systems. These products form part of the same industrial supply chain. The products in themselves have not been the subject of environmental controversy, although there has been recent attention to the environmental consequences of commonly used production methods in the industry in general.

With headquarters in North America and a workforce of some 55,000, HiTec has manufacturing and research facilities in more than 90 locations around the world. These operations are conceived as a "global village" in which activities such as R&D, design, and manufacturing take place, where expertise lies, and where it makes greatest economic and business sense. A complex network of reporting and operational relationships criss-crosses the globe.

HiTec is recognized as a leader and champion of more environmentally sound corporate practices. It has made extensive commitments to environmental management and, in recent years, has made great strides to improve its environmental performance. These activities form the core of HiTec's interpretation of sustainable development for the company.

The company does not have an explicit, stand-alone technology strategy for the products it manufactures and the processes it uses. Neither has it explored the parameters of sustainable technology in the context of its business. Rather, technological issues are entwined in a complex manner within the overall strategic management process. HiTec began to socialize the concept of sustainable development as a backdrop to its environmental management activities rather than using the concept as the driving force of those programs. Technology management and development are parts of a process of corporate transformation toward more sustainable management practice.

The company has a highly skilled and knowledgeable workforce committed to the company's core values which, at the time of the study, were

> We have only one standard—*Excellence;* we share one vision, we are a *team;* we create superior value for our *customers;* our *people* are our strength; *commitment*—we do what we say we will do; and we embrace change and reward *innovation.*"
>
> (HiTec, 1992)

These values are reinforced by HiTec's overall goal of establishing a leadership position in its industry. This philosophy infuses all aspects of company operations. In the case of the environment, this strategic goal translates into "environmental leadership."

HiTec's Approach to Sustainable Development

HiTec's response to the environment and sustainable development agenda has evolved since the early 1980s. It began with a Housekeeping strategy, through a Pollution Prevention approach to a Product Stewardship philosophy, as summarized in Table 7.1.

TABLE 7.1. EVOLUTION OF HiTec's ENVIRONMENTAL STRATEGY

	Stage 1: Housekeeping	Stage 2: Pollution Prevention	Stage 3: Product Stewardship
Time scale	Pre-1987	1987 to 1991–92	1992–93 and beyond
Strategy	"No more than required"	"Going the extra mile"	"(Low-key), environmental leadership"
Management	ad-hoc	Projects assume a life of their own once given corporate commitment and go-ahead; predominantly internal inputs	Programs and systems driven with corporate direction and expert guidance, internal and external inputs process
Management confidence in "value" of environment	Low	Low-medium	Medium-high
Technological focus	As required: ad-hoc, tidying up	Process technology: cleaning up production	Product and process technology: greening the design process
Initiatives and successes	Minor	Project specific, major and minor initiatives: Environmental Audits, Environmental Protection Program, CFC elimination, technology cooperation projects	Major, systems-based initiatives: Product Life Cycle Management, Design for Environment, Public Environmental Reporting Initiative, ongoing Stage 2 projects

(continues)

TABLE 7.1 (*Continued*)

Stakeholder involvement	Limited	Project specific and industry focused; government and academia	Suppliers and customers across the value chain; government and academia
Alignment with corporate strategy	Weak—legislative compliance, corporate responsibility	Weak—business efficiencies, emerging competitive advantage, corporate responsibility	Strong—industry leadership, competitive advantage, corporate responsibility

Stage 1: Housekeeping

Prior to 1987, environmental awareness at HiTec originated in health and safety programs aimed at employee well-being and in housekeeping initiatives focused on manufacturing efficiencies. Many of these activities are now labeled post-hoc by personnel as environmental initiatives and are used as evidence of the company's long-standing environmental credentials. Before formal environmental policies were established, environmental activities, such as office waste recycling and spill prevention, arose from the concerns and initiatives of employees or legislative requirements. They were not a result of a specific, overarching management commitment and direction. HiTec's early approach can be characterized as compliance-based. During this period, there were no major company-wide initiatives on environmental concerns, and stakeholder involvement in company environmental matters was limited to that demanded by legal requirements. Few, if any, links were made between the strategic direction of the company and environmental concerns.

Stage 2: Pollution Prevention

In 1987, HiTec established a corporate function responsible for environmental aspects of the company's business. This recognized that environmental concerns were becoming a critical element of HiTec's business environment, as was the need to increase the effectiveness and coherence of existing environmental activities. Senior management signaled their commitment to environmental concerns by launching a company environmental policy and minimum acceptable environmental standards, which manufacturing locations and operations were required to meet. Environment was conceived largely in terms of environmental protection. This is confirmed by the introduction early on of an Environmental

Protection Program that established a framework to enable the company to comply with environmental laws and evaluate its success against compliance.

HiTec also introduced an Environmental Audit program to establish a base line for its environmental performance and to determine areas where immediate action was required to bring the company into compliance both with legislation and corporate policy. The company treated the environment as a set of discrete issues for the business. It did not have a clearly articulated approach that infused all aspects of business decision making: Environment was not a strategic direction.

This stage was also characterized by greater involvement of external stakeholders in HiTec's environmental activities. These were generally limited to specific initiatives requiring government and technical academic input, especially in relation to technology development.

Stage 3: Product Stewardship

The success of the company's environmental initiatives and rising confidence in the value of environment to the company brought about a significant shift in HiTec's approach to environmental concerns. In contrast to the issue-specific or project-focused initiatives of earlier stages, Stage 3 is characterized by attention to product-based technologies and marked a move toward a more corporate-wide approach to the environment. Environment was conceived as an issue that impacts all aspects of business activities encompassing product and process technologies. HiTec's approach was underpinned by a new philosophy of product stewardship and guided by a goal of environmental leadership. Environmental leadership was seen as entirely consistent with, indeed an essential component of, the company's leadership strategy. Moreover, the company engaged with a wider range and greater number of stakeholders to fully assess and then address the environmental impacts of its products.

During this stage, HiTec revised its corporate policy for "Protection and enhancement of the environment." There is no direct reference to sustainable development in the policy, although HiTec is a signatory to the International Chamber of Commerce's Business Charter for Sustainable Development. Senior company personnel refer to the company policy as "incorporating the concept of sustainable development." The policy states:

> Recognizing the critical link between a healthy environment and sustained economic growth, [HiTec] bases its environ-

mental responsibility on the principle of product stewardship, being accountable for the environmental impacts of its products from their conception to final disposition.

(HiTec, 1993)

At this time HiTec's environmental activities are conceived against a corrupted agenda for sustainable development with an emphasis on product stewardship and environmental responsibility within a business framework of sustained economic growth. The company does not conceive policy in terms of an ethic of sustainability or recognize the fundamentally reforming nature of the sustainable development debate and its implications for the corporation. This observation is borne out by the approach the company has taken to more sustainable forms of technology management.

More Sustainable Technology Management at HiTec

HiTec has a substantial research and development subsidiary with operations in seven locations. This capability is responsible for the research, design, and development of the next generation of HiTec's products and technologies. In addition, the company has extensive engineering competencies at each manufacturing facility that are responsible for process developments to enable new product introductions.

As with many firms, HiTec has developed a concurrent engineering philosophy, to reduce the time to market for new products and to cut development costs. This led to closer relationships between design and manufacture under a "Design for Manufacturability" philosophy. At the time of the research, projects ran according to a staged design process. Each project had to achieve a number of standardized milestones before proceeding to the next stage in the design and development process. Recently, however, it was recognized that this linear conceptualization of design did not match the more systemic philosophy of Design for Manufacturability (DFM) and newer ideas surrounding Design for Recyclability (DFR) and DFE (described below). This mismatch prompted a comprehensive review of corporate design standards.

HiTec does not have a specific strategy for sustainable technology management, yet its technological activities do respond to the needs of the different stages of its environmental strategy. These developments are set out below.

Stage 1: Ad-hoc, Tidying Up

During Stage 1, environmental issues were almost entirely the concern of manufacturing engineering. Whereas legislative requirements and a desire to reduce manufacturing waste and minimize production hazards drove manufacturing changes, product designers were largely ignorant of the need to consider the environmental impacts of their designs and the design process. Product design was motivated by, for example, functionality, cost minimization, performance, and market requirements; environmental concerns were addressed as and when they arose, rather than in any strategic or systematic sense.

Stage 2: Cleaning Up Production

A major turning point in HiTec's approach to technology management and development was signaled in 1989 by a corporate directive to eliminate CFCs from manufacturing processes. This followed international concern over the ozone layer, as witnessed by the Montreal Protocol (Somerset, 1989). Backed by significant encouragement from regulatory agencies and strong commitment from the corporate environment department, HiTec adopted a leadership position and drove through an ambitious program to ensure that the company was "free [of CFC113] in three [years]."[6] It eliminated CFC113 in 1991, several years in advance of the requirements of the Montreal Protocol and ahead of many other companies and despite some views that the technical hurdles were insurmountable.

HiTec engineers explain their success in terms of five factors: First, each site was free to solve the problem according to its local idiosyncrasies and had total support from management in terms of motivation (the mandatory directive), money (several million dollars), and manpower (engineers were assigned full time to the project). Second, the company mobilized existing internal research and design networks where engineers from across the company shared ideas, problems, and solutions. Third, once in motion, the project took on a life and momentum of its own: HiTec engineers wanted to beat the competition and live up to the leadership goal of the company. Fourth, they worked in close cooperation with suppliers to test alternative, CFC-free products. Fifth, and perhaps most important, key corporate environment personnel established and maintained the program's legitimacy.

Internal legitimacy with senior management was secured by emphasizing the business benefits of the project. External validity was attained through strong relationships with government agencies. These agencies encouraged HiTec to increase the scope of its project and take onboard new projects. The company marked its achievement with a worldwide celebration, and employees continue to speak of their accomplishment with great pride.

Not content with this success, HiTec decided that its CFC-free manufacturing process technology and expertise should be shared with other organizations. The company spearheaded an international technology cooperation project to share its knowledge and technology for no monetary gain. And, directed by a senior environmental manager, five years after the company became CFC-free, HiTec engineers are still working with other companies and countries to achieve the goals of the Montreal Protocol. Across the company, employees felt that this was morally right, while acknowledging that economic benefits derive from the company's leadership strategy. For example, HiTec's image as a responsible corporation is enhanced, and the program continues to generate goodwill toward the company.

Stage 3: Greening the Design Process

Following this unprecedented technological success, the task for HiTec was to maintain and build on the momentum of the CFC initiative and capitalize on heightened environmental awareness across the company. Corporate environment recognized the need to shift the focus away from manufacturing alone to manufacturing and design. In general, designers were ignorant of the implications of environmental issues for design, above and beyond manufacturing concerns. Typically, HiTec's products and their design had remained unchallenged and unchanged despite the advent of environmental concerns within the company.

With the launch of a Product Life Cycle Management Program, HiTec signaled its commitment to "maximize the resource efficiency of products from design through to the end of their useful life" (HiTec, 1994). This developed into a major initiative to ensure that all products were "designed for the environment." At this early stage, DFE was seen as minimizing the environmental impacts of products and processes, rather than demanding a strategic reorientation in the company's product offerings in response to sustainable development. Business opportunities, competitive issues, and market requirements were the driving force of product design and selection, with environmental sensitivity a mediating, rather than motivating, factor.

During Stage 3, HiTec set about developing the tools and techniques to assist it to introduce the life cycle program and support a DFE philosophy. This process, ongoing at the time of the research, drew initially on the skills of a handful of experts around the company. It was driven almost entirely by senior environmental managers. These managers "cherry-picked" the knowledge and ideas of a tiny minority of engineers and senior technology managers who had begun to explore environmentally sensitive design options in isolation from, and independently of, corporate environmental initiatives. The strategy of the corporate environment team was to develop DFE tools and techniques while simultaneously socializing the life cycle concept with senior management. This interpretation of sustainable development at HiTec would be launched to the wider design community when the tools, techniques, and management commitment were in place.

Engineers in the company were largely unfamiliar with environmental concerns for design or corporate environment's philosophy, with the exception of senior technical managers in the research laboratories and the few designers who had taught themselves about environmental issues and made a personal commitment to more environmentally sensitive design. In fact, outside the relatively small (and select) network of experts, the DFE project was deliberately hidden from view. Many engineers were unaware that new personnel had taken over the direction of environmental initiatives since Stage 2. While these engineers held in high regard the key players (environmental managers) of Stage 2, they were quite dismissive of the abilities of the environmental management teams introduced across the company in Stage 3. The impression was that environmental managers should deal with manufacturing and housekeeping matters, leaving design issues to the technical experts.

Many design engineers and managers had no understanding of the impacts of their designs on the environment, while others spoke of the "natural" or "inevitable" miniaturization of their technology over time, which post-hoc could be interpreted as an environmental benefit. Few were aware of the words "design for environment," let alone their meaning. Many seemed unable to conceive of the company's product as part of a much wider value chain or as having any negative environmental implications, other than in manufacturing. Sustainable development was not a term they used. Neither did they refer directly, or indirectly, to the impact of their technology on issues such as equity and social well-being.

Avenues of Communication in HiTec's Network of Learning

During the initial stages of HiTec's environmental activities there was no formal environmental management structure within the firm other than that associated with the fledgling corporate environment team and health and safety experts around the company. The success of the CFC-free project is largely explained by the ability of two key corporate environment personnel to identify and then capitalize on a project which, once kick started, took on a life of its own. These "link" actors skillfully worked the company's internal and external networks to create a justifying "space" within which engineering actors were free to find solutions to the problems brought to them as a strategic response to legislation. These two personnel provided a link between the environmental community and the engineering community, internally, and between the corporation and the international community, externally. Indeed, one of the responsibilities of the corporate environment department today is to pick up environmental trends and feed them up to the Social Responsibility Committee of the Board, down to design, engineering, and management through the environmental management structure (described below), and horizontally to the company's Product and Service Delivery Group. This was the only mechanism identified during the research through which corporate environment formally participated in shaping strategic decision making.

At the same time, HiTec's engineering community has extensive networks of relationships across the company. Through these networks engineers share ideas, knowledge, technological solutions, and problems. These relationships include ad-hoc contacts between peers, internal and external to the company, and a more formal network of research councils, comprising experts from across the company. Together they form the engineers' network of learning.

Although the research councils meet several times a year, sometimes for a number of years, they are not part of HiTec's formal organizational structure. Rather, they emerge and fade as and when the need arises, springing out of the interest of a loose collection of like-minded individuals with shared interests or a common concern. Members of these groups have very similar understandings and interpretations of the implications of environmental concerns for HiTec's products and processes: They use a common (technical) language and hold similar (scientific) assumptions. The engineering community's networks have "mesh-like" properties— flexible enough to bend around obstacles, yet sufficiently rigid to pick up and run with a project, such as the CFC initiative. These technical relationships are essentially separate from the environmental community's networks, with the exception of senior management links, such as those identified in Stage 2.

Members of the engineering network learn about specific environmental concerns from directives issued from corporate environment and, importantly, through their own personal, technical networks. However, technological solutions to these environmental concerns emerge from within the internal design and engineering networks and through contacts in the company's supply chain. There are few, if any, nontechnical "outsiders" among these technology-based, knowledge relationships. Indeed, there is a sense of "them and us" dividing the two communities. Some engineers are of the opinion that they have little to learn from nontechnical people.

As the company's strategy evolved, a more formal environment management structure emerged, comprising around 50 personnel worldwide. This structure ensures that company policies, procedures, standards, and systems circulate throughout the corporation. Responsibility for the implementation of environmental programs lies with the local management at each site. However, there are marked differences in the level of awareness and commitment to environmental management across the company. The network of environmental specialists is mainly plugged into the manufacturing side of the engineering community rather than into design. Most engineers either did not know of, or were unable to identify, these specialists and rarely called on them for advice. This was of little consequence while HiTec regarded environment as a set of issues for manufacturing processes. However, the network gaps imply lack of awareness of the new product life cycle and design for environment philosophies being driven through the company. There is also a marked contrast between the "free-wheeling" characteristics of the original CFC project (Stage 2) and the more controlled and planned approach to the introduction of the new design philosophy (Stage 3), based on a more structured approach to communications between the two communities.

A number of engineers involved in the DFE initiative were skeptical about the company's continued willingness and commitment to change. Changes to date had required relatively minor product alterations, whereas the new DFE requirements had major implications for the company's products and could potentially call into question the fundamental characteristics of HiTec's technologies. There was little appreciation of the concept of sustainable development outside senior management levels, although many individuals expressed a deep concern about the need to protect the environment for their children and grandchildren. This sentiment originated from personal concern and external influences rather than corporate direction.

Perhaps the most remarkable aspect of HiTec's networks is the extent

to which actors are willing and able to share their knowledge. Many interviewees remarked how, time and time again, HiTec was teaching more
often than it was learning. However, the company did benchmark (and
therefore learned about) its environmental performance and practices to a
limited extent with other corporations to ensure that it remained a leader
in environmental initiatives in its industry.

Knowledge about technological issues relating to environmental concerns is shared in an ad-hoc manner between HiTec's manufacturing and
engineering personnel and members of the external engineering community who face similar problems. More formal interaction occurs through
the international technology cooperation projects spearheaded by the
company. In both cases, the flow of information is facilitated by the fact
that this technology is viewed as nonproprietary. As such the company
has felt a moral obligation to pass its expertise on.

Technology aside, HiTec has taken every opportunity to participate in
external business activities addressing managerial aspects of environmental concerns, such as the development of international standards and public reporting of environmental performance. Here, HiTec aims are to
ensure its views are heard and to influence the business and government
agenda. Environmental specialists at HiTec respond to requests for advice
from environmental managers in other companies. Indeed, following the
success of their technological cooperation projects and encouraged by
external stakeholders, there were suggestions that HiTec might initiate a
similar collaborative project to pass on its knowledge and experience
about environmental management systems.

Some indirect interfaces occur between HiTec's environmental managers and members of the external environmental community, although
environmentalists are specifically excluded from direct involvement in
the company's environmental decision making. To a limited extent,
HiTec's environmental managers discuss environmental concerns with
"moderate" environmentalists—more radical environmental activists,
such as Greenpeace, are not engaged in dialogue. Interfaces between
environmentalists and the engineering community are almost nonexistent
except for personal connections outside the workplace.

Unraveling HiTec's Network of Learning

This research sought to illuminate technology management in the context
of more sustainable management practice. It considered this from the perspective of actors in networks of learning within HiTec. This discussion

is presented in two parts: First, it describes the extent (and limit) of sustainable management practice at HiTec and highlights the factors that enable (and disable) the company's ability to learn (to be more sustainable); second, it explores islands of knowledge in HiTec's networks of learning, with particular attention to the connections (and gaps) between technology management, environmental management, and strategic management activities.

Sustainable Management Practice at HiTec

The management practices illustrated by HiTec are referenced to sustainable development. The concept of sustainable development is used as a backdrop to its management processes and company operations. HiTec is engaged in a process of learning about what sustainable development means for its organization and has changed that interpretation and continues to see it evolve. It has broadened the scope and deepened the conceptualization of its approach to more sustainable management.

HiTec conceives environment and sustainability as issues that can be accommodated by its existing management philosophy and culture, rather than as ideas that demand a fundamental transformation in that paradigm. However, it should be made clear that, in relation to the theoretical typologies proposed elsewhere (for example, Hunt and Auster, 1990; Roome, 1992; Steger, 1993), HiTec can be classified as a proactive or leading-edge company in its environmental management activities. Yet, it does not have an ethic of sustainability as the driving force of its overall operations. Table 7.2 summarizes HiTec's approach to more sustainable management.

HiTec has the capacity to learn to become more sustainable, since it is not handicapped by the nature of its product—its technologies have not come under great environmental scrutiny. This, together with HiTec's self-identified leadership position, means that it does not need to seek external legitimization for its activities—unlike a nuclear power station, for example. Indeed, external actors in the business community serve to reinforce its present philosophy and leadership position. However, the potential for HiTec to move beyond its Stage 3 interpretation of sustainable development is limited by its ability to break out of the boundaries circumscribed by its technology and the established relationships which constitute that technology across its value chain. HiTec's leadership position presents an opportunity for the company to "reengineer" itself in a

TABLE 7.2. KEY FEATURES OF HITEC'S APPROACH TO SUSTAINABILITY

Feature	HiTec
Management strategy	Leadership
Sustainability as…	Product Stewardship
Nature of learning process	Create a "space" in which to share knowledge about the way we do things and to learn how others do things.
Key internal drivers	Corporate Environment and environmental specialists, with the support and cooperation of senior management, in the context of environmental leadership.
View of technology	"We have a tenable technology which 'naturally' shapes more sustainable futures—the nature of our technology is not contested."
Sustainable technology management viewed as…	DFE/Product Stewardship with an emphasis on partnership projects built from in-house expertise. Large-scale environmental projects triggered by environmental managers.
Motivation for action	Business case for action balanced against the morally "right" thing to do.
Change process	From "free-wheeling" to "planned" change.

more sustainable form, as it has begun to do by adopting a Product Stewardship philosophy.

In certain respects, HiTec's relationships may be viewed as "weapons of leadership." The company purposefully and strategically manages its involvement with other predominantly business organizations and evolves its relationships with this community to further legitimize its leadership position and strategy and to pursue more sustainable forms of management practice. However, it does not need to seek out the support of actors outside this constituency, such as environmentalists.

Based on a technology that is relatively uncontroversial, HiTec's approach to sustainable technology management is founded on a philosophy of Product Stewardship, embodied in the notion of DFE. Indeed, the company's size and considerable technological and environmental management expertise enables it to define for others not only the philosophy of DFE but also the tools and techniques that comprise it. HiTec's contribution to the development of more sustainable futures lies in its willingness to share its nonproprietary knowledge and technology. This has the effect of influencing the actions of actors in companies not necessarily in its supply chain. It also serves to reinforce its Product Stewardship approach to sustainable development and leads to the adoption of this conceptualization of sustainable development by others. External support for its Product Stewardship philosophy internally validates this approach.

At the outset, it was suggested that an ethic of sustainability implies that companies wishing to implement sustainable technology management must fundamentally question the nature of their technology. HiTec does not appear to question the underlying assumptions embodied within its technology: The technology is viewed as environmentally uncontroversial (it has no direct and significant impacts); over time technological developments have had the effect of reducing these impacts (through miniaturization); and, by using DFE techniques, life cycle impacts may be reduced. The result is that HiTec is locked into its technology. Moreover, there is little evidence that technological decisions are made based on principles of sustainability, such as justice, equity, respect, precaution, and futurity, or that issues of redistribution of wealth and opportunity are explicitly considered by technology managers and designers. An exception is HiTec's decision to "freely" transfer nonproprietary environmental technology and knowledge. However, while those engaged in this process argue that it is morally justified, they rationalize it post-hoc as "good business sense" in aiding market entry and developing good will. Consequently, HiTec cannot be said to practice sustainable technology management.

Building (and Bridging) Islands of Knowledge at HiTec

HiTec's network of learning comprises three distinct communities: environmental, engineering, and strategic management. Within each community, different groups provide a heterogeneous character in relation to the knowledge base, beliefs, and assumptions. However, for simplicity of analysis, unless stated otherwise, each of the three communities is considered to be homogeneous.

The case study illustrates the different characteristics of the three communities. These are summarized in Table 7.3. The environmental community has explored the concept and meaning of sustainable development. Members of the engineering and strategy communities appear to have less knowledge in this area, with some having no knowledge at all.

Indeed, they rely on the environmental community for their knowledge of sustainable development issues. Aside from a tiny minority of experts, the engineering community has not considered to any great extent the environmental impacts of HiTec's technology (with the exception of its manufacturing processes). This contrasts with the activities of members of the environmental community who are champions of the DFE program, an initiative fully supported by senior management, although it has not had a marked effect on the strategic direction of the company—it complements rather than transforms it.

Both the environmental community and the engineering community have strong and extensive ties with outside individuals and organizations. However, the former has a greater diversity of connections (though excludes radical environmentalists) than the latter who typically do not engage with environmental interests. The engineering community has a built-in, dynamic, and emergent mechanism for the cross-fertilization of knowledge and ideas across the company. This contrasts with the environmental community's preference for structure and control and the strategic managers' formal structure for communicating environmental information. All three communities engage in ad-hoc sharing of knowledge among peers.

TABLE 7.3. CHARACTERISTICS OF DIFFERENT COMMUNITIES AT HITEC

Characteristic	Environmental	Engineering	Strategic Management
• Knowledge of sustainability	Moderate	Nil to limited	Limited
Product impacts	Driving DFE	Expert input to DFE	Supporting DFE
External ties	Extensive and inclusive	Extensive and exclusive	No data
• Mechanisms for information-sharing about environment	Structured and controlled	Dynamic and emergent	Formal
• Opinions of each other	Engineers are a source of expert knowledge; strategic management legitimizes our task.	Environmental specialists are best placed to deal with manufacturing issues. How far will management commitment go?	We fully support the activities of the engineers and environmental managers.

Finally, while the engineering and environmental communities enjoy full support from strategic management, engineers are somewhat skeptical of the abilities of the environmental managers—whereas the environmental community recognizes the need to enlist the expertise of the engineers and to inform them about environmental concerns.

Taken together, these differences suggest that HiTec's network of learning comprises three distinct islands of knowledge. The connections between the islands of knowledge have changed as HiTec has developed its response to the sustainable development agenda. During Stage 1, links were largely ad-hoc and formed as the need arose. The advent of Stage 2 led to the development of bridges between the three communities via two key managers. These managers were able to create a mechanism that, building on existing self-organizing structures within the engineering community, facilitated the transfer of ideas between the islands. However, the bias of the knowledge sharing was toward "familiar" business and technical relationships—between people who spoke a similar "language" and held similar assumptions.

During Stage 3, the momentum for this learning appears to have been lost with the introduction of a highly planned and thoroughly executed program of events. This has created the feeling that the engineers were in a state of "suspended animation," waiting for the environmental community to make the next move—despite the reality that the engineers had been the movers and shakers in Stage 2. The overall effect of the presence of the islands of knowledge is to create a separation between environmental management activities, technological development, and strategic decision making. This finding echoes the observations of Dermody and Hanmer-Lloyd (1995), who call for greater involvement of technical personnel in environmental management activities.

Conclusion

This chapter presents two models of technology: One assumes that technology is embodied in a social context, the other does not. The chapter develops the former perspective, reporting on research centered on an analysis of the environmental and technology management activities of the company HiTec, together with its network of learning and its social context. It is argued that this approach is consistent with the concept of sustainable development. If sustainable development is taken to be a socially negotiated concept and the management responses that result are embodied in, and derived from, environmental, economic, social, and political processes, then studies of sustainable technology must reflect this reality. It is suggested that researchers in this field should be willing to look inside the firm at the process of technology management and outside the firm to the network of learning which circumscribes that process.

For companies striving for sustainability, there is a need to articulate more precisely the meaning of sustainable development, as distinct from environmental protection, and to develop a language that more accurately describes management for sustainability and distinguishes it from environmental management. Moreover, if a philosophy of "Design for and with Society," beyond the bounds of the concept of "Design for the Environment," is to be encouraged, then there is a need for managers and researchers to have a greater understanding and awareness of the forces that shape organizational and technological choices. Critically, in learning to build sustainable industries for sustainable societies we must also learn what sustainable technology management represents and the factors that limit the decisions we make and must live with.

The evidence from the case study is that as HiTec has progressively moved to integrate environmental issues into its activities and explored the concept of sustainable development, it has broadened the way it thinks and operates and has extended the reach of its network of informants. This suggests that, as it continues to consider the meaning and implications of the sustainable development agenda, it has not seen the end of the expansion of its network.

What people understand by sustainable development is referenced to the relationships of which they are a part and through which they learn and are socialized and the sphere of control they have over either management systems or technology. This creates islands of knowledge within the network, each with its own set of beliefs, assumptions, values, and preferred style of learning. Within an expanding network, the number of islands of knowledge will tend to increase. Unless mechanisms are created to facilitate communication between these islands, it is difficult to conceive of a shared understanding of sustainable development and a common philosophy for more sustainable management practices.

The priorities must therefore be, first, to recognize that these differences exist within a firm's network of learning and, second, to provide individuals with the skills to communicate with people who perhaps speak a different "language" and certainly hold different beliefs and assumptions.

In the case of HiTec, two people (out of 55,000) triggered learning on a scale that achieved dramatic results. As firms move toward more environmentally benign technology, there is a need for a broader range of stakeholder involvement. This suggests a need for more bridges between islands of knowledge and a broader mix of people able to fulfill the role of "learning catalyst." In the absence of examples of sustainable technology and the lack of models of sustainable technology management, there is a need to develop processes that recognize the important role of open learning in organizations. This is seen as critical in guiding companies toward more sustainable practice.

NOTES

1. A version of this chapter was presented at the Fourth International Greening of Industry Conference, Research and Practice: Learning to Build Sustainable Industries for Sustainable Societies, Toronto, November 12–14, 1995.

2. Technology is defined here as "the sum of all objects, systems, and processes that can be materially described and that are created by man for his needs, making use of the possibilities offered by nature" (Roth, 1987).

3. This perspective has parallels with the work of sociologists of technology (reviewed by Williams and Edge, 1996).

4. Environmentally friendly technology is technology designed to meet human needs while considering and seeking to ameliorate its impact on nature.

5. Interview transcripts are held by the author.

6. Interview with senior environmental manager of HiTec, 03/22/94. Transcript held by author.

Part III
THE INDUSTRIAL ORGANIZATION IN SOCIAL CONTEXT

Chapter 8

Backcasting: An Example of Sustainable Washing

Philip Vergragt and Marjan van der Wel

The Challenge

Sustainable development has proved to be an elusive concept, inspired by the wish to combine environmental protection, global equity, and economic growth. The most cited definition of sustainable development refers to the fulfillment of the needs of present as well as future generations (Brundtland, 1987; Hogenhuis, 1997). Not only does sustainable development have a technological dimension that goes well beyond environmental care and end-of-pipe technological solutions—it directly connects technological innovation to broader issues of social change. The relationship of technological innovation to sustainable development has been the subject of a recent Dutch Government Research program. The basic idea for this Sustainable Technology Development (STD) program is to investigate how to steer technological innovation in such a way that big jumps in environmental efficiency might be brought about.

The possibility of steering technological innovation in socially preferable directions has been a long-standing research aim of what has become known as Technology Dynamics and Constructive Technology Assessment. Technology Dynamics concerns questions about the factors, actors, mechanisms, and choices made with respect to technological options. Research has shown that technology has a strong dynamic of its own and tends to become entrenched in society. This makes it difficult to steer. Yet, under certain circumstances, the preferences of societal actors can shape technological developments so that big shifts in technological trajectories have been observed (Nelson and Winter, 1982; Dosi, 1982; Kemp, 1994;

Schot et al., 1994). Technology and society should therefore be seen as interwoven into a seamless web (Hughes, 1983). Steering technological innovation toward social goals requires operating outside the normal processes of technology innovation. Consequently, any concern to steer technology developments in socially preferred directions presents a new and complex set of social and technological issues.

Constructive Technology Assessment (CTA) has a somewhat different orientation to the issue of the social embedding of technology. The dominant approach of CTA is to provide feedback from society on the perceived or expected negative consequences of technologies so that understanding of these issues can be included in the innovation process (Rip et al., 1995). One of the most promising ways to achieve this is to involve more social actors in the process of innovation. However, this is not always easy, because these processes often take place inside industrial research laboratories and are subject to commercial secrecy.

The wish to reduce or avoid the negative consequences of technological innovations, to steer innovation in the socially determined direction of sustainable development, and to broaden the decision-making process by including actors outside industry is at the root of the Dutch STD Program. However, the program includes other features: a commitment to taking a long-term perspective while placing human needs central to the process; the use of backcasting approaches; and a concern to explore new approaches by means of illustrative projects and processes (Vergragt and Jansen, 1993; Vergragt and van Grootveld, 1995).

Backcasting: The Dutch STD Program

The Dutch STD Program was created in 1993 by five Ministries of the Dutch Government (Jansen and Vergragt, 1992). It was inspired by the dominance of short-term responses to environmental issues prevailing at the time and by the wish to include global issues in the environmental debate. It was also inspired by the fact that solutions offered by technological development were not sufficiently valued as contributions to the solution of concerns about sustainable development. A further concern was the sense that solutions brought about through technological development alone were often not tractable because of the failure to develop the social and organizational setting in which those technologies would operate.

The mission of the STD Program is "to explore and illustrate, together with policy makers in government and industry, how technological development could be shaped by backcasting from visions of sustainable futures and to develop instruments for this." One of the program's explicit aims is to stimulate business to participate in long-term oriented innovation and to develop and use new creative methods and backcasting as part of their own "visioning" process.

The research question thus became "How can technology innovation contribute to sustainable development?" It was apparent that the challenge to technology from the demand for sustainable development over the next two generations (50 years) would be enormous. The same demands on technology arise from the calls for greater equity among members of the present generations. A simple calculation has shown that fulfilling the material needs of present and future generations on the basis of equity requires a jump in the environmental efficiency of technology by a factor of between 10 and 50 (say 20) over the next year (Weterings and Opschoor, 1992).

These jumps in environmental efficiency of technology cannot be brought about by technological innovations alone. The social conditions for these leap-frog technologies still have to be determined but will invariably involve significant structural and cultural change (Schwarz, 1997; de Meere and Berting, 1996).

To explain this further, technological innovations operating along existing evolutionary paths cannot bring about factor 20 improvements in environmental efficiency necessary for sustainable development. Instead of optimizing products and production processes, society must therefore aim for system shifts that include shifts from material products into service products. Cooperation between social actors or technological stakeholders will also be necessary to bring about these changes (Grin and Hoppe, 1995). For this to take place, a common conception of the direction we are heading is required. This means some shared vision of the future is necessary. Developing this vision in turn requires basic support for a process of social innovation within society.

The creation of a future vision (the challenge of the factor 20) and its translation into short-term actions and projects has been called "backcasting." Future visions are not enough here: Backcasting implies an operational plan for the present that is designed to move toward anticipated future states. Backcasting, then, is not based on the extrapolation of the present into the future—rather, it involves the extrapolation of desired or inevitable futures back into the present. This plan is built around processes characterized as interactive (many stakeholders are involved) and iterative (feedback is continuous between future visions and present actions).

The STD program started a number of projects (or illustrative processes) intended to show how big jumps in technology are both necessary and feasible. During these projects different methods were tested to find out which methodology was most effective. No systematic or comparative research has been carried out—the methods were developed by trial and error. Nevertheless, they were strongly influenced by the notions developed by Technology Dynamics and CTA, sketched above.

It is not the aim of this chapter to analyze all the methods that have been used in the STD program. Its more modest intent is to provide an example of backcasting applied to the field of "sustainable washing." The reason for focusing on this project is that it systematically included consumers and stakeholders as well as industry in processes that emphasized creativity.

Service Products

Before moving to discuss sustainable washing it is first important to discuss briefly the concept of a service product. The history of the environmental burdens of technological development has shown remarkable changes over the last 10 to 15 years, as good housekeeping and end-of-pipe technologies have been superseded by ideas of process integration and integral chain management (Tweede Kamer, 1989). In the last few years, environmental product development (ecodesign) has become prominent as a new tool based on the use of Life Cycle Assessment (LCA) techniques, to assess the environmental impacts of products from cradle to grave—or cradle to cradle (Brezet and van Hemel, 1997).

Other new concepts are now emerging that go beyond the cleaner production and cleaner products stemming from ecodesign. One of the more interesting concepts is "service products," the movement away from physical products toward services (Meijkamp, 1997a). The basic idea is that human needs will have to be fulfilled by services, with physical products appearing only as intermediates between need fulfillment and services. From the producer's viewpoint, providing a service must create added value, possibly more added value than through the production of a physical product.

Service products do not automatically diminish environmental burdens. However, the idea can be used to scan where service products offer these opportunities. An early example is a Dutch copying machine that was leased instead of sold. The take-back obligation compelled the producer to invest in end-of-life scenarios and recycling. A more recent example is the case of call-a-car services, where a car is shared by many users. This offers the opportunity of more efficient use of the car and also reduces unnecessary car journeys (because the car is less available). It reduces the environmental burden through more efficient use of the car during its lifetime and through car sharing (Meijkamp, 1997b).

The shift from physical products to services is viable in the present economy for reasons beyond the environmental arguments. The challenge here is how companies can create services that have added value, offer the consumer more comfort and better needs fulfillment, provide a reasonable profit, and improve the environmental burden.

Sustainable Washing: The First Phase

The project Sustainable Washing was inspired by the backcasting approach from the STD program as well as the Service Product concept. The starting point was the idea that the present household is becoming a small "factory," with many energy and materials-consuming appliances. The penetration of appliances into households continues: For instance in The Netherlands the clothes dryer is now quickly being adopted by households (Workshop, 1996). However, it is hardly conceivable that a sustainable society can fulfill its needs through the accumulation of appliances in individual households. Factor 20 environmental efficiencies cannot be reached through improvements in the present appliance-intensive approach to washing, cooking, and cleaning. To achieve the gains required in environmental efficiency of technologies, other social arrangements are necessary.

The point of departure of this project was the idea of combining the notion of a service product with an increase in scale of the operation of the apparatus. The hypothesis was that washing on a larger scale (say 10 to 50 households) might increase the environmental efficiency of the apparatus so that the required gains in environmental efficiency might be achieved. But this would require the consumer to be persuaded that washing as a service product is preferable to individual washing in individual households.

From this starting point the project group initiated the "Technical University of Delft Friday Washing Day project,"[1] which drafted several scenarios for washing services. In each of the scenarios the function of "laundry" was combined with some other function, say traveling, working, recreation, or shopping, in order to decrease extra transportation. These scenarios were developed in creativity sessions but at the time (early 1995) were not very well elaborated.

Up to this point the Friday Washing Day group was only exploring the options and potentials of service products combined with the up-scaling of technology. The STD program then provided the opportunity to organize a workshop involving industry and many other stakeholders. The STD program was examining approaches to include industry in long-term thinking, backcasting, and illustrative processes. Up until then, industry had showed some reluctance to get involved in STD activities. The notable exceptions were those projects that began from a technological starting point, such as Novel Protein Foods or Sustainable Chemistry. In these projects, industry was interested because of its concern for strategic technological innovation and the development of new research and development portfolios.

With this background a workshop was organized with participants from the washing powder industry, the washing machine industry, the organization of laundromats, as well as environmental, consumer, and housewives organizations, consultancies, large technological institutes and universities, service product organizations, and the government.[2] The disciplinary backgrounds of the participants varied from textile technology, washing powder technology, and energy technology to consumer research and environmental and energy research. Their common interest was in approaching environmental problems from new directions, including a commitment to cooperation with other stakeholders.

The workshops were organized around creativity sessions. The aim was twofold. The first was to start a collaborative process with the idea of creating interest and commitment to the idea of sustainable washing. The second aim was to generate new ideas and to test the ideas from the Friday Washing Day group. The method used was "Future Perfect," which is described elsewhere (Tassoul, forthcoming). The idea behind this method is that by focusing workshop participants on a common goal involving the long term (the "Sustainable Zoo"), participants would be removed from the overbearing influence of their day-to-day preoccupations, interests, and short-term commitments. This enables more creative thinking to enable new ideas to be accessed and developed.

The second aspect of Future Perfect is looking back from the imaginary future (the year 2040) and describing the route to the future situation, including the moments of major breakthrough. The third aspect was the "forced fit" of long-term ideas with the short-term challenges.

This approach proved to be very successful. A number of ideas about sustainable washing were generated, many of them quite futuristic. It appeared that most of these ideas did not fit into the scheme of the Friday

Washing Day scenarios: They ranged from a number of technological innovations (new textiles, new washing powder, new separation technologies, new drying technologies) toward more cultural options (throwaway clothing, detachable clothing, no clothing at all, less washing) (Vergragt et al., 1995).

The evaluation showed that the participants were satisfied, for two particular reasons. In the first place, they were confronted with new ways of thinking and addressing the problem as well as gaining insight to new solutions. In the second place, they found it interesting to meet other stakeholders in this field and found it useful to exchange opinions. They wondered if there could be a continuation of this activity and what follow-up steps might be taken.

Sustainable Washing: The Second Phase

The aim of the first phase of the project was to investigate how industry could be better involved in sustainable technological development. The results show that the crucial issue has less to do with the involvement of industry and more to do with the cooperation of a large number of stakeholders in a collaborative process. But this commitment to the process gave rise to the problem of how to continue the momentum of the collaborative, creative process once enthusiasm had been aroused.

The STD Program therefore continued the project to a second phase. In this phase, it was quickly decided to organize a second workshop with the same stakeholders, a year after the first one was held. This second workshop was oriented toward the implementation of concrete projects. Another decision was that research was necessary on a number of issues as an input to the second workshop. Three issues were given special attention: the elaboration of scenarios, the evaluation of the environmental gain arising from these scenarios, and the consumer acceptance of future washing practices.

Research was carried out by a student for a master's thesis at TU Delft. This involved close collaboration with many others (van den Hoed, 1996 and 1997). Scenarios were described for three washing situations in relation to three dates in the future. The first scenario was home washing, which served as a reference scenario. Home washing will be performed for sensitive and very personal washes in small appliances. The second scenario was neighborhood washing, a service in the neighborhood that did not require transportation by mechanical means. The third scenario was the washing service, which is a larger scale operation requiring transportation. The scenarios were developed in close interaction with technical experts and contain technological possibilities that are conceived as realistic in the middle to long term. A drawback of this approach is that new technological breakthroughs are not included in the scenarios.

Simplified LCAs were carried out for each of the scenarios. From these LCAs it appears that neighborhood washing and the washing service both lead to a reduction in the use of water and washing powder, but that the energy gain is zero or negative. This is caused by the need for transportation to the Washing Service and by the need for mechanical drying, for which no environmentally friendly solution has yet been found. The net environmental gain of forms of "collective washing" is therefore not so great as hoped for, which makes these options less attractive for policy makers. More research is necessary in three areas: new easy-drying textiles, sustainable energy sources for transportation or drying, and other techniques for drying. The use of low-temperature warmth can also be envisaged.

The third research project, on consumer acceptance, was carried out by researchers from the Universities of Delft and Wageningen (van der Wel and Nieuwenhoven, forthcoming). There was no possibility of carrying out a large-scale representative research project. Also, it is believed that the majority of consumers presently are not interested in collective washing. It is therefore necessary to see this as a niche market. The research has been carried out by in-depth interviews with 12 persons who were selected on the basis of their interest in environmental protection, technological innovation, and change of behavior.

The results show that the majority of the interviewees had a positive attitude toward Neighborhood Washing and to the Washing Service. This attitude was strongly reinforced by presenting realistic and detailed scenarios. For them the most important requirements were quality, consumer friendliness, professionalism, flexibility (no time constraints in bringing and returning washing), and a reasonable price structure. Information about the environmental gain is very important for this category of respondents. Other important aspects are hygiene, privacy (for underwear), textile wear, and speed of return. Most respondents were not very critical on these aspects. But as this was a nonrepresentative sample of the population, this could be quite different for other segments of the population.

The second workshop was held in September 1996, roughly the same time that participants were invited the previous year. Before the workshop took place a document was circulated in which the results of the investigations (the scenarios, the LCAs, and the consumer acceptance) were summarized (Workshop, 1996). The methodology was less innovative than in the first workshop. The aim was not so much creativity and new ideas but discussion about the possibilities of organizing a follow-up based on concrete projects.

In the morning the plenary discussion focused on challenges implied by the scenarios. These challenges were cultural, technical, enlargement of scale, and distribution. The discussion itself focused on the conditions for success, other possible scenarios (like other types of services, textile-leasing), missing knowledge, and the role of the government. In the case of missing knowledge, research on economic and organizational aspects was seen to be deficient at present. Consequently, consumer research needed to be extended to get a more detailed knowledge of the market issues of the scenarios. Research into new services is necessary in order to find out the synergy possible between different services. And research was also seen as important to assess technologies such as new textiles and new washing technologies.

Finally, research on energy aspects, to include the reduction of energy use, the use of solar energy, and the diminution of energy for transportation and drying was identified as necessary. The role of the government was discussed. In particular, participants felt that the government should play a much more critical role in stimulating the process and in helping to overcome financial barriers.

Four aspects were discussed in groups. These were the possibility of a pilot project, technological research, consumer research, and the organization of a forum within which the development of these ideas could continue. In each group very interesting suggestions were formulated, which are documented in the workshop report (Workshop, 1996).

The result of this second workshop was very positive, in the sense that the general idea of sustainable washing services became much more concrete. A number of proposals were formulated for research, for a pilot project, and for the forum. Also, the commitment of the participants seems to have grown since the first workshop. However, a negative aspect is that the activities thus far have not been taken up by the participants themselves. It appears that in this early phase of idea development and project statements the government is seen to have a crucial role. This poses severe problems, with the STD program and the STD project Sustainable Washing Services now coming to an end.

Results and Evaluation

The STD project "Sustainable Washing Services" shows that it is possible to interest industry in long-term oriented sustainable technology development and backcasting. From the first workshop it was clear that representatives from industry are willing to be involved in creativity sessions, to generate new ideas, and to cooperate with other stakeholders. Also, it was shown that this approach generates a common feeling that it is interesting to cooperate with other stakeholders in a search for new solutions. These involve a mix of technological solutions and nontechnological, more culturally oriented concerns.

Between the first and the second workshop, several research projects were carried out with respect to scenarios, LCAs, and consumer acceptance. These research projects contributed to the concreteness of the proposed scenarios and kept some of the participants involved. At the second workshop it was possible to present much more concrete proposals and research results as a consequence of these projects.

The second workshop reinforced the commitment of the stakeholders to the process and led to useful suggestions for follow-up projects: research, pilot projects, and the establishment of a more permanent forum. The only negative aspect is that while participants in the workshops regarded government involvement as indispensable in this phase, the government, for its part, will not continue the project.

A number of follow-up activities are proposed to take the project forward. These include:

- The organization of a permanent forum where stakeholders can meet, where information about projects and participants is available, and from where new activities may be organized.

- The organization of a pilot project aimed at testing the viability of a neighborhood service or washing service in a practical setting. Before starting such a pilot project research will be carried out, especially on the economic and organizational aspects of the service. Here again there is a role for government to take the lead in stimulating and financing the pilot project and related research.

- More research has to be carried out on the technological and consumer aspects of sustainable washing services. In the first place, research is needed on the environmental aspects of washing services, especially energy. Solutions will have to be found to the energy inefficiencies of the proposed services. Research is also needed on the consumer acceptance of specific services and the economic and organizational aspects of a washing service.

In conclusion, the project Sustainable Washing Services has been successful in mobilizing stakeholders, identifying and researching futures, and identifying areas for research and pilot projects. However, it has not been successful in gaining sufficient support to establish a follow-up to the project and has not influenced government policy making in the direction of sustainable service projects.

Discussion

The STD Program is a research program designed to investigate the contribution of technology to sustainable development. Its operational goal is the development of technologies that are a factor 20 times more environmentally efficient than existing technologies. From the beginning it was acknowledged that these "leap frog" technologies will also require large shifts in culture and structure—in the routines and habits of producers and consumers, and in the economic and institutional structure that endorses present practices.

The STD Project "Sustainable Washing Services" shows that it is possible to set up a technological trajectory that may lead to the implementation of factor 20 technologies. However, it also shows the importance of the coordination of research, policy, and action to effect substantive change. The project suggests a methodology that might be helpful for setting up similar projects. This methodology has been proposed in a joint project, "Sustainable Households," submitted for financing to the European Union. The methodology will be published separately by STD and will be further elaborated and investigated in the future.

In brief, the key elements of the methodology are:

1. Define a problem area for strategic research—for example, environmental pollution caused by the increased use of machinery and energy in households.

2. Design visions, or scenarios, of sustainable future situations, following the example of the washing service scenarios described in this chapter. More research has to be done on how to develop these

scenarios, how to organize endorsement of the process, and how to evaluate its effectiveness.

3. Identify the important stakeholders, which include the supply chain, distribution networks, retailers, users, governments (at all levels), advisors, technical and scientific experts, consumer and housewives organizations, environmental and financial organizations, and so on. From this make a social map of interests and aims as well as collaboration and antagonism to establish the general characteristics of the actor network.

4. Organize a creativity workshop with the aim of generating solutions to the defined problem. This needs to generate a common definition of the problem in the emerging network and evaluate existing and proposed solutions. Workshops of this kind can draw on the backcasting approach to move from a future vision toward short-term steps for implementation.

5. Improve the scenarios using the outcomes of visioning workshops and review the scenarios that are generated, using expert opinions.

6. Conduct environmental assessments of the scenarios by means of LCA, or similar techniques of environmental assessment. These environmental assessments will generally generate a research and development agenda for the improvement of environmental bottlenecks.

7. Conduct economic analysis of the scenarios to provide rough cost-benefit analyses of their short- and long-term implications and of the transition costs. At this point the economic and structural conditions under which the scenario might become viable should become clearer. At this stage the prices of environmental commodities—air, water, and energy—are crucial, as are the expected learning curves of the technologies with respect to their environmental benefits.

8. Develop consumer acceptance of the scenarios. This demands in-depth interviews with focus groups and others to find out the conditions for acceptance, motives for refusal, and the directions for experiments and pilot projects.

9. Conduct follow-up workshops to discuss the research results and action outcomes from items 6, 7, 8, and determine follow-up steps.

10. Follow-up steps may include: The technological research agenda needed to carry out the research necessary for the implementation of scenarios, a set of practical experiments to test the proposed scenarios, and a cultural research agenda to investigate social barriers to proposed scenarios.

The realization of this methodology requires strong coordination, preferably by a government agency, and enough resources to carry out the steps in a reasonable amount of time (2 to 3 years). Also, additional action research will be needed to evaluate new approaches in practice and to assess whether the process needs to be steered in other directions or with different emphasis.

The methodology outlined above is seen as one of the outcomes of the project Sustainable Washing rather than simply an input to the process. It was developed experientially—its effectiveness still has to be assessed in relation to future projects. Already it can be said that three elements are crucial for the success of projects of this kind, which were absent from the Sustainable Washing project:

- Coordination by a skillful project leader who has legitimacy from the stakeholders involved

- Sufficient resources and endorsement to carry the project forward as it develops its own agenda

- An outlook on implementation and follow-up

Because of the absence of these elements, the follow-up and implementation of proposed ideas and projects for sustainable washing has been frustrating for the participants. On the other hand, the methodology can only be developed by trial and error, because similar approaches do not seem to be available in the literature.

ACKNOWLEDGMENTS

The authors wish to acknowledge the ideas, cooperation, and continuous support of Rens Meijkamp of the group "Friday Washing Day." They also acknowledge the skillful and creative work done by Robert van den Hoed in the second phase of the project. Many of the ideas in this article are the result of our cooperative effort. Similarly, the authors thank the participants of the workshops and the other researchers involved in this project, in particular the facilitators of the first and second workshops: Marc

Tassoul, Coen Kleisen, and Anne Loeber. They acknowledge the endorsement of the first phase of the project by the Greening of Industry Network through Ellis Brand and Johan Schot. Last but not least, they wish to acknowledge the financial and moral support by STD, notably the director Geert van Grootveld.

NOTES

1. The members of the Friday Washing Day project were Rens Meijkamp, Marjan van der Wel, and Philip Vergragt, later joined by Robert van den Hoed.

2. The workshop took place on September 27–28, 1995, in The Hague.

Chapter 9

Thirty Cabbages: Diversity of Perspective to Catalyze Redesign in the Agrochemical Industry

William T. Vorley

The Prism of a Uniform Perspective

Homogeneity in the beliefs and underlying assumptions of an organization is the root of a tendency to *search for the familiar* in the face of ambiguity and uncertainty (Johnson and Scholes, 1993:63).

The emerging rubrics of "sustainable agriculture" and the "greening of industry" have confronted the chemical industry with plenty of ambiguity and uncertainty, and most pesticide manufacturers have indeed responded with a familiar immune reaction; a wall of information and public relations. Such information presumes that we share industry's perspective, and that we only need to be nursed from our irrational "unscientific" beliefs and be reminded of the contribution of pesticides to feeding a growing, hungry world to see their activities as entirely consistent with a goal of agricultural sustainability.

As part of these information campaigns, the industry has sought out and sponsored marginal groups to articulate and legitimize its own productionist perspective. Support for Dennis Avery and the Hudson Institute—respectively, author and publisher of *Saving the Planet with Pesticides and Plastic*—is a classic example of industry's response to uncertainty and unfamiliarity. Seeking out the familiar in this way only expands the contested area between the industry and its critics. It feeds the dangerous orthodoxy of the pesticides debate, consuming much of the political and institutional capital of both industry and environmental groups (Wolcott, 1993). It replaces debate with grand dichotomies and ridiculous choices: Bugs or people? Technology—friend or foe? High input agriculture or starvation? High input agriculture or wildlife? It locks industry's definitions of "sustainable agriculture" into defensive endorsements of the status quo. And, central to the theme of this chapter, it blocks meaningful discussion of the role of companies currently in the pesticides business toward the development of innovative products and services for more sustainable food and fiber production.

It is not only intellectual rigor and civil debate that suffer from a self-reinforcing uniformity of perspective. In an organizational culture dominated by one worldview, employees find it nearly impossible to legitimize any personal perspective other than the organization's worldview, and company recruitment obviously selects people who support that view or, more typically, can separate their personal and professional values.

Another cost of orthodoxy and gridlock is the massive level of state intervention it attracts. Most of this intervention takes the form of management and regulation of pesticides rather than research on less chemical-dependent farming systems. Pesticide regulation in the United States costs taxpayers and industry more than a billion dollars a year, while the US Department of Agriculture's budget for Integrated Pest Management (IPM) in 1995 was $192 million (Benbrook, 1996:213).

Rational discussion is not helped by a tendency of proponents of sustainable agriculture to define the term by what it is *not,* contrasting it to "conventional" agriculture—a construct of all that is perceived to be unsustainable in the modern agrifood system (reductionism, technological intensity, domination of nature, exploitation, dependence, competition, and so on). This "conventional" agriculture is probably not an accurate representation of most mainstream farmers (Beus and Dunlap, 1991). "Conventional" versus "sustainable" agriculture is another dichotomy that feeds orthodoxy and division.

The notion of sustainable agriculture has gained an unfortunate reputation of pointing an accusing finger at the faults of mainstream farming and its suppliers. It is therefore no surprise that most farmers around the world choose to align themselves more closely with pesticide manufacturers, who are at least producing something of use to them, than with the sustainable agriculture movement.

None of this would have much bearing on the greening of industry were it not for mounting evidence that an over-simplified reality and uniformity of perspective may leave an organization vulnerable to unforeseen breakpoints. An inability to innovate when confronted with historic opportunities will eventually affect a company's value to both sharehold-ers and stakeholders and can erode the credibility of statements on sus-tainable development. The leaders of large chemical corporations have recognized this point. In the buildup to the 1992 Rio "Earth Summit," the CEOs of Ciba-Geigy (now Novartis), DuPont, and Dow sat with 50 busi-ness leaders on the Business Council for Sustainable Development (BCSD) to prepare a global business perspective on sustainable develop-ment. The resulting declaration states that

> Progress toward sustainable development makes good busi-ness sense because it can create competitive advantages and new opportunities. But it requires far-reaching shifts in corpo-rate attitudes and new ways of doing business.

> (Schmidheiny and BCSD, 1992:xiii)

The need for new business opportunities is particularly urgent for the pesticide industry, despite continued growth in the global pesticides mar-ket—now valued at around $30 billion. The agrifood chain that links farmers and consumers is undergoing radical changes in power, with con-sequent shifts in the ability of players along that chain to extract value (Koechlin and Wittke, 1997). The customers of pesticide producers—farmers—are the sector of agriculture that is declining most steeply in OECD countries. Value is being added not on the farm but by food processors, retailers, and restaurants; these downstream players are increasingly involving themselves in the technical aspects of food pro-duction. The voice of the consumer, who has been consistently antipa-thetic to pesticide use in agriculture, is being heard more distinctly inside the farm gate.

This is not the only threat to the sustainability of the chemical pesticide industry. Research-intensive companies are realizing that the big-selling pesticides are becoming commodity products, and that price competition will increase further as patents expire and as seed-based biotechnological crop protection eats into valuable chunks of traditionally valuable chem-ical pesticide submarkets.

So the BCSD seems to be right. Shifts in attitudes and new ways of doing business are matters of survival for pesticide manufacturers as well as a means to walk the green talk. But which attitudes should be shifted, and how are those new perspectives introduced into a myopic corporate culture? What are the high-leverage points that can produce significant, enduring improvements (Senge, 1990:64–65)?

Divergent Perspectives and Leverage Points

These were the questions that a three-year project coordinated from Ames, Iowa,[1] set out to answer. Our hypothesis was that through divergent, constructive perspectives we have the chance to find innovative solutions in keeping with industry's sustainability talk. Our approach was to build those perspectives on what industry has already said, specifically the BCSD's comments on price correction and internalization of environmental costs, on an expanded definition of the role of stakeholders in corporate policy, and on the need to move beyond pollution prevention (Schmidheiny and BCSD, 1992:7). Hence our selection of environmental economists and stakeholder analysts as network partners, and our focus on redesign—confronting the causes of unsustainability—rather than ecoefficiency.

Before speculating about the future of an industry, it is vital to explore perspectives of its present. The pesticide industry justifies its contribution to sustainability in the language of demographics, hunger, efficiency, and human welfare—fewer farmers protecting more crops from the ravages of insects, fungi, and weeds in order to provide affordable food for growing populations. Is industry's demographic imperative correct, or are there other forces driving agriculture's dependence on pesticides?

Pesticides, Hunger, and Efficiency

In the 35 years since the publication of *Silent Spring,* the response by industry and some politicians and scientists to questions about the sustainability of agriculture's reliance on chemical pesticides has remained entrenched in what Bromley (1994) calls "the language of loss." The debate is framed in terms of the costs of pesticide bans—reduced yields, higher food prices, expansion of cropland into wildlife habitat, and world hunger—in the highly unlikely scenario of deleting pesticides from the existing mix of agricultural practices.

To see how the language of loss remains ingrained in the pesticide debate, we have to look no further than the US Agricultural Retailers Association (1996) *Food for Thought* calendar:

> Without pesticides and fertilizers, U.S. farm exports would fall to zero. Our balance of trade would drop by more than $4 billion, and millions of people around the world would starve.

> An estimated one-third of the world's food supply would be lost each year to weeds, insect pests, and diseases if crop protection chemicals were not used. This is enough to feed about two billion people.

By taking a hard look at the historical driving forces behind pesticide use, Pretty et al. (1997) conclude that the bulk of pesticide use has surprisingly little to do with "feeding the world" or keeping famine at bay. The largest markets for pesticide manufacturers—weed control with herbicides in OECD feedgrain crops—are means to substitute capital for labor, equipment services, and management in the low-margin, highly leveraged farming operations that have become the norm of OECD agriculture. Pesticides have been a factor allowing the revolutions of specialization and intensification in farming. They are a farmer's tool in securing a market for his food and fiber production in an extremely competitive global market, by meeting the demands of price and quality imposed by the gatekeepers of the agrifood system—the processors, the packers and the retailers. Pesticide use—especially in Europe and Japan—has also been stimulated by artificial price signals from high production subsidies.

Pesticides are feeding the feedlot more than they are feeding the world. A study for the US Farm Bureau (Porterfield et al., 1995) estimated that 61 percent of pesticides in the United States were used in crops primarily for animal feed rather than food or fiber. The global market value for pesticides used to protect national food security in developing countries (rather than to protect export feed, fiber, and plantation crops) is trivial by global standards. And much of the pesticide market for the most important food crop of the tropics—rice—has been shown to be an unnecessary hangover of the Green Revolution packages of high-yielding varieties, double-cropping, fertilizers, and pesticides.

Pesticides prop up other inherently unsustainable but superficially more "efficient" agricultural practices—simplified crop rotations, the separation of livestock and crop production, and the distancing of food and feed production from consumption. But pesticides are also widely used to prop up more sustainable farming practices, including soil-conserving low tillage systems in which herbicides are substituted for mechanical cultivation.

This perspective, which is absent from most rhetoric on both sides of the pesticide debate, highlights the synergism between pesticides and a raft of economic, technological, political, and commercial trends that have set agriculture into a pattern of chemical dependence. Pesticides may be the *cause* of some aspects of agriculture's unsustainability, but they are more likely to be a *consequence* of forces on agriculture that are generating a whole range of social and environmental outcomes seen by many observers to be inherently unsustainable. Although pesticides work in the initial benefit of individual farmers—allowing simplification of management and spread of management over more acres—they work against the interests of *farming.*

Pesticides are among the technologies that have contributed to an inexorable shift in agricultural activities away from the farm. The share of farming in value-added to agriculture has been in steady decline since at least 1920. The shift of agriculture from farm to nonfarm reduces returns to labor and requires farmers to either increase production or utilize their excess management and labor in nonfarm employment. Farm sizes have grown, not to achieve greater efficiency but primarily because expansion has been the only way to maintain income (Wessel, 1983:50).

Pesticides have also been one primary aspect of modern agriculture that has eroded the "social contract" between farming and nonfarming populations within the OECD, hastening the decline in agriculture's prestige and political bargaining strength.

These concerns challenge our definition of "efficiency" and "sustainability." We are obliged to question what we are sustaining, for how long, and for whose benefit. If we as a society are trying to sustain farmers (as well as agriculture's natural resource base), pesticides would be considered an extremely inappropriate and inefficient technology choice. There is a growing school of thought that, for the health of community and culture, we should have more people rather than less on the land, and a stronger link between the producers and consumers of food, our most basic need (Lewis, 1996).

The concept of efficiency is also challenged from another perspective, closer to classical economics: the theory of *externalities.* Pesticides have well-known environmental and health impacts, which market prices ignore. Prices reflect only those costs borne by the producer, or "internal" costs. Where the production activity creates costs borne by third parties, these "external" costs are not incorporated in the price, and the market has failed to allocate resources efficiently.

Leaders in the chemical industry, government, and environmental groups have an uncommon unanimity of perspective around the benefits of correcting prices to internalize external costs. The Council of Economic Advisers recently proposed to the US president that federal policy measures should be considered to incorporate environmental and public health values into farmers' decision making because: "When the application of fertilizers and pesticides imposes off-site costs, farmers can only be expected to make efficient decisions if they are themselves confronted with these costs" (Economic Report of the President, 1995:146).

It is clear the pesticide industry has made no systematic attempt to calculate the environmental and social costs of pesticide production, use, and disposal, even in their own agrochemical divisions and subsidiaries. The minute fees and taxes on chemical inputs in the US state of Iowa—introduced not as a full "polluter pays" but to fund research and extension on alternatives—was fiercely resisted by agrochemical interests (John, 1994). A healthy debate among all sectors of society on full-cost approaches, called for by Dow (Popoff and Buzelli, 1993), has not yet begun.

How would a full-cost perspective change the outlook of a pesticide producer toward the development and marketing of pesticides and their alternatives? A preliminary global analysis of the issue by Pearce and Tinch (1997) and a case study in the United Kingdom by Foster et al. (1997) point to both the weaknesses of methodologies applied to date and to the potential magnitude of corrections if pesticide prices were corrected to recognize and reflect the environmental and health costs of their use. A tax differentiated to reflect the differences between "soft" pesticides and products with high external costs would drastically affect the attractiveness of soft products relative to "bad actor" competitor products.

Science, Precaution, and Sustainability

Industry, science, and government have viewed sustainability in highly managerial and technocratic terms, defined by experts from the natural sciences or economics (Orr, 1992). The elevation of science as the grand arbiter in deciding what is and what is not sustainable has a long tradition. The answers science can provide are only as good as the questions asked of it; regrettably those questions are often confined to the narrowly defined physical hazards of individual pesticides or toxics. Science tells us that in 1996

A 150-pound adult would have to eat 3000 heads of lettuce each day for the rest of his or her life to ingest the amount of pesticide that is found to cause health problems in laboratory mice.

(US Agricultural Retailers Association, 1996)

And in 1891 science told us that

> A person would have to eat in one sitting 30 cabbages that had been dusted with paris green [copper aceto-arsenite] to get enough poison to hurt him.

(Gillette, 1891, cited in Porter and Fahey, 1952)

A green light from "expert" knowledge to eat 30 cabbages or 3000 lettuces per day completely misses the point of a perspective that represents the future-oriented, precautionary movement. This movement has been labeled "environmentalism" but is more accurately a broad range of concerns around the present and future well-being of people and planet, encompassing agrarianism and the reconnection of people with the land. A group labeled the "sustenance" group by Mayhew and Alessi (1997) questions the use of science, amid all the complexity and unknowns of the interactions between chemicals and living things, to serve as primary consultant to those making comprehensive decisions about the future. They feel that the deliberate release of biologically active chemicals into the environment in order to tip the "pest war" in humans' favor is inherently lacking in precaution. They view the technology of pesticides as flawed, because it is not durable—the more agriculture relies on pesticides, the less effective those chemicals become due to the evolution of resistant pest species and the decimation of natural control agents. The group points to disturbing evidence that the source of funding can dramatically affect the outcome of scientific studies on the safety of pesticides (Fagin et al., 1997). And, citing the 50 years it took to uncover DDT's impacts on the endocrine system of humans and wildlife, they feel that it is only a matter of time before science—retrospectively—finds associations between these chemicals and other symptoms of environmental stress, such as the epidemic of malformations in amphibians, or the slow epidemic of breast cancer in humans.

The "golden age" of accumulation in modern agrifood systems has been marked by an implicit coalition between agribusiness and science, because the high technology model was in the mutual interests of the scientific community and agroindustrial capital (Goodman and Redclift, 1991). The future-oriented "sustenance" group has been "triangulated" out of the dialogue, because its precautionary language threatens the stability of that coalition. From the perspective of a therapist, the exclusion of a third party is detrimental to finding innovative ways to unblock the impasse over pesticides and sustainability. If, however, science is positioned as a *consultant*—a *source* of information—instead of a primary arbiter, then space is opened for new information flows to emerge that can serve to stimulate innovative thinking (Mayhew and Allessi, 1997). An alliance between the pesticide industry and "sustenance" is essentially an attempt to balance interests in decisions over technology choice and corporate strategy; maximizing the value of the company to a diversity of stakes (including nature, and including future generations) rather than value to only shareholders.

The prospect of Dow or Bayer bringing deep ecologists into their process of strategic planning may seem ludicrous, considering the chemical industry's tradition of confusing dialogue with recruitment to their way of thinking (for example, Tombs, 1993), and considering environmentalism's adversarial history and aversion to sleeping with the enemy. But there are business opportunities in a more regenerative, less extractive agriculture; an alliance between industry and the sustainable agriculture movement could redefine a company's core competence, from chemistry to agriculture, or even to ecosystem management.

The two key prerequisites to a successful partnership between industry and "sustenance" are literacy and common vision.

Literacy and Learning

Without literacy, and the organizational learning that nurtures it, everything is viewed through the prism of an organization's dominant worldview, and "enlightening the public" continues to have precedence over enlightening a company's own personnel. Organizations must first seek literacy throughout their ranks before claiming the high ground with more "sustainable" technological and managerial fixes.

How can corporate literacy be achieved outside of the rarefied air of the boardroom? Companies could take the DuPont route, which has a slower pace of experiential learning, including a well-designed series of field trials that compare conventional agricultural systems with the best that reduced-input and organic agriculture can offer (for example, *Farm Journal,* 1994). These trials are an open collaboration with specialists in organic farming, such as the Rodale Institute, and seem to have successfully avoided the prejudgmental anti-organic sentiments of agribusiness. The French-based company Rhône Poulenc has also experimented with organic farming (Maitland, 1994).

Or companies can follow the lead of Monsanto, inviting the high priests "sustenance" to their headquarters to set management teams on the right path. Monsanto has seven Sustainability Teams totaling 140 staff members: the Eco-Efficiency Team, the Full-Cost Accounting Team, the Index Team, the New Business/New Products Team, the Water Team, and the Global Hunger Team (see Magretta, 1997). But note here the risk of constructing issues of sustainability within the existing technocratic. For instance, without a diversity of internal perspectives, a Global Hunger Team may easily construct world hunger as a technological (rather than a political) challenge, to be overcome by the export of genetically intensified US agriculture. Such an approach has the ingredients of the construction of world hunger in the 1970s—a shortage of protein—which led companies into commercially disastrous ventures in the 1970s with microbial proteins such as BP's "Torpina" and ICI's "Pruteen."

Monsanto's case is especially interesting. Distancing the new Monsanto from its notorious chemical legacy, CEO Robert Shapiro is gambling the future of the company on his own vision of sustainable development (Margretta, 1997) in which the "second curve" of biotechnology rescues society from the seemingly impossible task of producing more food from less land. Monsanto has invested more than two billion dollars over the past two years on access to biotechnology and to seed markets (Lenzer and Upbin, 1997).

Monsanto and Novartis have encountered strong resistance to food produced with the first generation of genetically engineered food products—bovine growth hormone to increase milk production per cow; soybeans resistant to Monsanto's "Roundup" herbicide; and maize, cotton, and potato varieties with a built-in biological insecticide—especially in Europe and Japan. Because these technologies are not *chemically* based (or at least reduce the use of persistent manufactured chemicals), Monsanto and other biotechnology firms have greeted hostility to these "biological solutions" with surprise, and with another "information"-based immune response. Yet in April 1997 the European Parliament voted for a suspension of genetically engineered corn pending a reassessment of risks.

These societal "revenge effects" are remarkably similar to the ecological revenge effects farmers experienced with pesticides—pest resurgences due to the evolution of resistant strains, and the creation of "secondary pests" that were previously regulated by naturally occurring predators and parasites (see Tenner, 1996). Both are symptomatic of direct head-on approaches that confront the symptoms rather than the cause of problems, whether those problems are crop pests or a low level of public legitimacy.

Consultation with representatives of "sustenance" is no substitute for a more profound and personal challenge to the institutional mind-set and, thereby, to a redefinition of the problem and an exploration of *redesign* strategies. For the kind of literacy that develops systemic thinking in a critical mass of a company's employees, a significant population—perhaps 5 percent of managers—has to become familiar with the perspectives of the practitioners of an agriculture which, according to existing mind-set, does not exist.

There are farmers, researchers, and advisors in industrial and peasant agriculture who, as pioneers and iconoclasts, are getting high yields and regenerating their natural resource base with few external inputs, and who are shifting from a consuming to a conserving agriculture (Pretty, 1995). These farmers and consultants see folly in the separation of "pests" from the rest of the farming system; they have a great deal in common with systems thinkers in business such as Peter Senge. If the pesticide industry is serious about moving from an antagonistic to a complementary role in sustainable agriculture, then companies (as well as regulatory agencies such as the US-EPA) should develop goals for *at least 5 percent of middle management to spend sabbaticals of up to one year on the farms and research stations of innovators in alternative agriculture.*

Uncommon Vision

The development of good solutions requires more than literacy in technological alternatives to controversial products. There is still a profound problem with balancing interests across sectors of society when decisions are made in the development process of new technologies and services (Linstone, 1989). "Solutions" that are seen to benefit only one sector of society are not solutions at all. They do not, in the words of Wendell Berry, "solve for pattern" (Berry, 1981).

Industry leaders and the BCSD have realized that a broader definition of "industry stakeholder" is essential. Schmidheiny and the BCSD (1992:86) state that "Prosperous companies in a sustainable world will be those that are better than their competitors at 'adding value' for all their stakeholders, not just for customers and investors." But there is still an entrenched tendency, especially in the US pesticide companies, to label nonfarming groups as outsiders in the debate over how food is produced and the land is managed, because they are not "in" farming and because they are not qualified scientists.

Taking a more systemic view reveals that there are no outsiders; "you and the cause of your problems are part of a single system" (Senge, 1990:67). One of the best ways to open up the potential of a single-system perspective—a perspective that is a far richer source of learning and innovation than the portrayed dualism between famine-fighting technologists and misguided public would have us believe—is *Future Searching.*

Future Search is a structured planning process that "gets the whole system in the room" (Weisbord and Janoff, 1995); 50 to 80 diverse stakeholders come together in retreat setting for two to three days. Rather than planning from the present through compromise and "agreeing to disagree," the search members agree on a preferred future, and then "backcast" from that agreed ideal future to plan the necessary actions of industry, government, and other stakeholders for creating that future.

Morley and Franklin (1997) describe such a search that took place in Minnesota, investigating options for the pesticide industry in sustainable agriculture. Over two days and two nights in the backwaters of rural Minnesota, a group of farmers, agribusiness representatives, scientists, NGO representatives, and members of the public built a dialogue around this controversial subject by asking, in the words of one participant, "What kind of future do we want?" rather than "How are we going to get a sustainable agriculture?"

It is fascinating to note how the Future Search conference described by Morley and Franklin quickly homed in on leverage points in the pesticides/agricultural sustainability issue, once the discussion had moved beyond the usual string of agricultural woes. Many of those leverage points were not found where the farmer or farm worker uses pesticides, or inside the gates of specific pesticide companies, or in the corridors of policy makers and regulatory agencies. Four points involved moving the goal posts at the marketing and consumption end of the agrifood chain through awareness-building or strengthened communities. Two more addressed other areas of public action: a need for greater democratic control over technology choice, and mechanisms for building trust among diverse stakeholders. An opportunity for business to develop a stewardship ethic received so many votes for the final "tasks/actions" stage of the Search that two groups were formed to tackle this issue. Only one area identified by the participants—watershed management—was primarily directed at farmers.

Clearly, this technique has the potential to bring industry and society together around a subject in which we are all stakeholders—the future of our food system. There is evidence that Future Search conferences of pesticide company employees, company shareholders, environmental groups, or the general public would all reach remarkably similar conclusions about what an ideal food system of the future would look like. This would make explicit the question of what is being sustained, for how long, and for whose benefit, and would explore the potential for agreement on how we get from our present condition to the preferred future.

If it is true that—by focusing awareness away from negative stereotypes and barriers of culture, personality, power, status, and politics toward shared goals—Future Search can uncover deep agreements on where our food system should be headed, then pesticide manufacturers would have an excellent reference point for selecting innovations that have a much more social consensus than the current basket of chemical and genetically engineered technologies.

Future searching is a powerful shortcut to bringing a wide diversity of perspective into a company's strategic planning. It reflects Handy's "second curve thinking," in which a company or organization is forced to challenge the assumptions that underlie its present strength by asking, "If we could reinvent ourselves, what would we look like?" (Handy, 1994:56). Systems thinking and future-oriented planning tools, when used by a literate and collegial organization, can provide a conceptual platform from which we can become active participants in shaping our reality, "from reacting to the present to creating the future" (Senge 1990:69). It is a way to build the ownership and unity of purpose necessary for the kind of corporate change that pushes beyond ecoefficiency toward deeper redesign of an organization.

This is a marked contrast to the visions foisted on corporations by born-again environmentalist CEOs, in which employees are "trained" in the vision until they "get it." A top-down vision in sustainable development is a contradiction in terms.

New Products and Services

Once companies are equipped with literacy and vision to move beyond reactive defense of the status quo, and once disincentives are reversed using green taxes on energy and chemicals, we may expect that a whole new range of opportunities will open up for the private sector to make money and walk their visionary talk in developing products and services for sustainable agriculture. Paul Hawken writes about chemical companies going back to the drawing board to "invent farming techniques that improve yield and enhance life" (Hawken, 1993:186).

An ecosystemic view can call into question the long-term market potential of "softer" chemical, biological, and biotechnological substitutions of current chemical pesticide products. If farming systems continue to depend on regular interventions with these new products, their market life will be drastically curtailed by resistance. But if farming systems are brought into equilibrium through ecosystem redesign and the use of selective chemicals, the market potential for these new products will rapidly shrink.

The received wisdom regarding "green" business is that industries can move to a dematerialized commerce, with cradle-to-grave product stewardship or ultimately a *knowledge-based* economy built on services rather than products. Sustainable agriculture is often described as "information-intensive," as opposed to "input-intensive" conventional agriculture. A pesticide company, realizing that it sold crop protection rather than chemicals, could therefore move into the farm services, crop insurance, or performance contracting businesses, and deliver the same end result (healthy crops) with far less material throughput and far less environmental impact.

The possibility that a "chemical" company could "extract value from a zero-input scenario" was floated by managers from DowElanco at a conference in 1995 (Burnside and Hoefer, 1995). The speakers presented a scenario of a shift from selling crop protection to selling Integrated Crop Management without a "product" bias.

But again, there are serious limitations to such a transformation. First, the farm services market is undervalued and distorted by extreme competition between chemical manufacturers and retailers, which leads to marketing practices that depress the perceived value of information services (Wolf, 1995); services such as pest scouting and soil testing are offered "free" or below cost to retain important customers, which makes farmers unwilling to pay independent consultants the full price.

Second, companies lack the credibility, tools, expertise, or organization—especially in terms of regional research infrastructure—to capture value from the service market. There is a danger that companies would package the skills and knowledge of sustainable farming into a "product" and "deliver" the technology in the same way that chemical inputs have been sold for the past three decades. Advocates of sustainable agriculture warn strongly against this cargo cult of purchased technologies and expertise (Röling, 1993; Ehrenfeld, 1993:170), proposing instead that agricultural development is built on participation with farmers and integration of local knowledge. Sustainable agriculture in its broad definition may not be a lucrative market for any purchased "inputs," be they chemicals or information.

Furthermore, the pesticide industry is experiencing a period of rapid change, as commodification and competition in high- and low-value markets (with generic chemicals and seed-based biotechnology, respectively) forces rapid consolidation to maintain profitability and to gain critical mass of technology and market access. Some companies are realizing that competence in crop biotechnology can open up completely new business opportunities. Markets are being created for preserved-identity grains and bio-industrial products such as lubricants, fuels, and plastics, as well as pharmaceutical products ("pharming" for "neutraceuticals"). But in general the late 1990s, when companies should be implementing their pledges of "far-reaching shifts in corporate attitudes and new ways of doing business," have turned out to be a far leaner and meaner era than the years leading up to the Rio Earth Summit. Sustainable development seems to have taken a back seat for many companies, while survival in this maturing industry is top of mind. Such conditions are considered far from ideal for the "greening" of corporate strategy (Walley and Whitehead, 1994).

Finally, there may be considerable shareholder resistance to companies diversifying into farm services; shareholders will not readily accept a decrease in the earning power of a company for a diversification they can effect more cheaply by buying shares of different companies.

Clearly a "simple" shift from selling chemicals to selling sustainability services is fraught with difficulty and risks of achieving neither the ecological benefits nor farmer acceptance (and hence profitability) that some business commentators have predicted. But literacy in sustainability through a diversity of perspectives, and a shared vision of a future agrifood system, provides the necessary ingredients for sustainable innovations.

Conclusions and Recommendations

It is tempting to attribute the different outlooks on pesticides to different moral positions. We could label agribusinesses as anthropocentric productionists, and label environmentalists as biocentric agrarians. But this would be to miss the point, that worldviews are not necessarily derived from core values but are a consequence of exposure to only one set of beliefs. Worldviews of organizations—from chemical companies to environmental groups—are self-reinforcing in that research is selectively funded, information is selectively acquired, and personnel are selectively hired in ways that reinforce the dominant paradigm. This dooms corporate visions for sustainable development to remain as sets of principles rather than catalysts for change.

The purpose of this chapter has been to explore how a greater diversity of views—views espoused by the leaders of industry but often distorted and refracted through the prism of the company's historical perspective—could throw new light onto the opportunities for business that adds value for shareholders *and* a wide range of stakeholders.

A systems perspective of the historical drivers, current markets, and technical alternatives for pesticides around the world challenges the demographic imperative that preludes most justifications of pesticide production. To see that pesticides are just one technological option for pest control—an option that may prop up other inherently unsustainable agricultural practices—is to revisit our tolerance for the associated risks of pesticide use to the health of humans and ecosystems. The evaluation of benefits relative to risks is further assisted by the perspective of environmental economics. If prices of pesticides were corrected to account for their full social and environmental costs, the merits of this technology relative to alternatives would be seen in a new light.

Internal learning has a relatively low cost compared to the expensive mistakes of tunnel vision. The failure to understand wider stakeholder perspectives and to balance the development of new technologies has had companies scrambling to relearn and to repair their image around the new technologies of genetically engineered seeds, as they have done with chemical technologies for the past 30 years.

An alliance with "sustenance" stakeholders could radically change a company's perception of what stake it has in the agrifood system. It can be the foundation of a new, more systemic means of technology assessment. Questions will be asked of new technologies such as, "Does it expand choices or create dependence? Does it attack symptoms or causes? Is it extractive or regenerative? Is it short term or durable? Is it head-on or lateral? Does it balance interests, benefits, and costs across society? Does it create a large opportunity cost in terms of technologies *not* developed?"

It is not only companies that learn from being brought face-to-face with other ways of knowing. Environmentalists come face-to-face with the constraints on companies, especially their need to protect shareholder value, which in turn tempers the tone of arrogance environmentalists have used when talking to business. Consumers come face-to-face with the fact that our choices have a direct impact on farmers' practices in terms of technology choice and landscape features. We are confronted with the fact that much of the pesticide use in developing countries is an extension of the North's ecological footprint, in its demands for feed grains for meat production, out-of-season fruits and vegetables, and cotton fiber and clothing. We see that what we do with our savings and pension funds, how we shop, how we eat, and how we vote, all contribute to the pesticide issue. All stakeholders learn to appreciate that the pesticide issue is not just about pesticides but is, in the words of Norgaard (1992), symptomatic of a society "stuck with ways of knowing, organizing, valuing, and doing things, with tightly intertwined roots of unsustainability."

NOTES

1. This chapter originated from a project coordinated from the Leopold Center for Sustainable Agriculture, Iowa State University, USA, linking CSERGE, EFTEC, and IIED in the United Kingdom, Ellipson in Switzerland, the ABL Group in Canada, and A&M Consultants in the United States. The work was funded in part by the Iowa Department of Agriculture and Land Stewardship through a grant from the US Environmental Protection Agency's Environmental Technology but does not necessarily represent the view of the agency.

Chapter 10

Sustainable Forestry Management as a Model for Sustainable Industry: A Case Study of the Swedish Approach

Susanne Östlund and Nigel J. Roome

Tachi Kiuchi, past Chairman and CEO of Mitsubishi Electric America, in a recent address to the World Future Society, argues that sustainable industry will need to learn by modeling itself on the design principles of the rainforest (Kiuchi, 1997). However, this challenging ecological metaphor has limitations. Certainly industry might usefully learn by applying ecological principles to its organization, but what ecological principles should industry draw on? A number of alternative conceptions can be used: the rainforest as a dynamic, homeostatic natural system; the rainforest as a system in punctuated equilibrium, where periods of relative stability are interwoven with the dramatic changes brought about by events such as forest fire, flood, or drought; the rainforest as a complex, open system made up of many self-organizing systems that together contribute to a relative dynamic order but where there is constant tension created by the potential for the system(s) to go through chaotic perturbations, which might generate transitions to a completely altered ecological state—for example, swamp, lake, or desert.

More important, sustainable development is not an exclusively ecological issue. Sustainable industry must operate in a human as well as ecological world. And, by implication, designing a sustainable industry involves learning through models that draw from activities where ecology, industry, and society come together. A model with this character is found in the sustainably managed forest—where forests are managed for productivity, with industry operating within ecological limits while taking cognizance of the broad set of other economic and social interests that are expressed in the forest. For its part, sustainable forestry has recently been seen as an important arena for the setting of industry standards. Sustainable forestry management standards are therefore an important issue not only for the forest products industry but as possible models for the design of industrial organizations as a whole.

This chapter explores the contribution of sustainable forestry management standards to thinking about sustainable industry. In particular, it draws on recent Swedish experience in establishing a sustainable forestry management standard and certification process. The chapter can therefore be read at two levels. At one level, it provides a case study of the development of the Swedish approach to sustainable forestry. It reviews the environmental problems of forestry and the forestry industry in Sweden and the solutions provided in the last decade. It also describes the transformation in the Swedish forestry industry toward a more sustainable approach to forestry, setting this in the context of the new thinking about sustainability, in forestry, that stemmed from the UN Conference in Rio de Janeiro in 1992. With this background, the Nordic forest certification program, with its aim of sustainable forest management, is described.

At the other level, the chapter considers what insight the case study provides into the contribution of sustainable forestry as a basis for the industrial organization of the future, not only in the area of forestry products but in sectors such as transport, domestic goods, or communications. The chapter suggests that industries committed to sustainable development could do well to follow the path provided by the process-based management approach of the sustainable forest rather than pursue the outcome-oriented approach of current environmental management systems (EMSs) such as BS 7750 (BSI, 1992) and the international standard ISO 14 001 (ISO, 1996).

This argument is consistent with recent criticisms of generic EMS standards—for example, the suggestion by Moxen and Strachan (1995) that EMS standards stress bureaucratic solutions to the exclusion of participatory forms of management and organizational change. In a similar way Spencer-Cooke in this book (Chapter 4) argues that standards such as ISO 14 001 and BS 7750 focus on environmental management rather than the broader range of economic, environmental, and social concerns of sustainable development. While EMS standards are designed to engineer environmental considerations and environmental information into the frame of the decision processes of industrial organizations, they do not help with the greater challenge of integrating industry into its dynamic, chaotic economic, social, and environmental context.

Forestry—Industrial Activity and Institutionalized Global Ecological Concern

People all over the world have become increasingly interested in, and concerned about, forests and issues related to forests since the early 1980s. Prior to the 1980s the main environmental focus of those concerned about the forest products industry was on pollution generated by the production processes for forest products. Emissions to water and air caused local and regional environmental problems and spurred the development of pollution control measures and regulations. The industrial response to these measures was often based on a blend of technical, economic, and political assessments. Factors included the availability of technology, the company's position in the investment cycle, the existing investment in plant and (the very expensive) pollution control or abatement equipment and machinery, and judgments on the political commitment to the enforcement of regulations. Over time, industry was encouraged to develop and invest in technology that lessened the impacts on the local environment so that many of the earlier local environmental problems were greatly improved.

In the 1980s the attention to ecological issues turned from its earlier local/regional perspective to a more global and system-wide view. Issues of resource conservation, the use of genetic resources and biological diversity, the contribution of forests to reduce global warming, the fate of indigenous forest dwellers, and international trade in forest products were hotly debated and discussed on a scale not seen before (IUCN, 1980). Deforestation and degradation of forest resources were a priority issue. And it became an even more critical concern through the 1980s. According to the Food and Agriculture Organization of the United Nations (FAO, 1995a), the annual estimated loss in natural forest area was 12.1 million hectares during the period 1980 to 1990. The largest losses took place in developing countries and were highest in Asia. The reserve of forest land became an increasingly important resource both as a source of forest products and as the other human and ecological functions it served.

The initial organizational response to this agenda was to initiate improved resource conservation. In the case of forest products companies, investments were made to improve the efficiency in the transformation of trees into lumber and fiber. Paper and board manufacturers, together with others, developed the logistics to use both increasing volumes of recycled post-consumer fiber and the new technology to adapt products to the new materials resulting from recycling. A number of new products were developed based on recycled paper. These quickly gained market share over products solely based on virgin wood fiber.

By the 1990s the agenda of issues for the forestry industry, raised by environmental activists and policy makers, included the forest as a resource base to maintain biodiversity. Environmentalists pointed to the importance of tropical rainforests for animal and plant life, as well as their role in climate systems. They also took up the issue of industrial cutting in the remaining stock of primary forest. These concerns were translated into action when large groups of consumers began to boycott products made with tropical timber and the products of companies known to be operating in virgin forest areas. Manufacturers and distributors of products made from tropical lumber saw many of their traditional markets disappear and undertook change programs aimed at replacing natural forest timber with farmed timber, recycled wood products, and other materials.

Forests also occupied a prominent position in the international deliberations at the United Nations Conference on Environment and Development (UNCED) held in Rio de Janeiro in June 1992. Prior to the conference, the issue of deforestation of the tropical regions had been an important concern but, at the conference, the focus turned to all types of forests, including natural and planted, in all geographical regions and climatic zones. Another major outcome was the acceptance of the principle of sustainable development[1] as a ground rule for future economic, ecological, and social development.

Sustainable Forestry—Intergovernmental and Governmental Pressures and Processes

Two parts of the international agreements signed at the Rio Conference were dedicated entirely to forests and their management: Chapter 11 of Agenda 21, "Combating Deforestation," and the non-legally binding authoritative statement of principles for a global consensus on the management, conservation, and sustainable development of all types of forests (UNCED, 1992).

The principles for the management, conservation, and sustainable development of forests stated at the conference related to issues of biological diversity, productivity, the regenerative capacity of the forests, vitality, and preservation of ecological, economic, social, and cultural functions of forests. Chapter 11 of Agenda 21 divided the measures for sustainable forestry into four programs:

1. Maintaining the different roles and functions of all kinds of forest and forest land

2. Improving protection, sustainable development, and preservation of all forests and new plantation of destroyed areas, by forest rehabilitation, regeneration, new plantation of forest, and other rehabilitative measures

3. Promoting an efficient utilization and effective evaluation to get the full value out of the products and services that derive from forests and forest land

4. Building up and/or strengthening capacity for planting, evaluation, and systematic observation of forests and related programs, projects, and activities, including trade and its processes.

Following the conference, governments engaged in a series of national, bilateral, and global initiatives. The UN agencies established special interagency arrangements for cooperation on forests and forestry issues. The UN Commission on Sustainable Development (CSD) established an intergovernmental forum focused on priority issues. The "open-ended ad-hoc Intergovernmental Panel on Forests" (IPF) came under its aegis. Here NGOs, industry, and other interest groups were invited to participate in the discussions about the implementation of the principles of Agenda 21 as they related to forestry.

In Europe, the Ministerial Conference on the protection of Europe's forests took up these principles for implementation at the national level. At the Ministerial Conference in Helsinki in 1993, four resolutions were adopted aimed at further developing regional and international forest collaboration. The sustainability principle is established by the first resolution (H1), which defines sustainable forestry as

> Management and use of forests and forest land in a manner and at a rate which preserves their biological diversity, productivity, capacity for regeneration, vitality, and potential now and in the future for meeting definite ecological, economic, and social functions at local, national and global levels without causing damage to other ecosystems.
>
> (Nordic Forest Certification, 1996a)

The second resolution (H2) gives guidelines for the preservation of the biological diversity of European forests. The third (H3) governs collaboration on forestry with countries in economic transition. And the fourth (H4) applies to the adjustment of the European forests to climatic change. Other national governments and regional blocks took similar action at ministerial levels, although the detail may vary between nations.

A meeting of European ministers in Geneva in 1994 followed up these resolutions by accepting criteria by which to measure compliance with the principles of sustainable forestry in the European countries. Criteria included the maintenance and development of the forest resources and their participation in the global carbon cycle; the health and vitality of the forest ecosystems; the forests' ability to produce timber and other products and services; the biological diversity of the forests; the role of the forests in water supply and protection against erosion; and, finally, the socioeconomic roles and functions of the forests. The criteria were largely modeled on the United Nation's principles for sustainable forests.

As forest issues developed in the sphere of institutionalized government and intergovernmental activity, awareness also grew that change in forestry management practices required the participation and involvement of other parties. Important actors included those involved in the production, distribution, and use of forestry products as well as nongovernmental organizations representing human and environmental rights. These actors formed an international membership organization, the Forest Stewardship Council (FSC), to promote "environmentally appropriate, socially beneficial, and economically viable management of the world's forests" (FSC, 1997). The involvement of the forest products industry in this process was important to the Forestry Stewardship Council. Active participation of industry was consistent with the pressure for change in forestry practices arising from governments, nongovernmental organizations, and consumers. It also was supported by the concern of industry to establish clear standards of practice and by the increasing interest in the lumber, pulp, and paper industries for forest products from sustainable sources.

The Forest Stewardship Council Initiative

The FSC was founded in September 1993 in Toronto, on the initiative of representatives of environmental and humans rights organizations, and timber users and traders from 25 different countries. The Forest Stewardship Council is an independent, international organization representing its members. Its headquarters are in Oaxaca, Mexico. The FSC operates a voluntary accreditation program for organizations and firms that provides for certification in the forestry sector. The FSC's Principles and Criteria contain overall guidelines that apply worldwide, but certification is adapted to comply with local conditions in each country. The Council sees one of its most important tasks as support for efforts to develop nationally appropriate FSC standards. However, the FSC itself does not undertake certification. Products certified in accordance with FSC standards are required to come from forests that are managed in a responsible manner, defined in environmental, social, and economic terms.

The General Assembly of the FSC is the organization's most important decision-making body and consists of three Chambers, for economic, environmental, and social interests, respectively. Each of these Chambers has one-third of the votes in the General Assembly. The FSC Board contains nine members, who are elected for a three-year term. Two members represent economic interests, while the remaining members represent environmental and social concerns. FSC is funded by membership fees, fees from accreditation and licensing, grants and donations, and returns from investments and services.

The Forest Stewardship Council has formulated 10 principles as the basis of its work:

1. Forest management shall respect all applicable laws of the country in which they occur, and international treaties and agreements to which the country is a signatory, and comply with all FSC Principles and Criteria.

2. Long-term tenure and use rights to the land and forest resources shall be clearly defined, documented, and legally established.

3. The legal and customary rights of indigenous peoples to own, use, and manage their lands, territories, and resources shall be recognized and respected.

4. Forest management operations shall maintain or enhance the long-term social and economic well-being of forest workers and local communities.

5. Forest management operations shall encourage the efficient use of the forest's multiple products and services to ensure economic viability and a wide range of environmental and social benefits.

6. Forest management shall conserve biological diversity and its asso-
    ciated values, water resources, soils, and unique and fragile ecosys-
    tems and landscapes, and, by so doing, maintain the ecological func-
    tions and integrity of the forest.

7. A management plan—appropriate to the scale and intensity of the
    operations—shall be written, implemented, and kept up-to-date. The
    long-term objectives of management, and the means of achieving
    them, shall be clearly stated.

8. Monitoring shall be conducted—appropriate to the scale and intensi-
    ty of forest management—to assess the condition of the forest, yields
    of forest products, chain of custody, management activities, and their
    social and environmental impacts.

9. Primary forests, well-developed secondary forests, and sites of major
    environmental, social, or cultural significance shall be conserved.
    Such areas shall not be replaced by tree plantations or other land uses.

10. (Draft principle for plantations, not yet ratified by FSC membership)
    Plantations should be planned and managed in accordance with prin-
    ciples 1 through 9 and the following criteria. Such plantations can
    and should complement natural forests and the surrounding ecosys-
    tem, provide community benefits, and contribute to the world's
    demands for forest products.

The Case of Swedish Forestry

The response of Swedish forestry products industry has taken place
against the backdrop of the international efforts in sustainable forestry
and the long history of forestry management in the development of the
economic and social fabric of the country. Indeed, the large forests of the
Scandinavian countries have been one of the most important resources on
which economic prosperity and wealth have been built and maintained.
Two-thirds of sparsely populated Sweden and Finland, and just over one-
third of Norway, are today covered by trees. This area contributes more
than half of Europe's forests, making the Scandinavian countries an
important supplier of wood and wood products to the European Continent
as well as to wider international markets. In addition to their economic
significance and environmental importance, the extremely long cultural
history of Swedish forests and the dynamics of environmental concern

about forests and their management has been critical to the discussion about sustainable forestry in Sweden.

Wood has been used for centuries as an important raw material in the construction of buildings, ships, furniture, and farming tools. It has also been used for fuel in homes and in mining as well as in the production of potash and charcoal. Today a range of products are made out of lumber or wood fiber. Out of the total harvest of wood, about 8 percent is used for energy and heating, while the rest is processed and used as input in the production of pulp, paper, and saw products (Swedish Forest Industries Association, 1997a). Paper, paperboard, and pulp amounts to the largest usage. Demand is rapidly increasing worldwide. According to a forecast made by FAO, which assumes the current growth rate, paper consumption will double in relation to today's consumption by the year 2010 (Swedish Forest Industries Association, 1997a).

In Sweden, forest products companies are highly integrated by ownership or cooperative arrangements. During the last 30 years the industry has undergone a change toward fewer production units with higher capacity. The number of pulp and paper mills have been reduced by half, while the total capacity has doubled; and the number of sawmills has been reduced by two-thirds while their output has increased five times (Swedish Forest Industries Association, 1997b). Over 85 percent of production is sold within the European Union.

A Hundred Years of Environmental Issues in the Swedish Forestry Industry

With industrialization the use of lumber increased, by the end of the 19th century many areas of Scandinavia experienced shortages of wood supplies. The forest area was diminished and regeneration was poor due to a combination of brutal logging, slash-and-burn agriculture, and livestock grazing over areas that were previously wooded. In response, Scandinavian countries began to take action in the early 20th century to halt the loss of forest cover. Silvicultural laws made forest owners responsible for ensuring that forests were tended with due regard to the long-term sustainable yield of the forest—the harvest was not allowed to exceed regrowth. At about the same time, a movement to replant trees in barren areas began. Many volunteers participated in this effort to "rebuild" the Scandinavian forests. As a result of the efforts of economic and community interests, the forests recovered. Today the region has twice as much standing forest as it did a hundred years ago (Swedish Forest Industries Association, 1997b).

Despite the substantial net growth of the forest area in the region, very little of the primary forest remains. New types of trees (with faster and higher yields more suitable for large-scale forestry) entered the Nordic flora. Together with new logging methods, these trees have had a profound impact on the ecosystems in the region. In particular, clear-cut methods created large areas without the trees needed to support animal and plant life and gave rise to large "wounds" in the landscape with reduced biodiversity. This loss of diversity was compounded by a trend toward even-aged monocultural plantations, where replanting did take place. Forestry management techniques have now become more sophisticated, with some companies relying on natural regeneration or replanting using seedlings grown from the genetic stock taken from the area before it was felled.

Not only have forestry methods given rise to environmental problems—the development of markets for processed and refined wood products during the last century also created problems. Developments in the chemical industry enabled new or modified fiber products to be produced. There was a general trend away from wood and wood fiber as natural resources were transformed through craft and manufacturing processes to the use of wood and fiber as inputs to many chemical processes. As a consequence, chemical pollution from the forest products industry increased. In the 1960s criticism of pulp and paper mills grew, especially over the often unrestricted emissions of chemicals and wood residues into air and water. There were concerns about emissions of dust, sulfur dioxide, and the characteristic odor of pulp mills, as well as the effluents from the pulp mills released into water. The chemical oxygen demand of these pollutants, together with the demands on the environment from waste fiber, had its effect on fish stocks and other aquatic wildlife and its related food web.

In Sweden, the threats to both nature and human health could not continue. One of the first tasks of the Swedish Environmental Protection Agency (SEPA), created in the late 1960s, was to introduce time-limited licenses to compel factories to limit their emissions to established threshold values. Every time the license was renewed, stricter thresholds were applied. As a response the industry began to reduce emissions by a combination of approaches based on "end-of-pipe" and "reduction at the source." Efforts were made to modify processes to use and waste less chemicals. Purification and cleaning methods were improved so that fewer and less chemicals were released to the environment. There was substantial investment in modern plant and technology to replace out-moded processing plants. Some of these new and improved processes were the outcome of pioneering forms of cooperation between forest products firms, their industry organizations, and chemical and equipment suppliers. The SEPA frequently intervened to encourage the strategy of joint development of pollution prevention approaches. This cooperative, multiparty approach involving business and regulators later became known as the Swedish Model.

Environmental improvements were brought about but new problems were encountered. In the 1980s attention was focused on the organic chlorine compounds (AOX) used in paper bleaching. These compounds have a tendency to break down into persistent, toxic compounds. New regulations were implemented that forced the industry to reduce the amounts of AOX. As before, the main strategy was to modify the cooking methods used in pulp and paper manufacture and to introduce more effective purification. Incremental reductions in AOX were achieved throughout the late 1980s.

This period saw a steadily growing environmental awareness penetrating markets, in addition to the longer standing concerns of environmental activists. There was increased customer demand for environmentally adapted products and processes. These pressures, acting together with stiffer emission requirements, led the industry into the transformation processes witnessed in the 1990s. New methods were adopted to measure and analyze environmental loads, and new generation technologies were developed and implemented for bleaching and cooking pulp and paper. These helped reduce energy consumption, reduce or phase out the use of chlorinated gas, improve chemical and fiber recovery, and enable improved environmental technologies to be used.

The change in processes in forestry products companies that accompanied these technological innovations and developments provided the ground within which the recommendations of the Rio Conference on the principles for sustainable development in the forestry industry could take root. As the industry was encouraged to consider its approach to pulp and paper manufacture in new ways, so it was encouraged to review the assumptions of forestry management and the practices that were employed.

The point of departure for the industry was to treat forests not as mined resources, exploited at will, nor as agricultural resources, to be harvested like an agricultural crop. Indeed, the forest could no longer be seen as simply an ecological resource. The Rio Conference laid the foundation to consider the forest as an economic, ecological, and social resource—invested with many human values—that should be available to this and future generations by maintaining the integrity of the forest's ecological properties and processes.

One outcome of this approach to sustainable forestry is the Nordic Forest Certification and a proposal for a Swedish Forest Certification process in line with the FSC principles described above.

Industrial Responses to Demands for Sustainable Forest Management

On August 1, 1995, the principal forest owners and the forest products industry established the joint Nordic Forestry Certification Project to investigate the prospects of concerted Nordic action on certification for sustainable forestry (Nordic Forest Certification, 1996a). The aim was to identify areas where environmental development was needed and to put in place a framework for collaboration among interests that would lead to sustainable forestry in line with the policies formulated by the United Nations and the Forest Stewardship Council.

A Swedish FSC Working Group was formed in February 1996 (FSC, 1997a). The members of the Working Group represent social, environmental, and economic interests. The Working Group is now preparing proposals to be submitted for approval by the FSC. These proposals cover standards for forest management, the application of standards, and include ideas about monitoring, evaluation, and the labeling of forest products.

The Working Group is using a consultative process built around questioning, seminars, and the circulation of information for comments. All interest groups have an opportunity to submit proposals in the areas covered by the Working Group, as well as the right to receive information about the ongoing process. The Swedish FSC Working Group has powers of decision in all matters involving the development of national standards. Decisions are based on consensus.

A number of subgroups have been established to support the process toward sustainable forestry management standards and certification. These include the Application Subgroup, which is concerned with the way future standards are applied; the Market Subgroup, which is preparing proposals for percentage-based FSC labeling for products of mixed origin; the Environmental and Biodiversity Subgroup, which prepares draft standards in the area of ecology and forests; the Saami People, Local Community, and Workers' Rights Subgroup, which is drawing up draft standards for human rights, especially for indigenous peoples, in relation to forests; the Production and Economic Subgroup, which is estimating the effects of various proposals made by the Working Group on production and the economy. There is also a Stakeholder Group attached to the Swedish FSC Working Group. The stakeholders have given written support for the principle of FSC certification and are participating in a broad consultative process in accordance with FSC requirements (FSC, 1997b).

At the heart of the Swedish certification project lies the importance of forestry to the Swedish economy and prosperity. In the project declaration it is stated that "Forestry offers both local inhabitants and society as a whole long-term benefits." [This is why] "the FSC process aims to promote the management and use of forests in ways that are ecologically, socially, and economically viable" (Swedish FSC, 1997).

In June 1997 the Swedish FSC submitted the draft Swedish FSC forest certification. Behind the draft were representatives from the forestry, forestry process, and furniture industries, environmental groups, and Saami people. The proposal states that forest certification should be a voluntary, market-oriented system. The responsibility for fulfilling the goals of the FSC rests with landowners, who undertake to manage their forests and demonstrate their ability to apply the principles in accordance with the applicable standard.

Forest owners who wish to receive certification for their forestry operations enter into agreements with the certification organization. Under such an agreement, the owner pledges to comply with the applicable standard by making specific undertakings regarding forest management. The certifier is responsible for ensuring compliance with the standard, for example by making random checks.

After certification of the forestry operation, products from the forest may be labeled with the FSC logo. The logo aims to ensure the credibility of the certification system by supplying a guarantee of the origin of the timber to indicate to buyers and consumers that the raw material concerned comes from forests managed in a responsible manner.

Draft standards, specified and applied to Swedish conditions, now cover all the FSC principles. Standards are specified for workers', indigenous people's, and local communities' rights as well as for ecological and economic areas. The overall standard also specifies model practices for labeling and certification processes for different categories of landowner.

Not surprisingly, the biodiversity and indigenous people standards were the hardest to agree on but were in the end agreed to the satisfaction of all parties. They recognize the historic rights of the Saami people and give consideration to them. Reindeer husbandry and the preservation of old natural forests are now proposed as part of the responsibilities of the forest owner.

Perhaps the most novel part of the principles concerns biodiversity. Never before have the responsibilities of forest owners been greater to protect and manage their forest resource in ways that maintain its ecological integrity. This now requires owners to develop and demonstrate a detailed knowledge of the land. For example, a specification has to be supplied on type and age of standing trees; dead trees; burning; valuable biotopes; montane areas; type of land; plantation forestry—nonnative species, treeless traditional cultivated landscapes; land management—soil scarification; genetics—clone forestry, provenance; fertilization and chemicals; landscape perspectives; roads; water—watercourses, wetlands; biofuel extraction; and last, conservation of historic sites.

Initially all forest owners were part of the Working Group, but one association, representing small family-owned forests, decided to withdraw from the certification project. That association represents roughly 25 percent of the forest area in Sweden (DI, 1997). Representatives from the association claimed that the costs for certification would be too high for its members. They pointed to the large areas of the forest that could not be used for logging but have to be protected for wildlife and plants; the restrictions on logging in forests close to mountain areas; and the responsibilities to negotiate with the Saami people, where reindeer husbandry is taking place. The owners of family forests claimed that the costs of these restrictions and the costs of managing the forest were higher for them than for commercial forest products companies because the family-owner had less flexibility over the forest lands at their disposal.

Another reaction to the project took place at the publication of the draft in June 1997. In the proposal for certification, forest owners retained the right to use fertilizer and to plant woods not indigenous to Scandinavian forests. In protest to these points Greenpeace decided to leave the working group (Greenpeace, 1997a). The draft of the certification program was sent out for consultation and comments, which were reviewed by the Swedish FSC Working Group. Minor revisions were made and a formal endorsement was sent to the International FSC in the fall of 1997.

Industrial Implications of the Sustainable Forestry Model

At the beginning of this chapter it was suggested that the case study of the Nordic approach to Sustainable Forestry was important at two levels: as an example of the response by the forestry industry to the demands for sustainable thinking and practices, and as a possible model that might be adapted to other industrial organizations, outside the forestry sector.

Sustainable Forestry as a Process Model for the Forest Products Industry

As far as the first level of analysis is concerned, the case study raises important points about the context, process, and output of the approach to sustainable forestry. In terms of context, the forest products industry is seen to have experienced a relentless expansion of the environmental agenda to which it has had to respond. The case study shows that the focus of the environmental concerns that constitute this agenda has shifted and can be expected to shift further as new issues come before the forest products industry. One characteristic of this unfolding environmental agenda is the move away from individual issues—for example dust, chlorine bleaching, and clear felling—and an increasing concern that industry should develop thinking and practice informed by principles like those of Agenda 21 and the FSC.

At the same time, the context within which the forest industry is operating has become increasingly multilayered, as decisions about the operating principles of forestry have been subject to pressure from a network of interests in forests. These operate at every level of organization—global, regional, national, and local. This pressure has been translated into operational practices in the forest, as companies (forest owners) are obliged to engage a wider set of interests in decisions about forestry management. The move toward cooperative, multiparty decision making over forest management extends the earlier cooperative model involving regulators, the forest industry, and equipment suppliers that led to breakthroughs in pollution control in the 1970s and early 1980s.

The same generic approach to the process of decision making has operated at each of these levels—whether it is the work at the Rio Conference, the activities of the FSC, at the Nordic or Swedish level, or in the development of forest management plans. This is based on the notion of inclusive, multiparty facilitated or mediated decision making. But there are critical differences at the local level. At the level of the forest, industry itself is responsible for the management of the process of multiparty or stakeholder engagement and dialogue through the obligation, on forest owners, to demonstrate that the forestry management plan is the result of a due process of consultation and discussion with interested parties. Unless this can be shown, the ultimate forest management plan, on which sustainable forestry certification depends, cannot be justified. At all other levels, industry is just one of the parties to decision making and can represent its economic position and perspective fully while recognizing that there are other interests to be taken into account and satisfied around the table.

Examining industry's responsibility for the process at the level of the forest enables a very important idea to emerge about sustainable industrial practices as they relate to process and output. Traditionally, the forestry products industry has seen forest ownership and forest management in terms of inputs and outputs. The demand for forest products is anticipated, output targets are specified, and this sets the demand for raw material inputs, within the constraints of production capacity and technical efficiency of the processing plant. Wood and fiber are either cut from owned sources or bought on the open market to meet demand. However, the preparation of a sustainable forest management plan obliges industry to engage the range of forestry interests and to operate within the forests' ecological limits. This implies that the outcome of the process—a sustainable forestry management plan specifying a socially and ecologically sustainable level of wood and fiber that can be harvested—can never be predicted with certainty by the forest industry at the outset of the process.

Each sustainable forestry plan will involve a process that combines the unique human interests and ecological or bioregional constraints operating in a specific area. For industry, the approach adds to its established focus on output—harvest goals and targets—by emphasizing a concern for process, ensuring that there is sufficient consent for the management plan so that a harvest can be agreed. It will be interesting to see how the forestry products industry adjusts to this move away from the certainty that has gone with earlier output-oriented forest management to the newer, process-based approach. It will also be interesting to see how the experience of the process-based management approach in forestry impacts the way that forest products companies operate their lumber, pulp, and paper manufacturing operations. Will the experience of this process of learning through consultation cause forest products companies to begin to mimic the fuller range of social and ecological properties of the forest, rather than seeing the forest in economic terms as a fiber and lumber factory? These issues will only become clear as the standards and certification programs become institutionalized in Scandinavia and elsewhere.

Sustainable Forestry as a Model for Industry

At the second level, what does the sustainable forestry management standard say to the issue of sustainable industry? First, it is clear that the approach can be applied to any industrial setting. The process approach is not restricted to forest management or even to companies that harvest living resources, such as agriculture and fisheries. Even companies that appear to rely on nonliving resources—minerals, metals, oil, and gas—or manufacturers of automobiles and communications systems, in practice have a wide range of impacts on living processes and bioregional resources as well as on the many human interests those resources support.

An issue here is how generalizable is the ecology-process approach of sustainable forest management. This can be considered against a complex industrial case—say, an automobile company with numerous parts suppliers around the globe; a number of automobile assembly plants, which receive parts; and a distribution system for the final product and spare parts that extend to many hundreds of dealers and many hundreds of thousands of automobile owners, on several continents. However, it is analytically more informative to consider the simple case—an industrial (say manufacturing) organization with a single site for manufacture of a single product, where it has a very short supply chain and distributes to local markets. Under these circumstances it is possible to conceive the company engaging in consultative processes with networks of stakeholders to ensure that its activities, and the environmental demands on resources that arise from those activities, are taken into account in setting output targets. The outcome of the consultative process would be a sustainable resource-development management plan that could then be verified and endorsed.

In practice, it is possible to extend the simple single producer/product case. But at each level of extension the level or scale of industrial operations adds information and consultation problems due to the interdependence of interests and the uncertainty about the precise nature of the bioregional impacts of industrial activity. This creates new complexity and risk to the process of defining a sustainable management plan.

But what does this say about the contribution of the ecology process-driven approach of sustainable forestry management to industry beyond the forestry sector? It implies that the standard is not robust in its application to industrial settings because its managerial value, as a decision-support tool, rapidly diminishes for industries that operate in a number of bioregions, or where resources or products are transported from one bioregion to another. This suggests that it is difficult to apply the sustainable forestry standard within the current industrial structure.

The problem with the robustness of the ecology-process approach can be viewed another way. Deficiencies in the wider industrial application of the approach are not seen as a result of failings in the ecology-process approach but as failures in the design of the structure and organization of existing industry. It can be argued that industry is prone to act unsustainable precisely because it has not been designed in accordance with the principles of the ecology-process approach contained in the sustainable forestry management standard. One way to judge this is to apply the precautionary principle, a key notion of sustainable development, to the information and consultation problems created by a moderately complex industrial or manufacturing organization.

The precautionary principle suggests that if the environmental and social implications arising from industrial activities cannot be determined, and if socially acceptable ways to manage those implications cannot be agreed, then industry should not operate beyond that scale. Instead, industry that wants to become sustainable should find ways to scale down its operations to a level where plans based on the ecology-process model of sustainable forest management can be applied.

Conclusion

This chapter set out to address the contribution of developments in sustainable forestry management standards to the forestry industry, in particular, and to industry more generally. The case study and analysis suggests that one of the most important characteristics of the sustainable forestry management approach is its emphasis on process rather than outcomes. Predetermined outcomes, in terms of forest yields, are not useful because they can rarely be specified before a management plan is agreed that respects the ecological limits and social interests expressed in a forest. The participative approach to resource management, and the concern for the intersecting interests of ecology, society, and economics, at the heart of the sustainable forestry management process, are also regarded as critical contributions made by the approach to sustainable development.

These aspects meet some of the criticisms of the more formal engineered approach to environmental management developed through system standards such as ISO 14 001.

Consequently, the sustainable forestry management process is seen as providing a powerful model for industrial organizations to adapt in formulating their approach to sustainable industry. More surprising, the model can be used to judge not only whether industrial activities are sustainable but also whether the structure of the industry itself is amenable to analysis from a sustainable development perspective.

NOTES

1. Although this term was used to connect economic, social, and ecological balance and justice in the Brundtland Commission Report of 1987, it was not until the Rio Conference that it was widely integrated and used in policy discussions. Sustainability was defined by the Brundtland Commission as, "Meeting the needs of the present without compromising the ability of future generations to meet their own needs" (WCED, 1987).

Part IV

THE INDUSTRIAL
ORGANIZATION IN GLOBAL CONTEXT

Chapter 11

Sustainable Production
Paradigms for Greenfield Economies

David Wallace

The Policy Background

The Earth Summit: Hope from Failure?

The 1992 Earth Summit (UNCED) has set the international policy framework for efforts to achieve environmentally and economically sustainable
development. The UN resolution that initiated UNCED set an objective of
identifying the actions required to reverse the environmental degradation
of the planet.

Two features of the resolution helped to ensure that the subsequent
process was unnecessarily polarized between North and South. First,
there was an underlying assumption that developing countries must
acquire environmentally sound technologies (ESTs).[1] Second, it called
for new and additional financial resources to be provided for developing
countries to participate in global environmental protection. In other
words, developing countries need to reach Western levels of technology,
and the developed countries should pay for this.

How realistic is the proposition that the West should pay for developing countries to acquire ESTs? The answer depends in part on the definition of an EST. Increasingly, businesses are realizing that their environmental impact is reduced by general improvements in the efficiency with
which new generations of technologies use resources, as well as by the
addition of dedicated "end-of-pipe" pollution control technologies. For

the most part ESTs are therefore synonymous with the latest technology.[2] It is not generally possible to clearly identify a proportion of the investment costs associated with better environmental performance, relative to earlier vintages of the technology. Taking this view of ESTs, UNCED was a mandate for developing countries to ask the West to underwrite their industrialization. In the run-up to UNCED, the fundamental tension between the developed countries' concerns for the global environment and the developing countries' need to industrialize became clearer.

One of the main outputs of UNCED was "Agenda 21," whose purpose was to outline mechanisms for addressing the twin objectives of environment and development. In Agenda 21, the inability to reconcile North and South is clear. In particular, it puts forward a broad definition of ESTs, encompassing the entire means of production in an economy, yet estimates that, globally, sustainable industry can be achieved at a cost of only $20 billion annually—remarkably cheap for an exercise that involves radically altering the momentum of two centuries of industrial development.

At UNCED, world leaders failed to come to terms with the huge economic forces driving industrialization in the developing countries. If they had, they would have been honest about the self-evident truth that the environmental consequences of these forces cannot be corrected by official development assistance. The only way to square the circle is to make the process of industrialization itself an agent for sustainable development.

Resources for Sustainable Production: Aid or Investment?

Predictably, Western governments choked on the overall estimate of $125 billion annually for their total contribution to Agenda 21 activities. In 1993, official aid to developing countries actually fell, to $55.2 billion from the 1992 peak of $59.5 billion. This includes all bilateral and multilateral flows, for all purposes (OECD, 1994). Prospects for "new and additional financial resources" from OECD countries are dismal, where reduction in public expenditure has become an overriding macroeconomic priority and aid for other countries is viewed by the public as undeserving by comparison with domestic healthcare, welfare, and education priorities.

Private financial flows to developing countries are rapidly becoming more important than official flows. In 1992 gross foreign direct investment (FDI) into developing countries from the OECD was around $40 billion. A trend of accelerating FDI suggests that this will be increasingly dominant as long as the conditions driving it prevail.

Other private financial flows to developing countries are comparable to FDI in scale, but not in effect. FDI involves active commitment of an investor in the host country, but purchases of bonds and equities and bank loans are passive investments with no significant impact on the management or governance of activities in the recipient country.[3]

Foreign Direct Investment by Western firms in developing countries is therefore potentially the largest financial resource available for implementing sustainable development. It outweighs many times over the official assistance available for sustainable industrialization of developing countries. The effectiveness of FDI as a force for sustainable industrialization depends on two factors: the influence of FDI relative to industrialization driven by a developing country's internal resources, and the political and commercial feasibility of integrating sustainability criteria into FDI decision making. To understand the possible influence of FDI we must first examine patterns of industrialization and identify the conditions under which radically different patterns of production—new industrial paradigms—can emerge.

Industrialization and the Environment

Environmental Consequences of Industrial Structure

Industrialized countries with similar levels of wealth and at similar levels of industrialization have varying impacts on the environment. For example, energy use per unit of GDP (energy intensity) in all industrialized countries reaches a peak during the process of industrialization and then declines steadily (Figure 11.1). Countries that industrialized later, such as Japan and France, peaked at lower energy intensities than their predecessors, such as the United Kingdom and the United States. Significantly, the energy intensity of these "follower" countries through their main period of industrialization was less than in their forerunners.

Clearly, over time less energy-intensive industrialization paths became available as more efficient vintages of industrial, domestic, and transport technologies became available on world markets. Meanwhile, older industrial countries maintained large stocks of older technology, so that the overall mix of the economy was less efficient.

Generalizations about developing countries are difficult, but the industrialization trajectory of some developing countries has resulted in

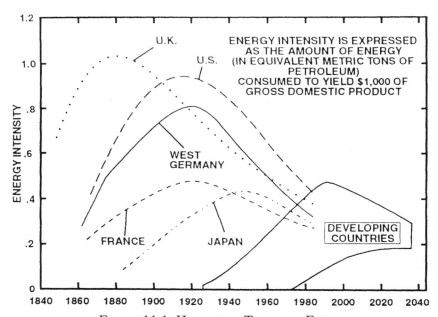

FIGURE 11.1. HISTORICAL TRENDS IN ENERGY
INTENSITY IN SOME COUNTRIES AND GROUPS OF COUNTRIES.
Source: A.K.N. Reddy and J. Goldemberg, "Energy for the Developing
World," *Scientific American* "International Edition," Sept. 1990: 64.

energy intensities exceeding current levels in major OECD countries and
surpassing the peak energy intensities that Japan and some others passed
through many decades earlier.

Other indicators of consumption show similar historical and cross-sec-
tional variations. For example, cement production per capita is increasing
in the poorer countries but generally declining in the richer countries
(Japan is a notable exception) (Janicke et al., 1994).

These observations suggest that there is no fixed relationship between
wealth and resource use, with its attendant environmental impacts. However, the empirical evidence for a rise and then decline of material
resource intensity (at least for some materials) as industrialization
proceeds is generally held to imply that industrializing countries will
inevitably go through a similar process, with massive impacts on the
environment. Alternatively, some argue that such observations set limits
on the degree to which developing countries should be "allowed" to
industrialize. Neither of these positions is compatible with sustainable
development.

Some people have tried to argue that there is no fundamental conflict between industrialization and the environment, citing as evidence the so-called environmental Kuznets curve (Figure 11.2).[4] The inverted-U shape of the Kuznets curve is said to describe the relationship between GDP per capita and measures of environmental quality, particularly air and water quality—for instance, sulfur dioxide (SO_2) concentrations. The relationship between development and the environment suggested by the Kuznets curve has gained wide acceptance, particularly following the publication of the 1992 World Bank Development Report. For example, a European Commission policy document portrays Kuznets curves unquestioningly as "stylized facts" of economic growth and the environment (Commission of the European Communities, 1994).

Both the World Bank and the European Commission acknowledge that pollution falls in higher-income countries only as a result of conscious environmental policies. However, some researchers have interpreted the Kuznets curve as proof that economic growth is the solution to environmental problems and that environmental policies are unnecessary. The Kuznets curve hypothesis distracts attention from the real reasons for differences in the environmental performance of different countries and hinders the promotion of less damaging industrialization trajectories.

In addition, the Kuznets relationship has not been unequivocally demonstrated. A comprehensive critique suggests that research in this area is troubled by favorable selection of environmental indicators, limited and unreliable data, contradictions among studies, and bias in the choice of "best-fit" curves (Ekins, 1995).

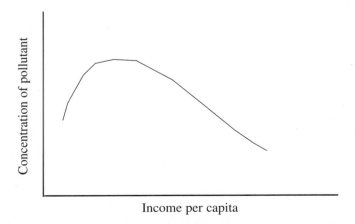

FIGURE 11.2. STYLIZED ENVIRONMENTAL KUZNETS CURVE.

The Conventional Response

With large-scale aid for technology transfer off the political agenda, the issue of transforming the pattern of industrialization in developing countries is being ignored, and the environment-versus-development impasse goes unresolved. Instead, piecemeal mechanisms for technology transfer through public sector initiatives are promoted. These fall into the categories of diffusion of information on technologies in the public domain; cooperation between technical and higher education institutions; replacing "outmoded technologies" with "environmentally sound technologies"; regulations to avoid dumping of dirty technologies in developing countries and standards to control technology imports; strengthening the role of the private sector and improving the incentive structure for participation in public sector initiatives (Munasinghe and Munasinghe, 1993). There is an increasing emphasis on soft technologies and technical capacity, as opposed to hardware.

This conventional response is inadequate, not just because sufficient financial resources do not exist, and are never likely to, but because public sector bodies are incapable of the task. The emphasis on soft technology is correct, but soft technology is not synonymous with levels of education and quality of institutions. Soft technology resides within firms, whose role must therefore be central to technology transfer, not ancillary to public sector efforts. This insight gives rise to a possible mechanism for an environmentally sustainable pattern of industrialization to emerge—a new paradigm for industrial production arising, as has happened in the past, from an evolution in the nature of firms.

The Evolution of Industrial Paradigms

How can the Western pattern of industrialization change sufficiently so that developing countries can industrialize without the massive environmental impacts that currently seem likely? Only a very different basis for the system of industrial production is likely to produce such a change.

Figure 11.3 represents the evolution of the dominant forms of industrial production in terms of a succession of dominant paradigms. The original industrial revolution in the United Kingdom relied on craft production techniques. This was based on a marriage of traditional skills with new sources of power and increased availability of raw materials.

Various technical and managerial innovations, such as the development of the principles of technical drawing (a prerequisite for the standardization of components) and Frederick Taylor's experiments on the organiza-

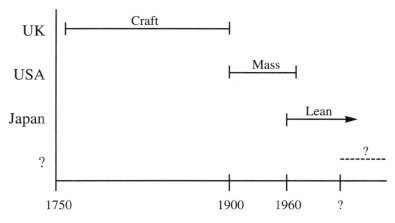

FIGURE 11.3. EVOLUTION OF PRODUCTION SYSTEMS.

tion of labor, laid the foundations for the mass production system.[5] This came to fruition early in the 20th century in the booming new economy of the United States of America, where an enormous and rapidly growing market allowed full advantage to be taken of economies of scale.

Henry Ford introduced the moving assembly line, with interchangeable parts and interchangeable workers doing simplified tasks with a minimum of training. Increasing specialization led to new professions of financial management and marketing to complement the engineering professions (Womack et al., 1990).

Finally, lean production is the current dominant model of industrial production. Its origins were in Japan in the post-war period, where a further series of management innovations led to more flexible production and working patterns. Once again the lead came from car manufacturing with one manufacturer, Toyota, pioneering just-in-time inventory control, "right first time," zero defects, worker cells, and worker control of the pace of the assembly line.[6]

These successive industrial paradigms are in effect the business community's set of automatic assumptions or beliefs about the best way to organize production. For most industrialists, bankers, politicians, or investors, the model they use to think about industrial organization is limited by the prevailing paradigm. In each case, economies and societies influence, and are themselves influenced by, the prevailing industrial paradigm and thus help to perpetuate it. Institutions that evolve in whole or in part to serve the commercial sphere, such as banks, labor unions, educational establishments, and public bodies, build in assumptions about the nature of these relationships. Change becomes an issue for individual firms or groups of firms and for society as a whole, but it is unlikely that the successive evolution of production paradigms has come to an end.

Toward a Sustainable Production Paradigm

In the evolutionary process described above, many features of the typical firm have adapted and evolved. Some of these have played a significant part in shaping the distinctive characteristics of each industrial paradigm, acting as internal evolutionary forces. Three of these forces are particularly relevant to how business deals with the environment.

Management of Physical Resources

Lean production, with its flexible manufacturing and just-in-time deliveries, avoids the problems of both craft production (lack of standard patterns for goods-generated unusable off-cuts and residues) and mass production (excess inventories and dumping of over-produced goods).

Further evolution in the management of physical resources is being driven by moves toward life cycle analysis (LCA)—where waste and product take-back regulations are playing a role—and price pressures such as environmental taxes on resources and waste, as well as risk and liability arising from environmental and health impacts. These forces are affecting firms' choices of materials at the design stage of the manufacturing process.

The Role of Workers in the Firm

The attitude of workers will be crucial to an intelligent, business-centered approach to sustainability. Lean production has pursued "empowerment" of workers who contribute to improvements in processes and procedures—for example through quality circles—and who determine the pace of the manufacturing process. This is partly a return to the status of the craftsman in the days before mass production and has been accompanied by flattening of managerial hierarchies and concentration on developing generic rather than task-specific skills.

Further evolution of this trend is already apparent in some firms, where employees are encouraged to engage with the community beyond their firm.

Expansion of the Boundaries of the Firm

The third internal evolutionary force concerns the boundaries the firm draws around those activities it feels it needs to manage and those it does not, or cannot. Lean production depends on close cooperation between firms in the chain of production and consequent integration of management functions, to maximize added value. Application of information technology to business processes has helped this process.

Possible further expansion of the firms' boundaries is illustrated in Figure 11.4. This shows the integration of management functions along the chain of production (dotted-line boundary). Impacts on the environment (horizontal arrows) are increasingly subject to regulations, pollution charges, and requirements for environmental reporting, thus distorting the simple, linear model of the lean production paradigm. This model may be increasingly inadequate for managing these environmental pressures, provoking a further expansion of the boundaries of the firm to encompass the environment and the community.

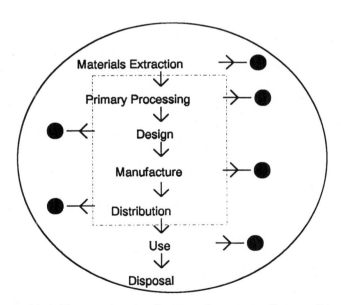

FIGURE 11.4. ENVIRONMENTAL IMPACTS ALONG THE SUPPLY CHAIN.

Sustainable Production Systems: Where and How?

Greenfield Economies and Sustainable Production

A significant evolution or revolution of the industrial paradigm might occur in countries that currently have low levels of industrialization. In Figure 11.3, it is striking that, following the emergence of the first craft production system, succeeding paradigms also emerged in "greenfield" economies—mass production in the industrializing United States and then lean production in the economic vacuum that was post-war Japan. New paradigms faced resistance and inertia from the socioeconomic structure associated with the old paradigms (it was not until 1980 that the UK car industry finally abandoned the piece-rate system of payments to workers—a legacy of craft production—in favor of the fixed hourly rates introduced by Henry Ford before World War II (Womack et al., 1990).

Industrialized countries will only slowly adopt new paradigms, and this is likely to occur at different rates in different industries. Many of the Asian "tiger" economies may already be too far along the path followed by the Western economies to be likely candidates for the emergence of a sustainable production paradigm. Moreover, much of their industrial development has been achieved through a static imitation of the Western economies as they were at some point in the last few decades.

By contrast, countries that are relatively nonindustrialized suffer no such problems. They offer the prospect of industrialization along an entirely different trajectory. And they offer perhaps the best chance for current best environmental, organizational, managerial, and technological competencies to combine to stimulate a sustainable system of production that at the national level has systemic environmental and economic advantages.

Multinationals as Agents for Sustainable Production

Multinational corporations (MNCs) can potentially play a critical role in creating a sustainable production paradigm. They have mastered the complexity of modern production; they are the repositories of knowledge about the most efficient business practices; and, uniquely, they have the capacity to spread this tacit knowledge to other firms (Kozul-Wright, 1995). Firm-to-firm transfer of leading edge managerial and technological expertise allowed Western European industry to close the productivity gap with the United States after World War II. Whereas portfolio investment had dominated capital flows before 1914, the increase in direct investments by American firms following World War II acted as a carrier of know-how, technology, and advanced capital goods (Abramowitz, 1995).

In addition, many (but by no means all) large Western firms are in the vanguard of developing corporate responses to environmental issues; these firms also dominate the ranks of Western MNCs. Legislative measures in Western countries have exposed firms to environmental pressures of increasing complexity, such as Integrated Pollution Prevention and Control. Environmental taxes and risk and liability arising from environmental impacts enhance the importance of the environment, elevating it to a core management issue for many.

Some firms have adopted responsible, proactive approaches to environmental issues. They are exploring new concepts such as design for the environment, eco-audits, life cycle analysis, cleaner and zero-emission production, industrial metabolism, and industrial ecology. Often it is the larger firms that have the resources and managerial competence to cope with the complexities of these issues.

However, these environmental pressures in Western countries are acting on firms that operate within fully industrialized and unsustainable economies. At best, Western economies face a slow and difficult process of transformation to sustainability. If the same pressures could be brought to bear in a greenfield economy, evolution of the environmentally promising features of lean production into a sustainable production system could happen as a natural part of the process of industrialization.

Catalyzing Sustainable Production

If a Sustainable Industrial Paradigm is to be a significant part of the means of achieving sustainable development in the developing world, how might this best be achieved? There is a need to identify credible policies that can overturn the mind-set that has created false expectations about the West's ability to pay for sustainable development in less developed countries (LDCs), which passively assumes the inevitability of the Western pattern of industrialization and which diminishes and sometimes demonizes the role of foreign direct investment in development. An alternative approach should have the following features:

- Developing country governments should be firmly in control of the policy agenda.

- The policies should operate through private industry, responding to clear commercial prospects.

- Social development associated with the private sector-led industrialization should be coordinated with the help of aid agencies.

The Starting Point—LDC Governments

The first step should be for LDCs to adopt and broadcast to investors a coherent and credible commitment to sustainability. An important element of this could be strict but general sustainability conditions on FDI, requiring potential investors to demonstrate the environmental and social benefits of their proposals.

Wherever possible, competition should be created among rival investors to offer help with capacity building—especially training, education, and assistance for local supplier firms—to work with local authorities to assist with planning, and providing any infrastructure, such as waste handling, connected with the business. This should operate in addition to selection based on the environmental impacts of the activities taking place within the confines of the proposed development.

Authorities should not be required to specify environmental performance in great detail—a problem for many LDCs where such expertise is limited. The purpose is to entice investors to offer their knowledge and expertise. Model tender documents that encourage foreign investors to consider these aspects in detail could be developed, perhaps with the help of aid agencies.

The ideal investor will be sensitive to wider social considerations as a result of working closely with the public and local and national authorities in developed countries. By tapping into this expertise and using it to guide infrastructure decisions—again perhaps supported by aid agencies—the host country might avoid the costly health and environmental pitfalls many Western countries are presently trying to correct at great expense.

Short-Term Advantages for LDCs

There should be immediate benefits of such a policy. It may increase the attractiveness of a country to many foreign investors. For multinational investors, particularly in industries with a long history of environmental constraints, coherent environmental policy is an increasingly important factor in investment decisions (along with political and economic stability, physical infrastructure, and an educated workforce). Firms are anxious to avoid sudden imposition of regulations a few years into an investment. This is driving some firms to apply developed country standards to polluting processes whenever they operate in developing countries. The UNCED process and the prospect of greater international efforts to limit environmental damage increases this concern.

Another benefit is that an investor who responds positively to an invitation to cooperate with the wider society outside the site of the investment is more likely to be a genuine long-term investor. The corporate sense of responsibility that gives an MNC the ability to make credible and detailed proposals to assist with capacity and institution building and infrastructure development implies other benefits. Such a firm can be accorded greater trust to engage in self-appraisal or monitoring of environmental impacts, therefore reducing demands on local bureaucratic institutions.

A general bias toward cleaner activities is also likely to mean a bias toward higher technology activities. There is the possibility that this, allied with corporate commitment to developing local skills and the opportunities of rapidly growing markets, will encourage the migration of the state-of-the-art in certain technologies to these LDCs.

Other significant and immediate advantages beckon. If the major aid agencies can be persuaded to buy into such an approach there is the possibility of attracting an increased proportion of the aid earmarked for environmental and general economic development purposes. In addition, it might become relatively easier for a country to introduce economic instruments, such as resource or pollution taxes. This would translate into a national advantage if, for example, a global regime to control carbon dioxide (CO_2) emissions was agreed. However, this advantage would only be preserved if an LDC was given credit for its efforts. An emission allocation based on the view that current consumption is determined solely by factors that have been beyond the control of policy makers (and the United States, for one, would surely advocate such a view) would deny such credit, and financial advantage, to an LDC that had adopted a more sustainable industrialization trajectory.

Spreading the Green Production Approach

If only one country, or a small set of countries, adopted such an approach it would be equivalent to "cherry-picking" of global FDI and/or aid. This might stimulate other countries to follow suit and compete to offer coherent sustainability strategies; but there are limits to this process if it is sustained only by a fixed pot of money. To significantly reduce the global environmental impact of industrialization in the developing world, the approach must in time spread to the majority of LDCs, as each enters the phase of rapid industrialization.

For this to occur, a sustainable industrialization strategy must give rise to a more efficient, competitive economy than other paths of industrialization. Efficiency might improve in various ways. MNCs and their local partner firms would have low waste and emissions, so waste treatment infrastructure can be avoided, freeing up resources for other investment. Low emissions mean reduced health impacts, higher labor productivity, freeing up of skilled labor for other activities, and reduced healthcare costs.

Expansion of management of human and physical resources beyond the chain of production—for instance, to include infrastructure planning—might be a logical further step, drawing in a wide set of stakeholders. The firm might evolve from being an organization that optimizes internal processes regardless of the externalities it creates toward being an organization that optimizes its output and impacts for a significant segment of society.

Over time it is likely that unforeseen synergies will emerge, and ways to avoid pervasive dead-weight activities and transaction costs that burden today's industrial societies should become apparent.

Policies for LDCs, Firms, and Aid Bodies

Policies for LDCs

A radical break from existing patterns of industrialization will require a high degree of commitment from any LDC government willing to take on this challenge. It will require political vision and leadership.

A key policy objective is to secure cooperation from MNCs. Some firms are socially and environmentally responsible purely out of altruism or because they are run by executives who respect some moral code. They are the exceptions. In general, firms that behave responsibly do so because of regulatory or institutional pressures. Pressure will be required to encourage firms in the right direction, without stifling their freedom to explore and test out new organizational forms and technologies.

For MNCs the main source of pressure could be the sustainability condition acting as an investment hurdle. This will be especially effective in LDCs where competition to invest is intense, such as China or Vietnam. To make this policy more effective, competition should be created between potential investors. Many developing countries already insist on competitive tendering for official projects, such as power generation contracts, and use their power to approve or deny direct investment to secure the best possible deal from a range of suitors in straightforward manufacturing sectors. For example, Volkswagen was "chosen" by the Chinese government to invest in car production primarily for the Chinese market.

This policy presupposes a greater openness to Western investors and abandoning of other policies such as import substitution—trying to develop domestic capacity in isolation from worldwide best practice. Increased openness to FDI is already apparent to a large extent, but in some countries ideological objections to foreign "economic imperialism" remain deeply ingrained.

A sustainability investment hurdle is likely to be most effective as part of a national plan for sustainable development that is based on a broad social consensus about sustainable development and expressed through long-term, comprehensive, and coherent goals. These features help to establish a high degree of political credibility for environmental policy, reducing resistance from firms and increasing their willingness to cooperate with official agencies and one another in finding solutions to environmental challenges. Models for this approach to creating a sustainable economy exist in the West, most notably in The Netherlands (Wallace, 1995).

The Dutch long-term plan uses national targets for pollution reduction as a framework for "voluntary" action by firms who cooperate to meet targets at an industry level. In developing countries, MNCs could play a vital role in coordinating similar industry-wide action and assisting domestic firms to minimize their environmental impacts without jeopardizing their competitiveness. This assumes that the MNC is not competing directly with domestic firms in identical lines of business— but this is unlikely for countries near the beginning of their industrialization and where the arrival of FDI is mediated by governments. Aid bodies could play a useful role in helping LDC governments to ensure that MNCs do not attempt to use such negotiated targets for their own narrow interests.

Strategies for Firms

In some cases there is already a good strategic fit between these conditions and the attitudes of firms to their subsidiaries in developing countries. Ford requires its suppliers in LDCs to improve product quality and processes and assists them in doing so (United Nations Industrial Development Organization, 1991). ABB, the Swiss-Swedish–owned engineering group that describes itself as a "multidomestic" firm, gives the same status to subsidiaries in developing countries as it does to its operations in its home countries and elsewhere in the OECD. In keeping with its sense of commitment to the countries it invests in, ABB has a deliberate policy of upgrading the technological capacity of LDC subsidiaries with the long-term aim of creating leading edge, R&D-based engineering facilities capable of exporting high-technology goods worldwide.

If developing countries do apply conditions, such as those outlined above, to foreign investors, many more MNCs can be expected to adopt similar strategies in developing countries. The far-reaching demands of a sustainability investment hurdle might also encourage firms to develop a consortium-based approach to bids, where several MNCs could collaborate to outline a possible sustainable development plan for an entire economic zone or region. From this process there might emerge firms specializing in associated services—such as assessing social and infrastructure needs, benchmarking the environmental, managerial, and technological status of indigenous firms, and organizing training—to meet their needs.

Aid Policies

For decades an unholy alliance of developing country governments, foreign contractors, and aid bodies have cooked up unnecessary and destructive mega-projects—roads to nowhere, dams in earthquake zones—in centralized drives to industrialize. Politicians gained power and patronage, Western contractors earned quick bucks, and aid agency officials earned brownie points for shoveling X-billion dollars out the door before the end of each financial year. A backlash by environmentalists and increasingly parsimonious lending governments has forced multilateral and even many bilateral aid bodies to reduce their involvement in the industrial sector, switching their attention to poverty alleviation, health, and education, and cutting out central government involvement wherever possible.

Coherent, credible commitments to sustainable development on the part of LDC governments could encourage aid bodies to support industrialization and take their lead from the priorities of the private sector. Aid bodies would need to appraise factors such as the political credibility of a national sustainable development plan and be clear about their own policies on support for projects inspired and perhaps even specified by private FDI-led investment. Industrial investments should be commercially attractive on their own terms. The best way of ensuring this is to have private firms lead such developments. But aid agencies might have political difficulties in supporting investments that would clearly benefit individual firms. Would negotiated, voluntary targets for environmental performance conflict with rigid administrative requirements in aid bodies, such as formulaic environmental impact assessments?

Ideally, the international donor community should somehow recognize or approve national sustainability plans. One key criterion for recognition should be that the plan imposes environmental and social conditions on FDI. Officially recognized LDCs would enjoy favored status for aid for industrialization. In this way aid agencies could play a key role in persuading an initial group of LDCs to make serious commitments to sustainable industrialization.

Epilogue

The 1990s have not been kind to those who expected official aid to play a significant role in establishing patterns of sustainable development in developing countries. Official aid spending has declined drastically as geopolitical spending, to prop up favored political regimes, and tied aid, to assist civil and military contractors in donor countries, has become unnecessary or unjustifiable. There is an increasing awareness that official aid can never again represent a significant proportion of the capital formation in the industrializing countries, and therefore it cannot have a direct impact on the course of industrialization. Foreign direct investment is one of the few potential policy levers available to Western countries. But the failure of imagination that allowed unrealistic expectations of aid mechanisms to dominate Rio lives on. Official statements from "Rio +5" at the United Nations in New York in June 1997 simply noted the scale of FDI, without even a hint of how it might be used to meet Agenda 21 objectives. Policy makers now need to recognize that, while the process of industrialization is the source of the greatest challenges to sustainability, it is also the best hope for a new, sustainable industrial paradigm.

NOTES

1. For example, the preamble states: "Conscious of the crucial role of science and technology in the field of environmental protection and of the need of developing countries, in particular, for favorable access to environmentally sound technologies, processes, equipment, and related research and expertise through international cooperation designed to further global efforts for environmental protection, including the use of innovative and effective means."

2. Some key readings on this theme of "clean" production can be found in Bruce Smart, *Beyond Compliance: A New Industry View of the Environment,* World Resources Institute, Washington, D.C., 1992; Tim Jackson, *Clean Production Strategies: Developing Preventive Environmental Management in the Industrial Economy,* Stockholm Environmental Institute/Lewis, London, 1993; Kurt Fischer and Johan Schot, *Environmental Strategies for Industry: Industrial Perspectives on Research Needs and Policy Implications,* Island Press, Washington, D.C., 1993.

3. Net flows of these types of investment totaled $42.6 billion in 1993 (OECD, 1994)

4. Kuznets looked at the proportions of GDP accounted for by manufacturing and agriculture in countries with different levels of GDP. The proportion of manufacturing in an economy tends to grow then decline slightly while agriculture falls sharply to very low levels and remains low. He used this as a classification system for the degree of industrialization of a country.

5. On Taylor's management-related innovations in the Bethlehem Steel yards in the United States at the turn of the century, see Carlota Perez, "Structural change and assimilation of new technologies in the economic and social system," *FUTURES,* October 1983, 357–75.

6. The classic exposition of the lean production paradigm is Womack et al., 1990. For an interesting critique of lean production see Robert H. Hayes and Gary P. Pisano, "Beyond World-Class: The New Manufacturing Strategy," *Harvard Business Review,* January–February 1994, 77–86. Reading between the lines, this was inspired partly by the failure of many US firms to grasp that lean production is an all-encompassing system as opposed to a menu of techniques such as just-in-time delivery or total-quality management.

Chapter 12

International Cooperation, Technology, and the Sustainability Challenge

David P. Angel

Changes in patterns of the development, transfer, and use of technology are a key part of any transition to sustainability. While changes in lifestyle, consumption patterns, and population growth are also required, a shift to green(er) technology may allow transitions that do not forsake improvements in socioeconomic welfare. Researchers and policy makers have called for the accelerated development and adoption of what have come to be known as green or environmental technologies (Angel and Huber, 1996; Ausubel and Longford, 1997; Heaton, 1992; Heaton et al., 1994)[1] in response to issues such as global warming, as well as to more localized but no less pervasive environmental problems, such as soil and water pollution and waste disposal. The purpose of this chapter is to explore the kinds of international policy interventions required to facilitate the technology transformations so that the forces of technology change are harnessed to the goals of sustainable development.

In practice there are multiple points of entry to this policy question. Much attention has been devoted to the micropractices by which firms, laboratories, and research organizations develop and modify products and production processes. There is a burgeoning literature on such topics as green product design and environmentally conscious manufacturing (Billatis and Basaly, 1997; Florida, 1996; Graedel and Allenby, 1995; US Congress, OTA 1992; and the contribution by Clarke in this book, Chapter 7). Other researchers have focused on national systems of innovation and the myriad ways in which national government policy, directly or indirectly, shapes processes of innovation and technology change (Nelson, 1993). Others have considered what level and type of government intervention is required in the technology development process. Should national governments, for example, change the incentives and risks for investment in green technology by creating guaranteed markets for green products or by changing the regime of appropriation for research and development (Romm and Curtis, 1996)? How can the process of environmental regulation be restructured to secure a more dynamic process of innovation? These and other related themes are critical issues in understanding the potential contribution of technology to sustainable development.[2]

Intergovernmental Response to the Sustainability Challenge

The focus here is on an aspect of the technology process that to date has received less attention—namely, the extent to which the accelerated development and deployment of green technology is best pursued as a collaborative international effort, as opposed to a series of primarily national technology initiatives. During and after the 1992 Earth Summit in Rio de Janeiro, there were repeated calls for increased international cooperation in addressing environment and sustainability concerns. Article 9 of the Climate Convention signed in Rio de Janeiro declares that:

> States should cooperate to strengthen endogenous capacity building for sustainable development by enhancing the development, adaptation, diffusion and transfer of technologies, including new and innovative technologies.

At a succession of international summit meetings, the leaders of Japan, the United States, and other industrial countries have repeatedly called for increased international cooperation in the development of technologies that alleviate and prevent environmental problems.

The motivations for an international, implicitly intergovernmental, response to the sustainability challenge, and more specifically international initiatives that accelerate green technology development, transfer, and use, are reasonably clear. First, the environmental challenges that have triggered much of the recent governmental response, especially depletion of the ozone layer, greenhouse gas emissions, and global warming, are intrinsically global processes. That is to say, actions (or lack thereof) in any one country are capable of impacting global environmental conditions. Moreover, the opportunities for responses, and the costs and benefits of responses, are distributed unevenly around the globe. This suggests that efficiencies may be gained through coordinated responses. This is the premise, for example, behind the Joint Implementation Program of the Climate Change Convention.

Second, science and technology development themselves are now seen as fundamentally international processes (Skolnikoff, 1993). Research outcomes, technology, and information diffuse rapidly around the globe. Informal collaboration among researchers is commonplace, and there are a large number of bilateral and multilateral international initiatives in technology development.[3] With few technical barriers to international cooperation, countries have become increasingly interested in synergies and efficiencies possible from collaboration, especially in areas of technology and science where costs are large and rapidly increasing (US Congress, OTA 1995a). Third, for many countries international cooperation in environment and technology is part of a broader geopolitical strategy. This is the case, for example, in the US–Japan Common Agenda initiative where cooperation in addressing global environmental challenges serves to counterbalance friction in other areas of the relationship, such as trade and investment.

In short, it is generally presumed that increased international cooperation in technology development and technology transfer is a significant part of the new institutional modality through which a sustainability transition will be achieved. But for all the enthusiasm for new and enhanced international collaboration and despite the scale of the challenge, the number and extent of new initiatives have been quite modest.

This chapter explores two key issues about these collaborative initiatives. First, what has been achieved through new international collaborative initiatives in green technology development and technology transfer, and what obstacles to expansion and intensification of these initiatives can be identified? Second, do these initiatives constitute a shift in the existing international regime of technology development, transfer, and use? In particular, most policy makers agree that sustainable development involves more than simply enhanced environmental management or the greening of industry, and this will likely require some transformation in long-standing modalities of North–South technology development, transfer, and use. In the words of one observer (Clarke, 1995), management for sustainability—as opposed to environmental management—requires:

> . . . policies and practices, underpinned by principles of justice, respect, equity, stewardship, precaution, and futurity which fundamentally question and reshape environmental, social, economic and political relationships and which enable the equitable redistribution of wealth and opportunity within and between generations.

This raises questions about whether the scope and consequences of recent international cooperative initiatives to support transformation in global patterns of technology development and use, discussed by David Wallace elsewhere in this book (Chapter 11), are sufficient to meet the challenge of the agenda of sustainable development or whether these initiatives only serve to reproduce existing patterns of international development.

International Cooperation in Green Technology

Over the last decade a wide variety of new and enhanced international and intergovernmental initiatives have been introduced with the goal of accelerated development and transfer of green technologies. Programs have been introduced by one country or another, on a bilateral or multilateral basis, that address all phases of the technology process, from basic research and development to product development, and from technology transfer to accelerated technology adoption and use. While a full review of these initiatives is beyond the scope of the current work, it is useful to outline examples of some of the more prominent programs.

One set of initiatives has the goal of accelerating the transfer of existing green technologies, or alternatively best-available technologies, from one country to another. The presumption here is that some degree of market failure exists in the linking of producers and users of technology. The Organization for Economic Cooperation and Development (OECD) has supported an initiative labeled "GreenTie" (see http://www.greentie.org). This involves a database of companies and products that bring together users and producers of green technology that may help to reduce greenhouse gas emissions. Similarly, the United Nations Development Program (UNDP), in cooperation with the government of Japan, has initiated an international clearing house for environmental technologies (see http://www.unep.or.jp). A similar clearing house is operated by the organization for Asia Pacific Economic Cooperation (see http://www.apec-vc.or.jp). Other groups, such as the US–Asia Environmental Partnership (http://www.usaep.org), have invested resources in the direct brokering of contacts between customers and suppliers of green technology.

A second set of international initiatives involves direct financing of industrial, energy, and infrastructure projects that improve the environmental performance of economies. Many bilateral initiatives involve linkages between industrialized and developing countries. Perhaps the most dramatic example of this is Japan's Green Aid Plan. In 1992—at the time of the Rio Summit—Japan announced that it would substantially increase its development assistance in the environmental sector. It pledged to spend $1 billion yen over the period 1992–97. In the end, Japan exceeded this goal by 40 percent. Among the many projects supported through this commitment are a variety of energy efficiency, clean coal, and thermal energy initiatives in China and Indonesia. A similar pattern of enhanced loans and investments is underway among other OECD economies, as well as multilateral lending agencies such as the World Bank and the Asian Development Bank.

Third, there are significant new cooperative initiatives in the development of green technologies. Japan and the United States have signed a series of agreements to cooperate in green technology research and development, including bilateral cooperation between Japan's Ministry for Trade and Industry (MITI) and the US Environmental Protection Agency. Finally, there are international cooperative initiatives deriving from specific treaties and agreements. The most prominent of these are the Global Environmental Facility (GEF) and the Joint Implementation (JI) program initiated under the Framework Convention on Climate Change. Joint Implementation creates a legal basis for one country to gain credit for reductions in greenhouse gas emissions achieved by another. Under the pilot program, for example, various electric power companies in Japan, Europe, and North America have cooperated to pay for and install home solar systems and energy efficient power generation equipment in Indonesia. In return for the investments made in these green technologies, the donor countries gain credit for greenhouse gas emissions saved through the projects against their own emissions targets.

Overall, a considerable degree of international cooperative activity is underway. At the same time, most observers agree that the level of international activity falls far short of what will likely be required to address global warming and other environmental concerns, and more generally, to build a new technological foundation for sustainable development. Where new agreements have been initiated, the scale of activity is often very modest and well below that initially proposed. Too often cooperation is limited to "information exchange" and does not carry through into project implementation. The disjuncture between expressed intent and action is partly a reflection of external constraints, such as economic recession or competing domestic and international demands for scarce governmental resources. But it also derives from perceived and real obstacles to international cooperation.

The two illustrative cases set out below enable identification of many of the obstacles and challenges that arise from these initiatives. These case studies draw on lengthy interviews with program officers and participating scientists and engineers in the United States and Japan.

Case 1: US–Japan Bilateral Cooperation in Technology Development

The urgent need to accelerate the pace of development of green technology, whether it be the incremental improvement of existing technologies (such as catalytic converters or solar cells) or the development of new breakthrough technologies (such as large-scale hydrogen energy carriers, or carbon dioxide fixation technologies), spurred this initiative. Much of the necessary research and development is likely to take place within the United States and other OECD economies. International cooperation provides an opportunity to share the costs of new technology development and foster synergy among different scientific communities. In this vein, the United States and Japan in February 1994 signed an implementing agreement for R&D cooperation in environmental and energy-efficient technologies, and later that year signed a second agreement for cooperation in Civil Industrial Technologies (many of which address environmental concerns). Both Japan and the United States have major government R&D programs in environmental and energy technology and significant opportunity for cooperation and synergy exists through these agreements.[4]

The technology cooperation agreements were signed under the auspices of the US–Japan Common Agenda. The Common Agenda for Cooperation in Global Perspective was launched in July 1993, as part of US–Japan Framework talks between President Clinton and Prime Minister Miyazawa. It is a geopolitical initiative that seeks to strengthen the alliance between the United States and Japan. While a significant motivation for the technology agreements was the desire to cooperate in addressing global issues and the interest in resource efficiency in research and development, the primary driver was a need to highlight aspects of strength in the US–Japan relation at a time of tension over trade deficits, investment, market access, and associated issues. The presence of this geopolitical concern was critical to the initiative, with environment and technology issues increasingly being addressed by both the United States and Japan in techno-nationalist terms. Indeed, the desire to promote the interests of US firms is clearly evident, for example, in President Clinton's Environmental Technology Strategy:

> America's principal trade competitors, Germany and Japan, have already positioned themselves to support environmental technology innovation and capture a leading share of the global market. The United States now has a limited window of opportunity either to strengthen its own presence in this market, or be left behind.
>
> (US EPA, 1994a:5)

The geopolitical commitment to a strong alliance between Japan and the United States serves here as a counterbalance to these technonationalist interests and allows R&D cooperation to develop.

What has been achieved to date through these cooperative agreements? In both the Civil Industrial Technologies agreement and the agreement in Environmental and Energy-Efficient Technologies, numerous structural and practical obstacles needed to be overcome as a precursor to actual research cooperation. Establishing ground rules for cooperation (addressing issues such as intellectual property rights, procedures for selecting projects, commercial applications of technology, and so forth) is one of the major accomplishments of these initiatives. These achievements provide a strong foundation for future cooperation. In the case of Civil Industrial Technologies, cooperation is limited to precompetitive research and development in areas of mutual benefit to the United States and Japan. In practical terms, the last condition meant the selection of a balanced portfolio of projects. In half of the projects the United States was perceived as the technology leader, and in the other half Japan was regarded as the more advanced. Among the projects currently underway are studies of environmental technology, synthetic membranes, and biomaterials, linking Japan's NEDO to the CST laboratory in the United States. Projects pursued under the environmental and energy-efficient technology agreement include studies of CFC incineration, biomass energy studies, methane conversion into hydrogen gas, and catalysis of chlorinated hydrocarbons. In general, these projects involve cooperation between government laboratories in the two countries, with twice yearly high-level group meetings.

The assessment of these agreements is mixed. On the one hand, they have met the geopolitical objective by strengthening operational ties between Japan and the United States. Indeed, the Common Agenda is widely regarded as a success by policy makers in both countries. In addition, the agreements have created a strong framework for international cooperation in research and development that addresses both structural obstacles, such as intellectual property rights, and some of the difficult practicalities of cooperation, such as language, housing, and so forth. On the other hand, the scale of the projects is quite modest. Indeed, in most cases the research agreements have fostered cooperation among existing projects, rather than initiating new research activities under the auspices of the agreements.

The lack of new resource commitments for research and development under the agreements has been a particular problem in the United States, especially as the agreements were launched at a time of funding cutbacks in many areas, such as renewable energy and environmental technologies. In Japan, by contrast, the international initiative coincides with a commitment to a major increase in government-funded research and development. Furthermore, these R&D agreements have not yet stimulated the level of industry participation that was anticipated.

These US–Japan international agreements have not, in sum, triggered the increase in green technology research and development that was hoped. Note that the argument here is not that international cooperation is necessarily the most efficient and effective approach toward developing green technology. Rather, it was hoped that broader geopolitical interests—in this case a strong US–Japan relation—could be leveraged to bring resources to bear that would not otherwise be available.

Case 2: International Environmental Technology Center

The second case study examines the other end of the technology process, namely, the accelerated transfer of existing green technologies to potential users. Over the past 10 years a significant number of international initiatives were launched with the goal of more effectively matching producers and users of green technologies, and enhancing the capacity of countries to assess needs and opportunities with respect to green technologies. One such initiative is UNEP's International Environmental Technology Center (IETC).

In the buildup to the Rio climate change conference, IETC emerged. As with Case 1, broader geopolitical interests were at work. In this instance, the establishment of IETC drew on Japan's interests in maintaining a higher profile in international environmental affairs. In an era of complicated post-Cold War politics, the Japanese government had clearly identified the global environment as a domain in which the country could establish itself as a "global leader." Two IETC offices were opened in Japan in early 1994, one located in Osaka and the other in Shiga prefecture. Under the agreement that established these centers, the government of Japan provides two-thirds of the operating budget, UNEP one-third. In addition, the host cities provide facilities, staff, and logistical support.

Both IETC facilities have the mission of promoting the transfer of environmental (green) technologies. The Osaka facility focuses on urban issues (such as energy use, drinking water, and waste disposal), and the facility in Shiga prefecture on protection of lake basins. In both cases green technology is defined broadly to include not just the technology as artifacts, but the know-how and management procedures necessary to make good use of that technology. Thus IETC is involved in both technology transfer and capacity building.

The principal tool used in technology transfer is the development of a searchable database (infoterra) of environmental technologies, as well as decision tools for the assessment of the applicability of technologies to local conditions. There are now in excess of 100 Internet-accessible databases of this kind providing countries with information on environmental technologies. In addition to governmental and international organizations, numerous databases are maintained by private business and NGOs. The UNEP IETC database is among the more innovative in that there is a strong commitment to the provision of technology assessment and decision tools, alongside the product/process database. In addition to the database activity, IETC engages in capacity building and institutional cooperation. Much of this activity is linked to urban Agenda 21 projects, involving regional and local workshops to enhance the capacity of countries to assess environmental technologies.

Within its stated terms of reference, the IETC has been reasonably successful. By stressing capacity building in developing countries over simple transactional brokering, IETC is focused on a longer term goal and distinguishes itself from commercial trade promotion programs (see Townsend, 1993). The center has gained legitimacy as a nonpartisan provider of technology information. At its founding, the United States and other countries feared that the center would favor Japanese manufacturers and Japanese technology, due to its location in Japan and the funding from the Japanese government. These fears have subsided as firms from the United States and other OECD countries have participated in various workshops sponsored by IETC. Private companies from the United States and elsewhere have benefited from the assistance provided by IETC. Indeed the weakness of the project has been the relationship to UNDP, rather than to Japan or other OECD countries. UNDP has persistently failed to generate its one-third share of the operating budget of the center. More generally, IETC has been marginalized relative to the overall program development activities of UNDP in the Nairobi headquarters and elsewhere.

Information exchange on existing technology is an important part of the overall matrix of international activities related to technology and sustainability. It is an activity, however, that is firmly rooted in the existing North–South political economy, facilitating the adoption of technologies developed in OECD countries by users in the developing world. It is also an activity that is dependent on patterns of funding and investment, and on development strategies in different countries.

Patterns of Technology Development, Transfer, and Use

The two case studies, one on cooperative research and development and the other on technology transfer, are illustrative of a multitude of international initiatives directed toward the accelerated development, deployment, and use of green technologies. Among the striking features of these two international initiatives is the degree to which they both remain deeply embedded in national political-economic concerns. Despite the high-minded vocabulary of international and global action, the modest scale and modality of activity is shaped very much by preexisting national geopolitical concerns. In the one case, the driving force for international initiative lay in a desire to strengthen a key bilateral alliance. In the other case, motivation arose from a desire to be seen as providing a leadership role in international affairs. The context within which international initiative of this kind take place is seen to shape both the micro impacts of individual projects and the overall modality of technology change and sustainability.

Micro Effects

The case of US–Japan cooperation provides a good example of the micro effects of geopolitical context. Recall that in the launching of this new cooperative R&D project the two countries sought to balance techno-nationalist concerns against a desire to strengthen the US–Japan alliance. Cooperation in green technology was seen by many policy makers in the United States as a dangerous pursuit that would only serve to facilitate the transfer of US technology to Japan, further undermining the competitive position of US firms in global markets. The resolution to this concern involved limiting US–Japanese cooperation to so-called precompetitive research and development—with no current or direct commercial application. In principle, this would seem to be a positive resolution to the problem of techno-nationalist concerns. The current tendency in much green technology research and development is toward near-term, incremental technology improvement (OECD, 1994). Working on precompetitive research and development, involving technologies that can be as much as 20 to 30 years from commercialization, provided an opportunity to support longer term technology projects in areas such as hydrogen fuels or large-scale renewable energy systems.

In practice, the competitive/precompetitive dualism is more problematic in that it is an economic concept that does not map simply and easily onto the real landscape of technology development. Engineers have no difficulty identifying examples of technology projects that are unambiguously competitive (such as improving the efficiency of a turbine blade) or precompetitive (such as power generation in space, or the use of hydrogen as a large-scale energy carrier). There are other technology projects, however, where classification within this duality is more complex.

Consider the case of renewable energy. Fuel cells and photovoltaics are already in limited commercial use within niche markets that are able to carry a higher cost of energy generation. These projects would consequently fail to meet the "precompetitive" criteria and, instead, would be classified as competitive technologies. Renewable energy R&D projects place a high priority on developments in energy efficiencies, storage and transmission capabilities, and other research that would allow fuel cells, photovoltaics, and other technologies to move from niche markets to widespread commercial use. This research and development is unlikely to impact directly the competitiveness of US firms, yet it is difficult to fund under current definitions of precompetitive technology. The adoption of a conservative definition of precompetitive research and development means that policy makers unnecessarily preclude a full and effective evaluation of priorities for green technology research and development.

Macro Effects:

It is also possible to identify a series of more general macro characteristics of international initiatives in green technology development, transfer, and use. Perhaps the most striking feature is the atomistic character of recent initiatives that tend to reinforce rather than transform the existing landscape of technology development and use. The concepts of sustainability that emerged from the Earth Summit in Rio de Janeiro clearly anticipated a change in North–South patterns of technology development and use. For example, at the Rio Conference it was widely suggested that much closer ties had to be forged between users and producers of technology, and that the technology needs of rapidly industrializing economies, such as China and India, had to play a greater role in shaping the technology development efforts of OECD economies. A sustainability transition required that the developing economies did not simply "catch up" to the techno-industrial foundation of the OECD economies, but used the opportunity created by new investment to forge a new, more environmentally benign, trajectory of industrialization. These concepts of sustainability are not addressed in any substantial way in the majority of international initiatives in green technology development, transfer, and use. Instead, "greening" of technology is wedded to the traditional geopolitics of national interest.

A second broad characteristic is the partial, rather than full, engagement in a new modality of public-private partnership. On this point David Wallace's contribution to the book (Chapter 11) discusses the potential for foreign direct investment by multinational corporations as a source of improved environmental practice in developing countries. To their credit, in both cases discussed above there is a specific commitment to engaging private business, NGOs, and other institutions in processes of technology development, transfer, and use. The ability to engage private business is one of the criteria cited for project selection in the Common Agenda, and a Common Agenda Business Council has been established in Japan. To date, however, success in leveraging international public policy into private initiative in green technology has been modest. Consequently, many of the emerging initiatives are vulnerable to the vagaries of government budgets. In fact for both the cases, government funding fell short of what was needed to fully implement the initiative.

Faced with limited budgets, international initiatives are liable to become part of a grand shell game in which commitments are fulfilled simply by moving existing projects from a "domestic" to an "international" umbrella. Perhaps the most critical arena within which the public-private modality needs strengthening is in the financing of green technology development, transfer, and use. As many researchers have noted, the scale of private investment in developing economies is far larger than that provided through development aid. Thus the critical policy question is how best to influence these private investment flows in ways that support a transition to greener production and sustainability. The principal policy instrument deriving from the Earth Summit that addresses this concern is the Global Environmental Facility (GEF). In 1990 the GEF was selected as the interim financing mechanism for the Climate Change Convention. The GEF operates by providing funding to cover gaps in cost between traditional and green technology projects. The institution remains mired in controversy over the types of projects funded and the closed-door process by which projects are selected through the main implementing agent, the World Bank.

The last broad area of concern is the technology itself. The contribution of technology to a sustainability transition will no doubt take a variety of forms, including incremental improvements in existing technology, more widespread adoption and use of best available technologies, development of "breakthrough" technologies that change the very foundation of economies, and shifts in the sectoral composition of economies. Any notion of a coordinated international initiative to shape the overall pattern of technology development activities is neither desirable nor feasible. And yet the lack of engagement with policy tools that might help to assess the contribution that technology initiatives are making to the sustainability transition is striking. The accelerated North–South transfer of existing green technology, for example, is accepted as a worthy goal in itself without much consideration of such issues as path dependency, system transformation, or life cycle assessment (see, for example, Chapter 8 by Vergragt and van der Wel in this book). Is a transition to sustainability supported by incremental improvements in existing technologies, or should the balance of research and development shift more toward emerging breakthrough technologies?

The significance of such questions is clearly evident in the anticipated large increase in the use of coal as a source of energy in China and other rapidly industrializing countries. To their credit, organizations like IETC have made a significant commitment to building local capacity for technology assessment based on the suitability of different green technologies to local economic and environmental conditions. There is a parallel need for meso-level and macro-level assessment of the impacts of international policy initiatives on trajectories of industrialization and development.

Conclusion

> International cooperation is frequently seen as being obviously good, and then frequently ignored.
>
> (International Energy Agency, 1994a)

Calls for increased cooperation among national governments are now a ubiquitous part of the policy dialogue surrounding global warming, the depletion of the ozone layer, deforestation, and other environmental concerns. Much has been achieved in this regard in the five years since the Earth Summit. There has been a modest increase in funding for green technology research and development, most especially in Japan but also in other OECD economies; international financing for green industry and infrastructure projects has increased substantially; and, perhaps most visibly, there has been a significant international initiative to accelerate transfer of green technologies to developing economies.

And yet at the 1997 Rio+5 meetings in New York, widespread disappointment was evident concerning what had been achieved to that date through international cooperative initiatives. Part of this disappointment derived from the modest scale and scope of multilateral and bilateral activity relative to the size of the sustainability challenge. More fundamentally, many delegates to the conference sensed that international efforts to accelerate the development and deployment of green technology served to reproduce rather than transform the existing North–South modality of technology development, transfer, and use. Rather than engaging fully with the challenge of a sustainability transition, most international policy initiatives implicitly grafted the greening of technology onto traditional national geopolitical agendas.

As the two case studies presented in this chapter demonstrate, on both a micro and a macro basis, international initiative remains tightly constrained by national geopolitical and economic concerns. The willingness of countries to participate in, and contribute resources to, international initiatives is circumscribed by domestic policy priorities. In many cases, of course, technology development is appropriately and most efficiently pursued as a national, regional, or local activity. But the very nature of the sustainability challenge requires a substantial transformation in existing patterns of technology development, transfer, and use. Perhaps the greatest challenge, and the greatest opportunity, lies in the rapidly industrializing economies of Asia and Latin America. If current growth rates of 8 to 10 percent annual increases in GDP continue in such countries as China and Indonesia, the vast majority of industrial stock in place 20 years from now will be new investment. The development of policy instruments that can shape this trajectory of investment and industrialization must be a key focus of future international initiatives in technology and sustainability.

NOTES

1. I use the term green technology broadly to refer to both "dark green" technologies that have been developed specifically to reduce environmental impacts (such as pollution prevention technology or renewable sources of energy) and "light green" technologies whose use does in fact reduce environmental impacts, even if this effect was not the primary goal of the technology (for example, sensors that allow more efficient heating and cooling of buildings).

2. The US strategy on these issues is described in US EPA 1994a, 1994b.

3. A good example of existing international initiatives regarding environmental technology are the various OECD implementing agreements in renewable energy (IEA 1996).

4. Total US federal government expenditures in green technology research and development and precommercial demonstration projects in 1994 were estimated to be between $2.5 billion and $3.5 billion (US Congress, Office of Technology Assessment, 1995b). Japan has launched an ambitious green technology R&D program under the auspices of the New Earth 21 initiative.

Conclusion: Implications for Management Practice, Education, and Research

Nigel J. Roome

This book began with a stark choice: Either we can accept the traditional principles of the market and the direction of economic and social change, or we can conceive the environmental and social consequences of industrial activity as a major challenge for the modernization of industrial organizations and their management over the next 20 years. The transition to sustainable development does not require business to forgo its motivation to seek profit and add to shareholder value. However, sustainable development, as envisioned in this book, obliges industry to adopt a much more flexible, socially and environmentally responsive mode of operation. Indeed, sustainable development ultimately defines a new position for industry in society, a new industrial structure, and new understandings of the responsibilities and skills of managers.

Some might believe that these changes can be brought about through strategic formulations and plans that are given direction by senior managers in industry and decision-makers in society. But progress toward sustainable industry, as part of a sustainable society, is characterized here as a significantly more complex social and industrial project, involving continuous and unpredictable patterns of learning and change. Many actors will be involved in this process. And, it requires leadership at many levels so that the vision, values, and activities of industrial organizations are developed, articulated, and harmonized with the actions of other actors in society.

The book also began with some specific questions about the future of industrial organizations and their contribution to the attainment of a more sustainable world. These questions invited the reader to identify the differences between environmental management and sustainable development; to assess the progress of companies toward those concepts; to consider changing social expectations and environmental limits and how companies might fashion their response(s) to them. The questions asked what these changes mean for the governance and management of industrial organizations: How should industry manage technology and its relationships with others in society over the next 10 to 20 years? What skills and understanding will we need to manage the process of change that is anticipated? And finally, how will these changes impact the identity of organizations?

In addressing these questions the book leads to a critical conclusion— managers of industrial organizations are constrained in their move toward sustainable development by the conceptual frame that shapes their thinking and the contextual frame that determines the overall setting within which they act. Unless we can break free from the prison of these frames and develop new frames that relate business more closely to sustainable development, a sustainable industrial society will remain a chimera.

Conceptual Frames

It is the contention of this book that environmental management, involving adherence to standards such as ISO 14 001 or concepts like ecoefficiency, does not provide a secure basis for the transformation of industrial activity and society toward sustainable development. Many contributions to the book point out that sustainable development is different from the ideas that have informed industry and business since the beginning of the industrial revolution. And that it is different from the ideas that have shaped industry's recent response to environmental management. The connection here is that during the last 10 years the so-called proactive companies have learned how to accommodate environmental concerns within their dominant framework. In contrast, the challenge of sustainable development is precisely that; it is a new paradigm within which business thinking and practice must fit if it is to become a guide for the future. Some of the distinctions between the characteristics of the paradigm for business environmental management and for sustainable development that help to differentiate the two concepts are summarized in the accompanying table.

This table identifies the substantive differences between environmental management in business and sustainable development. Six frames are set out that differentiate the way environmental management is currently

FRAMING ENVIRONMENTAL MANAGEMENT AND SUSTAINABLE DEVELOPMENT

Environmental Management	Framing	Sustainable Development
Business and economics as dominant systems with environmental impacts	Mental frame	Business and economics embedded in and dependent on social and environmental systems
Accommodating environmental values in business	Decision frame	Evaluating and integrating economic, environmental, and social outcomes of business choices
Company and its supply chain	Organizational frame	Economic, institutional, social, and environmental systems and networks that shape production and consumption
Determined by the life of products/services, processes, and technologies	Time frame	Intergenerational
Utilitarian with attention to product stewardship	Values frame	Utilitarian + stewardship limited by principles of respect, justice, equity, inclusiveness, and precaution
The company and its supply chain, technology, processes, products, and services	Change frame	Limitless—up to reinventing organizations, institutions, and society

conceived in business and how sustainable development is constructed in this book. These frames impact the nature and scope of managerial choice and industrial practice. The first of the frames centers on the mental model used by managers as their reference for "sense making" when interpreting change in the world.

Current conceptions of environmental management view environmental concerns within a box determined by business and economic systems. Environmental concerns are included in this frame when they align with the purposes and trajectories of these systems—for example, when environmental improvements bring about efficiencies in resource use or provide market opportunities. In contrast, sustainable development sees those same business and economic systems as embedded in broader social and environmental systems. In this conception business operates within the "bounded freedom" provided to organizations by legal codes as well as the social mores and limits imposed directly or indirectly by the resource endowments and environmental processes of the planet. Sustainable development identifies a responsibility of all actors in society, including industry, to respect these social and environmental limits.

The second frame—the decision frame—follows exactly from these two alternate conceptions of the position of business and economic systems in relation to social and environmental systems. The decision frame determines the scope of the information required for industrial decisions and management choices. In the case of environmental management, choice is informed by a concern to accommodate environmental issues within the dominant framework of current business thinking. As a result, the environmental impacts of products, processes, and activities are assessed by industry managers using an array of environmental management techniques. The decision whether to act on these impacts is evaluated and then justified against conventional business drivers—such as, efficiencies in resource use, cost savings, new market opportunities, or corporate positions around industrial leadership or company and brand identity. Environmental actions are legitimized in terms of conventional business rationality.

Sustainable development takes a different position. It assumes that businesses committed to sustainable practices are concerned with evaluating and integrating the economic, social, and environmental consequences of managerial choices. Sustainable development emphasizes evaluation above valuation. Valuation implies that the social and environmental dimensions of choice, if measured at all, are reduced to economic terms. They are subordinated to economic metrics, whereas evaluation recognizes that social and environmental consequences are not reducible to economic metrics. Evaluation places the real complexity of choice before decision-makers. It establishes that they are responsible for the integration of the economic, social, and environmental consequences that follow from the choices they make. Choice framed in this way demands much more sophisticated and broad-based decision support systems that cover measures of economic, social, and environmental change. It also calls for clear guidelines on the principles and values that define the criteria used to guide choice.

The emphasis attached by sustainable development to the satisfaction of needs, within environmental limits and social expectations, implies that industry should consider the relevance and overall need for products and services as well as the efficiency with which those products and services are made. As a result, the decision frame for sustainable development goes well beyond the issue of whether products and services are more or less environmentally friendly, functional, and cost-effective. It requires complex economic, social, and environmental data and a more integrated and transparent decision system.

The third frame relates to the limits of the organizational field within which the industrial firm operates. This determines the depth and breadth of the organizational interactions that are ordinarily incorporated within managerial choice. Current conceptions of environmental management have begun to deal with issues of integrated supply chains, where a number of organizations are involved in concerted responses to environmental concerns. Integrated supply chain management involves the coordination of different industrial organizations that are linked through the supply of a product or service. Sustainable development pushes this organizational frame to its limit. It recognizes that the technologies that define products and services are themselves embedded in social and institutional systems. Sustainable development is therefore concerned with the economic, social, and environmental issues that arise from the relationships between technology, products and services, and the social system. It is concerned with more than the organizational issues that arise from a supply chain. Instead, sustainable development is concerned with value chains and the overall pattern of production and consumption to which they contribute.

The distinction between supply and value chains can be illustrated through the example of automobile and transport services. Integration of the activities of different industries to improve the environmental performance of the automobile supply chain involves vehicle designers and manufacturers working together with component suppliers, from paint to windshield manufacturers, as well as oil and gasoline companies. Coordinated activity in this supply chain is difficult but not as demanding as the integration needed to improve the environmental performance of the overall value chain of the automobile. This value chain includes automobile and automobile parts manufacturers, sales outlets and service centers, oil and gasoline companies, road construction companies, automobile users, and planners—both city planners, who design urban systems, and transport planners, who determine highway infrastructure from road surfaces to street lighting. The sustainable development issues—economic, social, and environmental—of the automobile value chain include not only a wider set of concerns than those required to improve the environmental performance; there is also a larger constituency of interests involved. The sustainable development issues of the transport service value chain are more demanding still because it is concerned with the economic, social, and environmental performance of transport services, in which automobiles and their core technologies are only one product. In addition, there are manufacturers of bicycles, trains, buses, trucks, and airplanes, together with the suppliers of the components and technologies for these products, as well as those who provide transport infrastructure, transport users, and those subject to the economic, social, and environmental consequences of transport.

Ultimately, sustainable development is concerned with ways to improve the contribution of, say, transport services to sustainable lifestyles and sustainable patterns of production and consumption. In doing this it must overcome significant information problems and the problems of social and institutional inertia. From this vantage point, sustainable development is concerned with whole systems and the networks of organizations and social actors who shape those systems. This can not be brought about by industry alone. It requires complex multiparty learning and action.

The time frame within which these issues are set and managed expands as we move from environmental management to sustainable development. Environmental management normally operates around time frames that are determined by the character of the environmental impacts of products/services, technologies, and processes. These can be extremely long, as is the case with the half-life of many irradiated by-products of the nuclear power industry. However, sustainable development is framed in terms of intergenerational time lines, even though there is no firm agreement on the number of generations that should be considered. The principles discussed in the values frame nevertheless imply that no reduction in opportunities should be imposed on future generations as a result of actions in the present.

This brings us to the critical question of the values that guide managerial choice. Here environmental management is seen to proceed by reference to a utilitarian values system, where the value of resources, products, and services is uniquely defined by those who use them and those who produce them. More recently, some companies have adjusted these dominant values to accommodate the notion of "product stewardship."

This means that it is not always possible for them to exploit the full range of economic opportunities because of the self-imposed responsibility of stewardship.

Sustainable development broadens the values that are routinely used in managerial choice. And, when sustainable development is viewed as a socially negotiated and constructed pathway for development, it implies that managers also need to take into account the values of other actors in the choices they make. The industrial and social process of choice are therefore governed by principles such as inclusiveness and respect for different perspectives and values, while the subjects of choice need to be judged against values that include utility, justice, equity, and the need to act with precaution.

The last of the six frames concerns the process of change itself. The scope of change for environmental management is set in terms of the company, the supply chains it contributes to, and its processes, products, and services. We are beginning to see some industries considering the impacts of their technologies in terms of the environment. In contrast, nothing is beyond the scope of critical reexamination, revision, and reinvention for sustainable development. No artifact, activity, organizational system or entity, social or institutional structure can be assumed to be permanently sustainable. An example discussed in the book is the position the forest products industry faces over the sustainable yield of forest material. It would be wrong to think that there is a fixed sustainable volume of lumber and fiber that can be taken from a forest. Sustainable yield is determined in part by ecological limits, which are subject to the possibility of change as a consequence of events—such as forest fires, climate change, pests, and disease. In part, it is determined by reference to the overall set of human interests in the forest, which include use and nonuse values as well as cultural, religious, and intrinsic values. None of these values can be regarded as fixed or permanent. They are subject to change as new and emerging interests impact the overall value of the forest, the nature of forest management, and the yield that might be taken.

Taking these six frames together characterizes sustainable development as a more fundamental, organizationally complex, and open process than present-day approaches by business to environmental management. Moreover, the transition from environmental management to sustainable development suggested in the preceding table will itself need to involve processes that incorporate more views and values than has been customary in traditional environmental management. It suggests that you can not move toward a new paradigm without adopting something of the character of that new paradigm. It will only come about by circumscribing managerial choice with principles that reflect this broader range of values and social interests and respecting environmental limits as well as the efficiencies in the resources used for products and services.

A number of authors in this book suggest that engagement and dialogue between industry and a wide range of stakeholders provide important opportunities for learning, innovation, and change beyond the limits of current technologies and social structures. New approaches to governance are required to reinforce the principles or values that guide industrial decisions toward sustainable development; to ensure that industrial organizations act in ways that are consistent with these principles and ever changing limits and expectations; and to provide opportunities for stakeholders to engage in those governance structures. Indeed, engagement between industrial interests and stakeholders should inform change in corporate governance as well as bring about the social and institutional changes that allow new technology and organizational innovation to take root.

Sustainable development emphasizes organizational learning from the future. Scenarios and backcasting techniques are regarded by many of the contributors to this book as a way to develop visions of the future that enable industry and other actors to identify the steps needed to realize sustainable development. Scenarios can be used to address technological needs and opportunities and to specify the new relationships between industrial organizations and other social institutions and actors. Involving managers in this type of learning requires a substantial commitment to engage in more open-ended, creative, and inclusive forums for change.

The book also emphasizes that sustainable organizations of the future will commit to the continued dematerialization of products. One consequence of dematerialization is a move from a focus on products and services to a focus on human processes. The shift from "management of throughput" to "management of process" brings with it a loosening of managerial control over resources, the shape of products, and the level of output of those products. It becomes more and more difficult to specify the material requirements of production with precision. Instead the resources available for production, the various value chains that meet human needs, and the products and services that make up those value chains are determined through socially negotiated future search processes in which industry is just one partner. Sustainable development is consistent with a less technologically deterministic and rigid industrial system emphasizing instead shared governance to shape the emerging social, organizational, and technological systems that determine the pattern of production and consumer choice.

These points suggest that the transition from present-day environmental management practice to more sustainable forms of development requires a complete reorientation of thinking about the role and operation of industrial organizations in society. This reorientation will not be easy. It will take place through a series of complex social and industrial experiments. As with all well-fashioned human experiments, it will be guided by principles that limit risk and maximize learning.

Contextual Frame

The move toward sustainable development is also constrained by the contextual frame within which managers operate. This contextual frame is defined by the overall system within which industrial decisions and managerial choices are made. This system is shaped through the dynamic interplay of natural systems, with their endowments of natural resources and processes, and human systems. Human systems—economic, political, cultural, and institutional—are seen as a tyranny of the many small decisions we all make as consumers, as producers, and as citizens. Although there are powerful individual forces in these human systems, the overall direction is determined through the cumulative effects of choice and the overall trends in human history. These trends have the potential to yield both good and bad. Viewed in this way the agenda of sustainable development is a "global institutional response" to the outcomes of recent human development. The success of that agenda in reshaping industry and society will be determined more by the direction of economic, social, and political trends than it will by the demands for a more sustainable society. Let us explore these ideas further.

This book argues that the move toward sustainable development must play out against the historical trends of global change. The transition to a sustainable industrial and social system consequently must overcome the concepts of human systems and natural systems planted in our minds through our experience of industrial development. This transition is made more difficult because not everyone sees sound justification to change the course of development away from the present unsustainable modes of production and consumption—especially when the consequences of our behavior are remote or vaguely seen, or where the advantages that are seen to arise from the present system are risked by change. Yet managers can only begin to reshape their context after they redefine the concepts used to understand industry, society, technology, and the relation between economic, social, and environmental change. Leadership and vision to communicate these concepts, a commitment to values and self-reflection, and a recognition of the need to alter the direction of change are preconditions without which the prognosis for the long-term survival of humankind is bleak.

Sustainable development will not come about if it runs counter to the trends in context and widely held conceptualizations of context. The emergence of the preconditions for sustainable development therefore rest on the extent to which social, cultural, political, and economic trends support thinking and practice that is consistent with sustainable development. A clear tension is perceived between two possible trends: (1) A global political economy, based around present-day concepts—more products and more consumption, unfettered wants, global markets, and open trade; or (2) the emergence of more localized markets, in which producers and manufacturers are expected to meet diverse needs, expressed at the local level. If the emerging global marketplace fragments into myriad locally distinct markets, then industrial managers will be propelled to act as facilitators of local actors and stakeholders and to meet their needs through the development of services within the context of their local conditions. In this way, the sustainable industrial enterprise would resemble a continuously entrepreneurial firm—forever changing to develop new products and services and building the relationships needed to make those products or services work for consumers and society. This move toward more localized global markets would promote economic, cultural, and social diversity that mirrors and reinforces environmental diversity.

Within this second scenario, the successful industrial enterprise will be the one that is most in demand as a social partner and most able to respond rapidly to social and community-based needs. In order to be a partner of choice, enterprises will strive for trust and credibility through adherence to a strong and transparent set of values. They will be keenly aware of and responsive to a plurality of needs and perspectives whether within the organization or its extended stakeholder set. The organization itself will become more ephemeral as stakeholders are linked into coproduction as well as consumption. This will involve moving from formal, hierarchically patterned interactions to networked relationships with governance responsibilities spread throughout the organization and its many partnerships.

The managers of the future will correspondingly need to draw on a multiplicity of experiences to enable them to work with diverse local partners. They will need to be skilled in project facilitation and able to act as project analysts who can identify expert knowledge and relate technology development to local needs. They will have the capacity to relate to many types of social partner, their organizational settings, knowledge, and capabilities, and to act as communicators and interpreters between groups. Where managers work for large corporations, they will be organizationally "branded entrepreneurs" who use their own discretion within the values and intent of the organization they represent.

Implications for Management Education

The preceding discussion pinpoints the changes in industrial structure and management practice anticipated by the move toward a more sustainable industrial and social system. But what does this mean for those preparing future managers for their role in a sustainable society?

Management education provides a basis for the (professional) development of managers and for their capacity to support organizational change. It provides managers with the skills demanded by the industrial organization of today as well as the sustainable enterprise of tomorrow. In terms of today's agenda, environmental concerns and environmental management practices have become sufficiently important to industrial thinking and practice that they will continue to gain ground in management education programs. These programs will develop environmental literacy and expose management learners to the skills, tools, and techniques that will help organizations to incorporate environmental considerations into their decision systems and structures. This will improve the environmental profile of companies, their products, services, and industrial processes. But this alone will not equip future managers for the transition toward sustainable industry.

Management for sustainable industry is fundamentally about strategic organizational development and change. Its strategic orientation stems from the system-spanning character of sustainable development with its implications for the way that members of the organization envision their role and responsibilities, manage technology, and shape the relationships between the organization and other industries in its institutional field and society at large.

The emphasis on change and process management implies competence in the "soft skills" of group leadership, network support, communication, integrative skills, and visioning. Those with narrowly functional or uncritical perspectives of the industrial firm and its role in society will find it difficult to contribute to the transformation required for sustainable development. In contrast, those with broad experiences of different groups and sectors of society, who are able to synthesize alternate perspectives and communicate with professional cadres, experts and nonexperts alike, will be leaders in this transformation. They will recognize the need to continuously revise their assumptions and practices and will have the capacity to unlock the creativity of others.

In matching the needs of sustainable development management, learners must be encouraged to view human beings as more than simple economic actors—as beings capable of broader moral reflection and purposeful action based on different ethical systems. This requires management education to expose learners to people who may be working toward many different goals. It means developing an appreciation of the limits of technical knowledge so that judgment and skepticism can be coupled together with the ability to adapt and change in the light of experience and in the light of anticipated futures. It requires an ability to address the values that underscore choices and the experience of tools that measure social and environmental performance, financial and economic outcomes, and the quality of collaborative processes.

Education for sustainable development emphasizes relatively new forms of educational approach and pedagogy. Experiential learning is key, with management faculty taking a role as facilitators of learning (as opposed to instructors in the traditional sense). But experiential learning is not enough to shape new concepts that support sustainable development as a new paradigm. Management education for sustainable development at its core is a subversive process. It demands a fundamental, critical analysis of the traditional purpose and values of business that are often taken for granted in management education. It rejects unidimensionality in favor of multidimensionality. It rejects case studies in favor of a mix of cases, role playing, and group consulting projects. It matches short time horizons with the capacity for longer term visions of change. It rejects universal management prescriptions in favor of creative experimentation and adaptive learning. It replaces economic explanations of the firm with deeper contextualizations of the firm in economic, social, and environmental systems. It complements analytic skills with the capacity for dialogue and joint action. After all, by challenging the current norms of business thinking and practice, sustainable development challenges the norms of management education.

Behind these comments is the idea that teachers and learners will need to develop a deeper basis for discourse across disciplines and values systems, establishing a richer, more comprehensive picture of industrial organizations and their context and bringing more diversity into the learning process. While environmental management can ostensibly be integrated across the management curriculum, by extending traditional areas of management sustainable development places paradigm redefining courses at the very core of the management curriculum. This has clear consequences for how learners are received and employed by industry.

Implications for Management Research

Sustainable development as a complex series of social and industrial experiments creates conditions in which management education and research are integral to the system of knowledge development and knowledge in action. Researchers are not neutral observers and research institutions are not observatories of development—they are part of the process that moves us toward or away from a sustainable society. Researchers are part of the industrial and social transformation for sustainable development. Researchers have a responsibility to construct bridges between theory, concept, method, and practice and should be critically engaged in the processes of organizational learning, progress, and change for sustainable development.

What are the main areas for research beyond the responsibilities of researchers to engage in praxis rather than purely fundamental research? The following priority areas are identified for research and action.

Change

Understanding the processes, mechanisms, drivers, and resistances to change is vital to the field of sustainable development. Sustainable development involves change continuously informed by the dynamic interplay of current and future needs. It is also a new paradigm that is unlikely to be brought about through regulation or intervention by the state. While it is possible to ensure that incentives and instruments create the ground for sustainable development, it is not possible to force the concepts or values that drive sustainable development. By its nature sustainable development involves systems change that affects many parties, at many different scales and levels, and in many ways. It requires consent and cooperative action within the framework of competitive economic systems. Research on sustainable development as change must span internal organizational issues and institutional and social fields, identifying the factors that encourage or discourage the direction of change. The study of change agents and their role within formal structures and looser networks is particularly important.

Learning

It is necessary to better understand the mechanisms of learning and the way that learning is influenced by the trends and forces of global and local change. An important vein of research on organizational learning concerns the role of formal structures and informal networks as conduits of learning and the development of competence for the new paradigm(s) of sustainable development. There is a need for more research on how managers learn through encounters with other actors and how that learning translates into organizational change, new practices, and technological and social innovation.

It is important to evaluate the contribution made by tools and techniques that measure the environmental and social changes provoked by industrial decisions—not only the way data from these tools and techniques are used but their effects on organizational thinking and practice.

Research is also needed on the content, structure, and performance of management education programs for sustainable development and on the effects of these programs on industrial management.

Integration

Studies are required on how industry and its managers understand and operationalize the integration of economic, environmental, and social aspects of choice and how those choices impact industrial activities. What is the scope of the tools, techniques, and mechanisms used for integration, and how are they embedded within organizational thinking and practice? How do mainstream business systems and processes change in response to environmental management and sustainable development frameworks? To what extent do these changes support or inhibit sustainable development? For example, as companies move toward activity-based costing systems, does it become easier to determine product-specific measures of economic, social, and environmental impacts? Are businesses extending their paradigm to make sense of their economic, environmental, and social responsibilities under sustainable development?

A number of other areas for study cut across the issues of change, learning, and integration. These are discussed below.

Dematerialization

The organizational challenges of moving from products to services and the dematerialization of the product component of services is important to the transition to a more sustainable pattern of production and consumption. It is necessary to understand the way dematerialization is understood and realized in organizations and the consequences of dematerialization on supply and value chains, the overall pattern of production and consumption and lifestyles. The approach to research that is followed by industrial ecologists—with their concern to understand the potential for more efficient energy and material flows between producers—is important to a better appreciation of the physical limits of production systems. However, it is also necessary to expand the current concept of industrial ecology toward a human industrial ecology model of sustainable production and consumption systems. This would permit a wider examination of the acceptability of dematerialized products to consumers and other actors in society—for example, the consequences that arise in terms of employment and the changes in social structures that accompany the acceptance of new products and services.

Interfirm Collaboration, Industry/Society Projects, and Partnerships

Sustainable development leaves no illusions about the importance of developing multiparty collaborative structures to complement the power of competition. Research into emerging forms of collaboration and their influence on mainstream organizational thinking and practice is needed. Research should involve study of the many new industry-to-industry partnerships found in industrial ecological systems, as well as industry-to-society/community partnerships that provide a basis for learning and the development of products and services to meet real needs.

Future Scenarios and Backcasting

More case studies and researcher involvement are required in the development of future scenarios and backcasting that includes industry and other stakeholders. The work by Philip Vergragt and Marjan van der Wel, set out in Chapter 8 of this book, indicates many of the challenges of this research—not least the need to secure resources and to establish the legitimacy of this approach to research in action. However, their work also indicates the need to use techniques that assess the environmental and social impacts of new technologies and the way that research and development is stimulated through work on scenarios. This type of research in action provides an important opportunity for researchers to facilitate dialogue and stimulate change for sustainable development.

Technology Innovation

Technology stands at the heart of the strategic direction of industrial firms, their market position, products, and services. Technology, including the knowledge and structures that are required for technological artifacts to find application, is at the core of sustainable development. Research on technology innovation has an important place in the sustainable development research agenda. Moreover, the issues of learning; change; integration; dematerialization; interfirm collaboration; and broader society/business partnerships, scenarios, and backcasting; as well as social and environmental assessments all come together at the interface between technology innovation and the contribution of industry to a sustainable society. Technology management and the influence of technology on social and institutional structure and systems are therefore critical research topics.

At the more macro level, there is a need for research into trends in social behavior as discussed below.

Sustainable Consumption and Production

No research on sustainable development and industry would be complete without a much more robust analysis of the trends in consumption and production at the global, regional, and local scales together with a much improved understanding of the factors—communications, media, advertising, images of lifestyle—that are shaping these patterns. There is also a need for research that considers the contribution of individual industries to the overall pattern of production and consumption and the bottlenecks that constrain change at the systems level.

Global Changes and Trends

Behind the pattern of consumption and production and its influence on progress toward sustainable development, there are the subtle, yet significant, global trends in social expectations, patterns of relationships, and shifts in culture and ideas in economics. These are shaping the canvas on which sustainable development is being drawn—for example, the move toward open economies and trade, the merging of cultures, and the development of global communications. What is needed here is research that is better able to detect the direction of these changes and to develop and assess the institutional and other mechanisms that might be used to resist the worst effects of change while supporting the benefits that change might bring.

Governance

A recurring theme of this book is the notion that the structures by which society and industry have been governed are inadequate given the direction of change and the demands for sustainable development. New forms of governance are discussed that incorporate a broader set of values, wider constituencies of interests, and longer time horizons, giving rise to more flexible and precautionary approaches to industrial decisions and policies. In line with the ideals of sustainable development, responsibility for governance needs to be dispersed more widely within social and industrial systems. This provokes the need for research to address *inter alia* how the span and scope of governance is changing; what paradigms, ideas, and information are used to inform governance; what justifications and arguments are used to legitimize decisions; and the extent to which decisions are becoming more transparent and decision-makers more accountable. Researchers should also be interested in understanding the implications that arise where responsibilities for governance are more broadly shared and decentralized within industrial systems and the institutional fabric of society.

Final Word

Sustainable development is seen as a new paradigm for industrial organizations that is not usefully informed by looking back at the experiences of an unsustainable past. Rather it will involve industrial organizations working with other actors and stakeholders to identify what sustainable futures might look like and to agree how to progress toward them. This will not be an easy process.

Considerable effort will be required to break with past concepts, conventions, institutional relationships, and established power structures. New and powerful visions of the future are necessary, together with agreement on the direction for change and a firm belief that progress is possible. This will demand leadership and a commitment to processes that bring actors together in constructive discussion and shared action. Leadership is important to establish the ground for learning and innovation for sustainable development. These processes will enable a shift away from technology that shapes social and environmental futures to a position where social and environmental futures provide the space to identify technological needs, economic opportunities, and the organizational structures and institutional arrangements needed to create that future.

Creating a sustainable future will require the commitment of many groups and actors to processes that emphasize the importance of the environmental, social, and economic dimensions of industry in society. For industry, a serious commitment to sustainable development implies a shift in the definition of its core purpose and the sense making frame of its managers. It will see itself as more than an efficient and effective machine, adding value to materials through human knowledge and ingenuity. Sustainable industries will see themselves as embedded in social and environmental systems, providing the basis for economic venture, social value and innovation, and environmental maintenance and restoration. In this way managers will assume, and share, responsibilities for the governance of economic change and technological innovation jointly with other social actors—governance designed to ensure that the satisfaction of individual economic needs does not jeopardize the quality of life and well-being of the community and the environment either now or in the future.

References

Introduction

Brundtland, G-H. (1987), *Our Common Future—The Report of the World Commission on Environment and Development.* New York: Oxford University Press.

Carley, M., and J. Christie (1992), *Managing Sustainable Development.* London: Earthscan.

Ditz, D., J. Ranganathan, and R. Banks, eds. (1995). *Green Ledgers: Case Studies in Corporate Environmental Accounting.* Washington, D.C.: World Resources Institute.

Earth Council (1997), *Compilation of Reports From Rio+5 Consultations in Western Europe.* New York: Earth Council.

European Partners for the Environment (1994), *Toward Sustainability.* Brussels.

Fischer, K., and J. Schot (1993), *Environmental Strategies for Industry: International Perspectives on Research Needs and Policy Implications.* Washington, D.C.: Island Press.

Gladwin, T., et al. (1995), "Shifting Paradigms for Sustainable Development: Implications for Management Theory and Research." *The Academy of Management Review* 20(4):874–907.

Green, K., P. Groenewegen, and B. Vorley, eds. (Forthcoming), *The Greening of Industry Case Book.* London: Earthscan.

Groenewegen, P., et al., eds. (1996), *The Greening of Industry Resource Guide and Bibliography.* Washington, D.C.: Island Press.

Hall, S., and N. Roome (1996), "Strategic Choices and Sustainable Strategies." In *The Greening of Industry Resource Guide and Bibliography* (eds. P. Groenewegen, K. Fischer, E. Jenkins, and J. Schot). Washington, D.C.: Island Press.

Hart, S. (1997), "Beyond Greening: Strategies for a Sustainable World." *Harvard Business Review,* Jan-Feb:67–76.

Kuhn, T. (1962), *The Structure of Scientific Revolutions.* Chicago: University of Chicago Press.

Magretta, J. (1997), "Growth Through Global Sustainability: An Interview with Monsanto CEO, Robert B. Shapiro." *Harvard Business Review,* Jan-Feb:79–88.

O'Connor, M., S. Fauchaux, G. Froger, S. Funtowicz, and G. Munda (1996),

"Emergent Complexity and Procedural Rationality: Post-normal Science for Sustainability." In *Getting Down to Earth* (eds. R. Constanza, O. Segura, and J. Martinez-Alier). Washington, D.C.: Island Press.

Roome, N. (1997a), "Corporate Environmental Responsibility." In *Business and the Natural Environment* (eds. P. Bansal and E. Howard). Oxford: Butterworth-Heinemann.

———— (1997b), "Learning to Integrate Environmental Concerns into Business Organizations." *American Academy of Management,* 1997 Meeting, Boston.

Starik, M., and G. Rands (1995), "Weaving an Integrated Web: Multilevel and Multisystem Perspectives of Ecologically Sustainable Organizations." *The Academy of Management Review* 20(4):908–935.

Chapter 1

Adriaanse, A., S. Bringezu, A. Hammond, Y. Moriguchi, E. Rodenburg, D. Rogich, and H. Schütz (1997), *Resource flows: The material basis of industrial economies.* Washington, D.C.: World Resources Institute.

Barber, B.R. (1995), *Jihad vs. McWorld.* New York: Random House.

Barth, S. (1998), "1998 VIP predictions." *World Trade,* February:24.

Bateson, G. (1978), *Mind and Nature: A necessary unity.* New York: Dutton.

Berkes, F., C. Folke, and M. Gadgil (1994), "Traditional ecological knowledge, biodiversity, resilience and sustainability." In C.A. Perrings, K.G. Mäler, C. Folke, C.S. Holling, and B.O. Jansson, *Biodiversity Conservation: Problems and policies,* pp. 269–287. Dordrecht: Kluwer Academic Publishers.

Boeing Commercial Airline Group Marketing (1997), *Current Market Outlook.* Seattle: Boeing.

Botkin, D.B. (1990), *Discordant Harmonies: A new ecology for the twenty-first century.* New York: Oxford University Press.

Boyce, J.K. (1994) "Inequality as a cause of environmental degradation." *Ecological Economics* 11(3):169–178.

Bright, C. (1996), "Understanding the threat of bioinvasions." In L.R. Brown et al., *State of the World 1996*, pp. 95–113. New York: W.W. Norton.

Brown, L.R. (1998), "The future of growth." In L.R. Brown et al., *State of the World 1998.* New York: W.W. Norton.

Chichilnisky, G. (1994), "North–South trade and the global environment." *American Economic Review* 84(4):851–874.

Clark, I. (1997), *Globalization and Fragmentation: International relations in the twentieth century.* New York: Oxford University Press.

Costanza, R., and H.E. Daly (1992), "Natural capital and sustainable development." *Conservation Biology* 6:37–46.

Costanza, R., B.G. Norton, and B.D. Haskell, eds. (1992), *Ecosystem Health: New goals for environmental management.* Washington, D.C.: Island Press.

Costanza, R., J. Audley, R. Borden, P. Ekins, C. Folke, S.O. Funtowicz, and J. Harris (1995), "Sustainable Trade: A new paradigm for world welfare." *Environment* 37(5):16–44.

Costanza, R., et al. (1997), "The value of the world's ecosystem services and natural capital." *Nature* 387 (May 15):253–260.

Daily, G.C., ed. (1997), *Nature's Services: Societal dependence on natural ecosystems.* Washington, D.C.: Island Press.

Daily, G.C., and P.R. Ehrlich (1992), "Population, sustainability, and Earth's carrying capacity." *Bioscience* 42:761–771.

———— (1996), "Impacts of development and global change on the epidemiological environment." *Environment and Development Economics* 1(3):311–345.

Daly, H.E. (1994), "Operationalizing sustainable development by investing in natural capital." In A. Jansson, M. Hammer, C. Folke, and R. Costanza, eds., *Investing in Natural Capital: The ecological economics approach to sustainability*, pp. 22–37. Washington, D.C.: Island Press.

———— (1996), *Beyond Growth: The economics of sustainable development.* Boston: Beacon Press.

Durning, A.B. (1990), "Ending Poverty." In L.R. Brown et al., *State of the World 1990*, pp. 135–153. New York: W.W. Norton.

Ehrlich, P.R., G.C. Daily, S.C., Daily, N. Myers, and J. Salzman (1997), "No middle way on the environment." *The Atlantic Monthly*, December:98–104.

Eskeland, G.S., and A.E. Harrison (1997), "Moving to greener pastures? Multinationals and the pollution-haven hypothesis." *World Bank Policy Research Working Paper* No. 1744, March.

Esty, D.C. (1994), *Greening the GATT: Trade, environment, and the future.* Washington, D.C.: Institute for International Economics.

Flavin, C. (1997), "The legacy of Rio." In L.R. Brown et al., *State of the World 1997*, pp. 1–22. New York: W.W. Norton.

Fowler, C., and P. Mooney (1990), *The Threatened Gene: Food, politics, and the loss of genetic diversity.* Cambridge: Lutterworth Press.

French, H.F. (1993), "Costly tradeoffs: Reconciling trade and the environment." *Worldwatch Paper* No. 113, March.

———— (1997), "Privatizing international development." *Worldwatch* 10(3):8–17.

George, S., and F. Sabelli (1994), *Faith and Credit: The World Bank's secular empire.* Boulder: Westview Press.

Gladwin, T.N. (1992), *Building the Sustainable Corporation: Creating environ-*

mental sustainability and competitive advantage. Washington, D.C.: National Wildlife Federation.

Gladwin, T.N., and N. Wasilewski (1986), "Environmental interdependence and organizational design: The case of the multinational corporation." In R. Lamb and P. Shrivastava, eds., *Advances in Strategic Management*, pp. 229–277. Greenwich, Conn.: JAI Press.

Gladwin, T.N., J.J. Kennelly, and T.S. Krause (1995), "Shifting paradigms for sustainable development: Implications for management theory and research." *The Academy of Management Review* 20(4):874–907.

Gladwin, T.N., T.S. Krause, and J.J. Kennelly (1995), "Beyond Eco-efficiency: Toward socially sustainable business." *Sustainable Development* 3(April): 35–43.

Gladwin, T.N., W.E. Newburry, and E.D. Reiskin (1997), "Why is the northern elite mind biased against community, the environment, and a sustainable future?" In M.H. Bazerman et al., eds., *Environment, Ethics and Behavior*, pp. 234–274. San Francisco: Jossey-Bass Publishers.

Govindarjan, V., and A. Gupta (1998), "Setting a course for the new global landscape." *Financial Times,* February:3–5.

Greider, W. (1997), *One World, Ready or Not: The manic logic of global capitalism.* New York: Simon & Schuster.

Hawken, P. (1993), *The Ecology of Commerce: A declaration of sustainability.* New York: Harper Business.

Hobsbawm, E. (1994), *The Age of Extremes: A history of the world, 1914–1991.* New York: Pantheon.

Holling, C.S. (1986), "Resilience of Ecosystems: Local surprise and global change." In W.C. Clark and R.E. Munn, eds., *Sustainable Development of the Biosphere*, pp. 292–316. Cambridge: Cambridge University Press.

——— (1992), "Cross-scale morphology, geometry, and dynamics of ecosystems." *Ecological Monographs* 62(4):157–178.

Holmberg, J., K.H. Robert, and K.E. Eriksson (1996), "Socio-ecological principles for a sustainable society." In R. Costanza, O. Segura, and J. Martinez-Alier, eds., *Getting Down to Earth*, pp. 17–48. Washington, D.C.: Island Press.

Kellert, S.R. (1993), "The biological basis for human values of nature." In S.R. Kellert and E.O. Wilson, eds., *The Biophilia Hypothesis*, pp. 42–69. Washington, D.C.: Island Press.

Korten, D.C. (1995), *When Corporations Rule the World.* San Francisco: Berrett-Koehler.

Krauss, M. (1997), *How Nations Grow Rich: The case for free trade.* New York: Oxford University Press.

Lélé, S., and R.B. Norgaard (1996), "Sustainability and the scientist's burden." *Conservation Biology* 10(2):354–365.

Mander, J., and E. Goldsmith, eds. (1996), *The Case Against the Global Economy and for a Turn Toward the Local.* San Francisco: Sierra Club Books.

Matson, P.A., W.J. Parton, A.G. Power, and M.J. Swift (1997), "Agricultural intensification and ecosystem properties." *Science* 277(July 25):504–509.

McKinsey Global Institute (1994), *The Global Capital Market: Supply, demand, pricing and allocation.* New York: McKinsey.

Meyer, N. (1995), Plenary on sustainable consumption. *The Balaton Bulletin*, Fall:28–31.

Meyer, W.B. (1996), *Human Impact on the Earth.* Cambridge: Cambridge University Press.

Mittleman, J.H., ed. (1996), *Globalization: Critical reflections.* Boulder: Lynne Renner Publishers.

Nader, R., et al. (1993), *The Case Against Free Trade: GATT, NAFTA, and the globalization of corporate power.* San Francisco: Earth Island Press.

Norgaard, R.B. (1988), "The rise of the global exchange economy and the loss of biological diversity." In E.O. Wilson, ed., *Biodiversity*, pp. 208–210. Washington, D.C.: National Academy Press.

Norton, B.G. (1991), *Toward Unity Among Environmentalists.* New York: Oxford University Press.

Odum, H.J. (1971), *Environment, Power and Society.* New York: Wiley.

Organization for Economic Cooperation and Development (1996), *Trade liberalization and changes in international freight movements.* Restricted paper COM/TD/ENV (96):73, prepared for the OECD Joint Session of Trade and Environment Experts.

——— (1997), *Economic Globalization and the Environment.* Paris: OECD

Postel, S. (1994), "Carrying Capacity: Earth's bottom line." In L.R. Brown et al., *State of the World 1994*, pp. 3–21. New York: W.W. Norton.

Princen, T. (1997), "The shading and distancing of commerce: When internalization is not enough." *Ecological Economics* 20:235–253.

Rapport, D.J. (1997), "Is economic development compatible with ecosystem health?" *Ecosystem Health* 3(2):94–106.

Redclift, M. (1996), *Wasted: Counting the costs of global consumption.* London: Earthscan.

Ruggiero, R. (1997), "The high stakes of world trade." *Wall Street Journal*, April 28.

Soros, G. (1998), "Toward a global open society." *The Atlantic Monthly*, January: 20–32.

Stern, P.D., O.R. Young, and D. Druchman, eds. (1992), *Global Environmental*

Change: Understanding the human dimensions. Washington, D.C.: National Academy Press.

Swanson, T.M. (1992), "The Global Conversion Process: The fundamental forces underlying losses of biological diversity." *CSERGE Working Paper* GEC 9241. London: Centre for Social and Economic Research on the Global Environment.

United Nations Department for Policy Coordination and Sustainable Development (1997), *Critical Trends: Global change and sustainable development.* New York: United Nations.

United Nations Environment Programme (1995), *Poverty and the Environment.* Nairobi: UNEP.

———— (1997), *Global Environment Outlook.* New York: Oxford University Press.

Vitousek, P.M. (1994), "Beyond global warming: Ecology and global change." *Ecology* 75(7):1861–1876.

Vitousek, P.M., H.A. Mooney, J. Lubchenco, and J.M. Melillo (1997), "Human domination of Earth's ecosystems." *Science* 277(July 25):494–499.

Von Weizsacker, E., A.B. Lovins, and L.H. Lovins (1997), *Factor Four: Doubling wealth, halving resource use.* London: Earthscan.

Wackernagel, M., and W. Rees (1996), *Our Ecological Footprint: Reducing human impact on the Earth.* Philadelphia: New Society Publishers.

Wilson, E.O. (1992), *The Diversity of Life.* Cambridge: Harvard University Press.

Woodley, S., J. Kay, and C. Francis (1993), *Ecological Integrity and the Management of Ecosystems.* Waterloo, Ontario: St. Lucie Press.

Woodwell, G.M., ed. (1990), *The Earth in Transition: Patterns and processes of biotic impoverishment.* Cambridge: Cambridge University Press.

Chapter 2

Associated Press (1991), "Presbyterians Ratify Teaching On Sex, Ecology." *The Boston Globe,* June 9:4.

Beck, U. (1992), *Risk Society: Toward a New Modernity.* Newbury Park, CA: Sage Publications.

Bookchin, M. (1990), *Remaking Society: Pathways to a Green Future.* Boston: South End Press.

Boulding, K. (1966), "The Economics of the Coming Spaceship Earth." In H. Jarrett (ed.) *Environmental Quality in a Growing Economy.* Baltimore: Johns Hopkins University Press.

Brundtland, G-H. (1987), *Our Common Future—The Report of the World Com-*

mission on Environment and Development. New York: Oxford University Press.

Buttel, F. (1992), "Environmentalism: Origins, Processes, and Implications for Rural Social Change." *Rural Sociology* 57(1):1–27.

Buttel, F., A. Hawkins, and A. Power (1990), "From Limits to Growth to Global Change: Constraints and Contradictions in the Evolution of Environmental Science and Ideology." *Global Environmental Change* 1(1):57–66.

Calvin, W. (1994), "The Emergence of Intelligence." *Scientific American* 271(4):101–107.

Capra, F. (1982), *The Turning Point.* New York: Bantam Books.

Carson, R. (1962), *Silent Spring.* Boston: Houghton Mifflin Co.

Catton, W., and R. Dunlap (1978), "Environmental Sociology: A New Paradigm." *The American Sociologist* 13(Feb.):41–49.

Colby, M. (1989), *The Evolution of Paradigms of Environmental Management in Development.* SPR Planning Paper No. 1 (Washington, D.C.: Strategic Planning and Review Department, The World Bank); see also Colby, M. (1991), "Environmental Management in Development; The Evolution of Paradigms." *Ecological Economics* 3:193–213.

Commoner, B. (1990), *Making Peace With the Planet.* New York: Pantheon Books.

Daly, H. (1991), *Steady-State Economics.* Washington, D.C.: Island Press.

Daly, H., and J. Cobb (1994), *For the Common Good.* Boston: Beacon Press.

Dassman, R. (1976), "Bioregional Provinces." *Coevolution Quarterly* Fall:32–37.

Dembner, A. (1994), "Movement Is Strong on Campus." *The Boston Globe,* November 12, p. 28.

Devall, B., and G. Sessions (1985), *Deep Ecology.* Salt Lake City: Peregrine Smith Books.

Dowie, M. (1995), *Losing Ground: American Environmentalism at the Close of the Twentieth Century.* Cambridge: MIT Press.

Downs, A. (1972), "Up and Down With Ecology: the Issue-Attention Cycle." *Public Interest* 28:38–50.

Dubos, R. (1976), "Symbiosis Between the Earth and Humankind." *Science* 193:459–462.

Dunlap, R. (1991), "Trends in Public Opinion Toward Environmental Issues: 1965–1990." *Society and Natural Resources* 4:285–312.

Egri, C., and L. Pinfield (1994), "Organizations and the Biosphere: Ecologies and Environments." In Clegg, Hardy, and Wood (eds.), *Handbook of Organization Studies.* London: Sage Publications.

Ehrenfeld, J., and A. Hoffman (1993), *Becoming a Green Company: The Impor-*

tance of Culture in the Greening Process. Paper presented at the Greening of Industry Conference, Designing the Sustainable Enterprise, November 14–16, Boston.

Ellul, J. (1964), *The Technological Society.* New York: Vintage Books.

Evernden, N. (1985), *The Natural Alien.* Toronto: University of Toronto Press.

————— (1992), *The Social Creation of Nature.* Baltimore: The Johns Hopkins University Press.

Fligstein, N. (1993), *The Cultural Construction of Political Action: The Case of the European Community's Single Market Program.* Unpublished manuscript. Berkeley: University of California.

Fox, W. (1990), *Toward a Transpersonal Ecology: Developing New Foundations for Environmentalism.* Boston: Shambhala.

Gladwin, T. (1995), *Sustainable Development and Sustainable Enterprise.* Presentation at the Management Institute for Environment and Business Conference, Austin, Texas, July 19–21.

Gladwin, T., T. Freeman, and J. Kennelly (1994), *Ending Our Denial and Destruction of Nature: Toward Biophysical Sustainable Management Theory.* Unpublished manuscript. New York: Stern School of Business.

Gladwin, T., J. Kennelly, and T. Krause (1995), "Shifting Paradigms for Sustainable Development: Implications for Management Theory and Research." *Academy of Management Review* 20(4):874–907.

Hannan, M., and J. Freeman (1977), "The Population Ecology of Organizations." *American Journal of Sociology* 82:929–964.

Hart, S. (1995), "A Natural-Resource-Based View of the Firm." *Academy of Management Review* 20(4):986–1014.

Hirschman, A. (1977), *The Passions and the Interests.* Princeton: Princeton University Press.

Hodgkinson et al. (1993), *Non-Profit Almanac.* San Francisco: Jossey-Bass Publishers.

Hoffman, A. (1993), "The Importance of Fit Between Individual Values and Organizational Culture in the Greening of Industry." *Business Strategy and the Environment* 2(4):10–18.

————— (1994), "Organizational Change and the Greening Process: A Case Study of the Amoco Corporation." *Total Quality Environmental Management* 4(1):1–21.

————— (1996), "Environmental Management Withers Away." *Tomorrow* 6(2):60, 61.

————— (1997), *From Heresy to Dogma: An Institutional History of Corporate Environmentalism.* San Francisco: The New Lexington Press.

Jacobs, M. (1993), *The Green Economy: Environment, Sustainable Development and the Politics of the Future.* Vancouver, B.C.: UBC Press.

Jonas, H. (1973), "Technology and Responsibility: Reflections on the New Tasks of Ethics." *Social Research* 40:31–54.

Jubeir, J. (1995), "Educating Environmental Managers for Tomorrow." *EPA Journal,* Washington, D.C.

Kuhn, T. (1970), *The Structure of Scientific Revolutions.* Chicago: The University of Chicago Press.

Leopold, A. (1949), *A Sand County Almanac.* London: Oxford University Press.

Lewis, C.S. (1953), *The Abolition of Man.* New York: The Macmillan Company.

Lowe, P., and J. Goyder (1983), *Environmental Groups in Politics.* Boston: Allen and Unwin.

Makower, J. (1993), "Business Schools Get in Line." *Tomorrow* 3(3):50–53.

Mangan, K. (1994), "The Greening of the MBA." *The Chronicle of Higher Education,* November 2: A19, A20.

Marsh, G. (1965), *Man and Nature.* Cambridge: Harvard University Press.

Merchant, C. (1980), *The Death of Nature: Women, Ecology and the Scientific Revolution.* New York: Harper & Row Publishers.

Morrison, C. (1991), *Managing Environmental Affairs: Corporate Practices in the U.S., Canada and Europe.* New York: The Conference Board.

Olson, M. (1965), *The Logic of Collective Action: Public Goods and the Theory of Groups.* Cambridge: Harvard University Press.

Patterson, O. (1991), *Freedom in the Making of Western Culture.* New York: Harper Collins.

Pfeffer, J. (1982), "The External Control of the Organization." Chapter 5 in *Organizations and Organization Theory.* Boston: Pitman.

Pham, A. (1994), "Business Schools See Green." *The Boston Globe,* June 28:35.

Piller, C. (1991), *The Fail-Safe Society: Community Defiance and the End of American Technological Optimism.* Berkeley: University of California Press.

Porter, M. (1980), *Competitive Strategy.* New York: The Free Press.

——— (1985), *Competitive Advantage.* New York: The Free Press.

Rockefeller, S., and J. Elder (1992), *Spirit and Nature.* Boston: Beacon Press.

Roome, N. (1994), *The Environmental Agenda: Taking Responsibility—Management and Business.* London: Pluto Press.

Schnaiberg, A. (1980), *The Environment: From Surplus to Scarcity.* New York: Oxford University Press.

Schnaiberg, A., and K. Gould (1994), *Environment and Society: The Enduring Conflict.* New York: St. Martin's Press.

Smart, B. (1992), *Beyond Compliance: A New Industry View of the Environment.* Washington, D.C.: World Resources Institute.

Wagner, B. (1994), "The Greening of the Engineer." *US News & World Report,* March 21:90,91.

Woodward, K., and R. Nordland (1992), "New Rules for an Old Faith." *Newsweek,* November 30:71.

Zald, M., and R. Garner (1987), "Social Movement Organizations: Growth, Decay, and Change." In Zald and McCarthy (eds.), *Social Movements in an Organizational Society.* New Brunswick: Transaction Books, pp. 121–142.

Zald, M., and J. McCarthy (1987), " Resource Mobilization and Social Movements." In Zald and McCarthy (eds.), *Social Movements in an Organizational Society.* New Brunswick: Transaction Books, pp. 15–48.

Chapter 3

Bebbington, J., and R. Gray (1996), "Sustainable Development and Accounting: Incentives and Disincentives for the Adoption of Sustainability by Transnational Organisations," In *Environmental Accounting and Sustainable Development—The Final Report.* Final Report of the EMAA Workshop, Limperg Instituut, Chartered Association of Certified Accountants, Institute of Chartered Accountants, Instut der Wirtschaftsprüfer & Koninklijk Netherlands Instutuut van Registeraccountants.

Callens, I., and D. Tyteca (1995), "Toward Indicators of Sustainable Development for Firms—Concepts and Definitions." *Fourth International Research Conference of the Greening of Industry Network,* November 12–14, Toronto, Canada.

Eden, S. (1994), "Business, Trust and Environmental Information: Perceptions from Consumers and Retailers." *Business Strategy and the Environment* 3(4):1–8.

Ellger, C., and J. Scheiner (1997), "After Industrial Society: Service Society as Clean Society? Environmental Consequences of Increasing Service Interaction." *The Services Industries Journal* 17(4):564–579.

Gladwin, T.N., T.S. Klause, and J.K. Kennelly (1995), "Beyond Eco-Efficiency: Toward Socially Sustainable Business." *Sustainable Development* 3(1):35–43.

Gray, R.H. (1994), "Corporate reporting for sustainable development: accounting for sustainability in 2000 AD." *Environmental Values* 3(1):17–45.

Green, K., B. Morton, and S. New (1996), "Purchasing and Environmental Management: Interactions, Policies and Opportunities." *Business Strategy and the Environment* 5(3):188–197.

Irons, K. (1994), *Managing Service Companies—Strategies for Success.* Wokingham, England: Addison-Wesley Publishing Company.

ISO (1997), *ISO14031 (draft)—Environmental Performance Evaluation.* International Organization for Standardization.

James, P., and M. Bennett (1994), *Environmental-related Performance Measure-*

ment in Business; From Emissions to Profit and Sustainability? Ashridge Management Group Publication.

Lundgren, M. (1996b), *The White Collar Business' Ecological Footprints.* School of Business, Stockholm University, Sweden, unpublished.

Morton, B., K. Green, S. New, and C. Miller (1997), "Negotiating Environmental Improvement: The Emerging Role of Environmental Supply Chain Management and NUS Services Ltd." *Business Strategy and the Environment Conference Proceedings* September 18–19, Leeds, UK, pp. 167–172.

Normann, R. (1984), *Service Management—Strategy and Leadership in Service Businesses.* Chichester, UK: John Wiley & Sons.

Norwegian Ministry of the Environment (1994), *Symposium: Sustainable Consumption.* Oslo, Norway, 19–20 January.

——— (1995), Oslo Roundtable Conference on Sustainable Production and Consumption, Oslo, Norway.

Robins, N., and S. Roberts (1997), *Changing Consumption and Production Patterns: Unlocking Trade Opportunities.* International Institute and Development and UN Department of Policy Coordination and Sustainable Development.

Roome, N. (1997a), "Corporate Environmental Responsibility." In *Business and the Natural Environment* (eds. P. Bansal and E. Howard). Oxford: Butterworth Heinemann.

——— (1997b), "The Role of Meaning, Communities of Knowing and Action Learning in the Integration of Business and the Environment—A Theory of Action Learning Networks." *The Sixth International Research Conference of the Greening of Industry Network.* November 16–19, Santa Barbara.

Rydberg, T. (1995), "Cleaner Products in the Nordic Countries Based on the Life Cycle Assessment Approach—the Swedish Product Ecology Project and The Nordic Project for Sustainable Product Development." *Journal of Cleaner Production* 3(1,2):101–105.

Salim, E. (1994), "The Challenge of Sustainable Consumption as Seen from The South." In *Symposium: Sustainable Consumption.* Oslo, Norway, 19–20 January.

Shrivastava, P., and S. Hart (1995), "Creating Sustainable Corporations." *Business Strategy and the Environment* 4(3):154–165.

Starik, M., G.M. Throop, J.R. Doody, and M.E. Joyce (1996), "Growing an Environmental Strategy." *Business Strategy and the Environment* 5(1):12–21.

Stead, W.E., and J.G. Stead (1992), *Management for a Small Planet—Strategic Decision Making and the Environment.* London: Sage Publications.

van Someren, T.C.R. (1995), "Sustainable Development and the Firm: Organizational Innovations and Environmental Strategy." *Business Strategy and the Environment* 4(1):23–33.

WBCSD (1996), *Sustainable Production and Consumption—A Business Perspective.* World Business Council for Sustainable Development, Geneva, Switzerland.

Welford, R.J. (1996), *Corporate Environmental Management: Systems and Strategies.* London: Earthscan.

———— (1997), *Hijacking Environmentalism: Corporate Responses to Sustainable Development.* London: Earthscan.

Ytterhus, B.E., and S.J. Refsum (1996), *The GRIP Barometer—A Mapping of Environmental Adaptation in the Manufacture of Furniture, Building and Construction, Banking and Insurance, Advertising, Tourism and the Wholesale and Retail Trade.* Center for Research in Environmental Management, The Norwegian School of Management, Norway, unpublished.

Chapter 4

Brundtland, G-H. (1987), *Our Common Future—The Report of the World Commission on Environment and Development.* New York: Oxford University Press.

Commission of the European Communities (1992), "Towards Sustainability: A European Community Programme of Policy and Action in Relation to the Environment and Sustainable Development." COM (92) *23 final—Vol. II, Brussels.*

European Partners for the Environment (EPE) (1994), *Toward Sustainability.* Brussels.

———— (1996), *From EMAS to SMAS: Charting the Course from Environmental Auditing and Management to Sustainability Management.* Brussels.

Investor Responsibility Research Center (IRRC)/Global Environmental Management Initiative (GEMI) (1996), *Environmental Reporting and Third Party Statements.* Washington, D.C.

Senge, P. (1990), *The Fifth Discipline.* New York: Currency Doubleday.

Spencer-Cooke, A. (1997), "From EMAS to SMAS." In Sheldon (ed.), *ISO 14001 and Beyond.* Sheffield: Greenleaf Publishing.

United Nations Environment Programme (UNEP)/SustainAbility Ltd. (1996), *Engaging Stakeholders*, Vols. 1 and 2, London.

Chapter 5

Belz, F. (1995), *Ökologie und Wettbewerbsfähigkeit in der Schweizer Lebensmittelbranche.* Bern, Stuttgart, Wien.

Belz, F. (1997), "Swiss Business Environmental Barometer." In F. Belz and L. Strannegård (eds.), *International Business Environmental Barometer 1997.* Oslo, pp. 95–119.

Belz, F., and L. Strannegård (1997), "International Comparison." In F. Belz and L. Strannegård (eds.), *International Business Environmental Barometer 1997,* Oslo, pp. 141–169.

Belz, F., et al. (1997), "Von der Öko-Nische zum ökologischen Massenmarkt im Bedürfnisfeld Ernährung. Konzeption eines Forschungsprojektes." Discussion paper no. 40 of the Institute for Economy and the Environment at the University of St. Gallen (IEE-HSG), St. Gallen.

Berkhout, F. (1995), "Life cycle assessment and innovation in large firms." Paper presented at the Fourth Greening of Industry Network Conference in Toronto, Canada, November 12–14, 1995.

DOW Europe and SustainAbility Inc. (1995), *Who Needs It? Market Implications of Sustainable Lifestyles.* London.

Enquete Commission (1993), *Responsibility for the Future. Options for Sustainable Management of Substance Chains and Material Flows.* Bonn.

——— (1994), *Shaping Industrial Society. Prospects for Sustainable Management of Substance Chains and Material Flows.* Bonn.

Friends of the Earth Netherlands (1994), *Sustainable Netherlands. Aktionsplan für eine nachhaltige Entwicklung der Niederlande.* Frankfurt.

Hammer, M., and J. Champy (1993), *Reengineering the Corporation. A Manifesto for Business Revolution.* New York.

Hopfenbeck, W. (1993), *The Green Management Revolution. Lessons in Environmental Excellence.* Hertfordshire.

Hummel, J. (1997), *Strategisches Öko-Controlling am Beispiel der textilen Kette.* Wiesbaden.

Jungk, R., and N.R. Müller (1991), *Zukunftswerkstätten: Mit Phantasie gegen Routine und Resignation.* München.

Keller, W. (1991), "Die Sanierung der Glatt als Beispiel erfolgreicher Kooperation im Umweltschutz." In T. Dyllick (ed.), *Ökologische Lernprozesse in Unternehmungen.* Bern, Stuttgart 1991, pp. 185–198.

Keynes, J.M. (1930), "Economic Possibilities for Our Grandchildren." In J.M. Keynes (1972), *Collected Writings, No. 9.* London, pp. 231–332.

Kirchgeorg, M. (1995), "Kreislaufwirtschaft—Neue Herausforderungen für das Marketing." In *Marketing ZfP* 17 (4):232–248.

Linnanen, L., et al. (1994), "Life Cycle Management: Integrated Approach Toward Corporate Environmental Issues." Paper presented at the Third Greening of Industry Network Conference in Copenhagen, Denmark, November 13–15, 1994.

Max Havelaar (1996), *Max Havelaar-Stiftung Jahresbericht 1995.* Basel.

Neale, A. (1997), "Extending the Scope of Environmental Management: The Case of Company-Assisted Travel in Britain." In *Business Strategy and the Environment* 6(1):9–17.

Pichel, K. (1993), *Die Einführung integrativen Umweltschutzes durch ein Instrument der Organisationsentwicklung. Möglichkeiten und Grenzen von Zukunftswerkstätten in Betrieben.* Berlin.

Roome, N., and S.F. Clarke (1995), "Exploring the Sustainable Enterprise: A Journey through Theory and Practice." Paper presented for the Third Greening of Industry Network Conference in Copenhagen, Denmark, November 13–15, 1994.

Roome, N., and M. Hinnells (1993), "Environmental Factors in the Management of New Product Development: Theoretical Framework and Some Empirical Evidence from the White Goods Industry." In *Business Strategy and the Environment* 2(2):12–27.

Schaltegger, S. (1997), "Economics of Life Cycle Assessment: Inefficiency of the Present Approach." In *Business and the Environment* 6(1):1–8.

Schneidewind, U. (1994), "Mit COSY (Company Oriented Sustainability) Unternehmen zur Nachhaltigkeit führen." Discussion paper no. 15 of the Institute for Economy and the Environment at the University of St. Gallen (IEE-HSG), St. Gallen.

Schneidewind, U, J. Hummel, and F. Belz (1997), "Wettbewerbsgerechtes und nachhaltiges Umweltmanagement: Von der Vision zur Transformation—Initiierung ökologischer Wandlungsprozesse durch COSY-Workshops." Discussion paper no. 43 of the Institute for Economy and the Environment at the University of St. Gallen (IEE-HSG), St. Gallen.

Steger, U. (1996), "Managerial Issues in Closing the Loop." In *Business Strategy and the Environment* 5:252–268.

SustainAbility (1993), *The LCA Sourcebook: A European Business Guide to Life Cycle Assessment.* London.

WBCSD (1995), *Eco-Efficient Leadership for Improved Economic and Environmental Performance.* World Business Council for Sustainable Development, Geneva.

Welford, R. (1995), *Environmental Strategy and Sustainable Development. The Corporate Challenge for the 21st Century.* London, New York.

Zinn (1995), "Wie umweltverträglich sind unsere Bedürfnisse? Zu den anthropologischen Grundlagen von Wirtschaftswachstum und Umweltzerstörung." In S.M. Daecke (ed.), *Ökonomie contra Ökologie? Wirtschafsethische Beiträge zu Umweltfragen.* Stuttgart, Weimar, pp. 31–62.

Chapter 6

Arogyaswamy, B., and C. Byles (1987), "Organizational culture: internal and external fits." *Journal of Management Studies* 13(4):647–659.

Bate, P. (1994), *Strategies for Cultural Change*. Oxford: Butterworth-Heinemann.

Bennis, W., and B. Nanus (1985), *Leaders: Strategies for Taking Charge*. New York: Harper & Row.

Burlingham (1988), "This woman has changed business forever." *Inc.* June, p. 42.

Child, J. (1984), *Organization: a guide to problems and practice,* 2nd ed. London: Harper & Row.

Clarke, S., and S. Georg (1995), Summary Report: 1994 Greening of Industry Conference, Copenhagen.

Coulson-Thomas, C. (1992), "Strategic vision or strategic con?: Rhetoric or reality?" *Long Range Planning* 25(1):81–89.

Crane, A. (1995), "Rhetoric and reality in the Greening of Organizational Culture." *Greener Management International* 12:49–62.

Denison, D. (1990), *Corporate Culture and Organizational Effectiveness*. New York: Wiley.

Denison, D.R., and A.K. Mishra (1989), "Organizational culture and organizational effectiveness: a theory and some preliminary empirical evidence." *The Academy of Management,* 1989 meeting, Washington, D.C.

Feenberg, A. (1986), *Lukács, Marx and the Sources of Critical Theory.* Oxford: Oxford University Press.

Gabriel, Y. (1991), "Organizational stories and myths: why it is easier to slay a dragon than to kill a myth." *International Sociology* 6(4):427–42.

Gladwin, T. (1993), "The meaning of greening: a plea for organizational theory." In *Environmental Strategies for Industry* (eds. K. Fischer and J. Schot). Washington, D.C.: Island Press.

Green, S. (1988), "Strategy, Organizational Culture and Symbolism." *Long Range Planning* 21(4):121–129.

Halme, M. (1994), "Managerial processes behind organizations' environmental transformation efforts." 1994 Greening of Industry Conference, Copenhagen.

Hanson, K.O. (1996), *Social Evaluation. The Body Shop International 1995.* The Body Shop, Watersmead.

Harrison, R., and H. Stokes (1992), *Diagnosing Organizational Culture.* San Diego: Pfeiffer and Company.

Hoare, Q. (1977), *Selections from Political Writings 1910–1920,* A. Gramsci, ed. London: Lawrence & Wishart.

Inzerelli, G. (1980), "Some notes on culture and organizational control." Center for the Study of Organizational Innovation, University of Pennsylvania, discussion paper 84, September.

Jones, D.R. (1996), "The Sustainable Enterprise—Leaning into the Future." 1996 Greening of Industry Conference, Heidelberg.

Klyn, B., and K. Kearins (1995), *A case for marketing education: but will The Body Shop's bubble burst?* Hamilton: Univ. of Waikato.

Martin, J., and D. Meyerson (1988), "Organizational cultures and denial, channeling and acknowledgment of ambiguity." In *Managing Ambiguity and Change* (eds. L.R. Pondy et al.). New York: Wiley, pp. 93–125.

Mathews, M.C. (1988), *Strategic Intervention in Organizations: Resolving Ethical Dilemmas.* Newbury Park, Calif.: Sage.

Meima, R. (1994), "Making sense of environmental trends, paradigms, culture and the fragmentation of metaphor." 1994 Greening of Industry Conference, Copenhagen.

Metcalfe, L., and S. Richards (1987), "Evolving Management Cultures." In *Managing Public Organizations: Lessons from Contemporary European Experience* (eds. J. Kooiman and K. Eliassen). London: Sage, pp. 75–86.

Mintzberg, H. (1987), "Crafting Strategy." *Harvard Business Review,* July-August.

Murphy, P. (1989), "Creating ethical corporate structures." *Sloan Management Review* 30(2):81–87.

Newton, T., and G. Harte (1994), "Green Business: Dream or Reality?" 1994 Business Strategy and the Environment Conference, Nottingham.

Perrow, C. (1972), *Complex Organizations. A critical essay.* Glenview, Ill: Scott Foresman.

Peters, T.J., and R.H. Waterman (1982), *In Search of Excellence.* New York: Harper & Row.

Reed, M., and P. Anthony (1990), "Professionalizing management and managing professionalization: British management in the 1980s." Employment in the Enterprise Culture Conference, Cardiff.

Roddick, A. (1991), *Body and Soul.* London: Elbury Press.

Roome, N., and S. Clarke (1994), "Exploring the sustainable enterprise: A Journey through theory and practice." 1994 Greening of Industry Conference, Copenhagen.

Schein, E. (1983), "The role of the founder in creating organizational culture." *Organizational Dynamics,* Summer.

Smircich, L. (1983), "Concepts of culture and organizational analysis." *Administrative Science Quarterly* 28.

The Body Shop (1993), *The Green Book 2.* The Body Shop, Watersmead.

———— (1994a), *Interim Financial Report.* The Body Shop, Watersmead.

———— (1994b), *Values and Vision Report.* The Body Shop, Watersmead.

———— (1994c), *L.A. News* No.11. The Body Shop, Watersmead.

———— (1996a), *The Body Shop Social Statement 95.* The Body Shop, Watersmead.

———— (1996b), *HR Vision 2000.* The Body Shop, Watersmead.

Ward, S. (1994), "Shares rally in Body Shop fight back." *The Independent,* September 2.

Welford, R. (1997), *Hijacking Environmentalism: Corporate responses to sustainable development.* London: Earthscan.

Welford, R., and D.R. Jones (1994), "Report on measures of sustainability in business." Center for Corporate Environmental Management, Huddersfield University, Huddersfield.

Chapter 7

Bijker, W.E., and J. Law, eds. (1992), *Shaping Technology/Building Society.* London: MIT Press.

Burall, P. (1996), *Product Development and the Environment.* Aldershot, England: Gower.

Clarke, S.F. (Forthcoming), "Unraveling networks of learning: An international study of more sustainable technology management." Dissertation. York University, Ontario, Canada.

Clarke, S.F., and S. Georg (1995), *From Greening to Sustaining: Transformational Challenges for the Firm.* Summary Report of the Third International Research Conference of the Greening of Industry Network. Lyngby, Denmark: Technical University.

Clarke, S.F. (published as Winn) and N.J. Roome (1993), "R&D Management responses to the environment: Current theory and implications to practice and research." *R&D Management* 23(2):147–160.

Cramer, J., and W.C.L. Zegveld (1991), "The Future Role of Technology in Environmental Management." *Futures* 23(5):451–468.

Dermody, J., and S. Hanmer-Lloyd (1995), "Greening New Product Development: The Pathway to Corporate Environmental Excellence?" *Greener Management International* 11:73–88.

Eden, S. (1996), *Environmental Issues and Business: Implications of a Changing Agenda.* Chichester, England: John Wiley & Sons Ltd.

Foray, D., and A. Grübler (1996), "Technology and the Environment: An Overview." *Technological Forecasting and Social Change* 53:3–13.

HiTec (1992), Annual Report.

———— (1993), Environmental Policy.

———— (1994), Environmental Progress Report.

Hunt, C., and E. Auster (1990), "Proactive Environmental Management: Avoiding the Toxic Trap." *Sloan Management Review* 31(2):7–18.

Irwin, A., S. Georg, and P. Vergragt (1994), "The Social Management of Environmental Change." *Futures* 26(3):323–334.

Kemp, R. (1994), "Technology and the Transition to Environmental Sustainability: The problem of technological regime shifts." *Futures* 26(10):1023–1046.

Perrings, C. (1994), "Sustainable livelihoods and environmentally sound technology." *International Labour Review* 133(3):305–326.

Roome, N.J. (1992), "Developing Environmental Management Strategies." *Business Strategy and the Environment* 1(1):11–24.

Roth, A.W. (1987), "The Choice of Technology for the Future of the Human Race." *International Journal of Technology Management* 2(3/4):329–335.

Roy, R. (1994), "The evolution of ecodesign." *Technovation* 14(6):363–380.

Schot, J., R. Hoogma, and B. Elzen (1994), "Strategies for Shifting Technological Systems: The Case of the automobile system." *Futures* 26(10):1060–1176.

Somerset, M.E. (1989), "An attempt at stopping the sky from falling: The Montreal Protocol to protect against atmospheric ozone reduction." *Syracuse Journal of International Law and Commerce* 15:391–429.

Steger, U. (1993), "The Greening of the Board Room: How European Companies are dealing with Environmental Issues." In K. Fischer and J. Schot (eds.), *Environmental Strategies for Industry.* Washington, D.C.: Island Press, pp. 147–166.

Williams, R., and D. Edge (1996), "The social shaping of technology." *Research Policy* 25(6):865–899.

Chapter 8

Brezet, H., and C. van Hemel (1997), *Ecodesign: A Promising Approach to Sustainable Production and Consumption.* Paris: UNEP.

Brundtland, G-H. (1987), *Our Common Future—The Report of the World Commission on Environment and Development.* New York: Oxford University Press.

de Meere, F., and J. Berting (1996), "Maatschappelijke Veranding en Technologische Ontwikkeling: A Culturele Analyse van het DTO Programma." Delft, DTO Work document CST6.

Dosi, G. (1982), "Technological Paradigms and Technological Trajectories." *Research Policy* 11:147–162.

Grin, J., and R. Hoppe (1995), "Toward a Comparative Framework for Learning from Experiences with Interactive Technology Assessment." *Industrial and Environmental Crisis Quarterly* 9:99–120.

Hogenhuis, C.T. (1997), "Sustainability and Technology from a Cultural Perspective: Analysis of the Concept of Sustainability and Positioning of the STD Program." Delft: DTO Work document CST8.

Hughes, T.P. (1983), *Networks of Power: Electrification in Western Society 1880–1930.* Baltimore: The Johns Hopkins University Press.

Jansen, J., and P. Vergragt (1992), "Sustainable Development: A Challenge to Technology: Proposal for an Interministerial Research Program." Unpublished document.

Kemp, R. (1994), "Technology and the Transition to Environmental Sustainability: The Problem of Technological Regime Shifts." *Futures* 26(10):1023–1046.

Meijkamp, R. (1997a), "Changing Consumer Needs by Eco-efficient Services: An Empirical Exploration on Car Sharing." *Proceedings of the Second International Conference Toward Sustainable Design.* London: The Centre for Sustainable Design.

———— (1997b), "Breaking Through Habitual Behavior. Is Car Sharing an Instrument for Reducing Car Use?" Paper for 25th European Transport Forum, Uxbridge: Brunel University.

Nelson, R., and S. Winter (1982), *An Evolutionary Theory of Economic Change.* Cambridge: Harvard University Press.

Rip, A., T. Misa, and J. Schot (1995), *Managing Technology in Society: The Approach of Constructive Technology Assessment.* London: Pinter.

Schot, J., R. Hoogma, and E. Boelie (1994), "Strategies for Shifting Technological Systems: The Case of the Automobile System." *Futures* 26(10): 1060–1076.

Schwarz, M. (1997), "Maatschappelijke Levensvatbaarheid en Duurzame Technologieontwikkeling: Schets van het Project Maatschappelijke Contexten." Delft: DTO Work document CST1.

Tassoul, M. (forthcoming), "Future Perfect: A Process to Make Sense of the Future Through Creativity—Background and a Practical Case." Delft: Technical University of Delft paper.

Tweede Kamer (1989), *Nationaal Milieubeleidsplan 1988–89,* numbers 1 and 2. The Hague: SDU.

van den Hoed, R. (1996), "Future Vision." In *Toward Sustainable Clothes Washing: Technology, Services and Culture in the Future.* Technical University of Delft Sustainable Washing Project Workshop Briefing Paper, September 1996.

———— (1997), "Sustainable Washing of Clothes: In Search of Factor 20 and the Service Approach as an Innovation Strategy." Paper given at the Second International Conference Toward Sustainable Design. London: The Centre for Sustainable Design.

van der Wel, M., and G. van Nieuwenhoven (forthcoming), "Consumer Aspects of Upscaling." Paper of the Technical University Delft, Sustainable Washing Project.

Vergragt, P., and J. Jansen (1993), "Sustainable Technological Development: The

Making of a Dutch Long Term Oriented Technology Program." *Project Appraisal* 8(3):134–140.

Vergragt, P., and G. van Grootveld (1995), "Sustainable Technology Development in the Netherlands: The First Phase of the Dutch STD Program." *Journal of Cleaner Production* 2(3,4):133–137.

Vergragt, P., M. van der Wel, R. Meijkamp, and M. Tassoul (1995), "Involving Industry in Backcasting Scenario Building." Paper for the Fourth International Conference of the Greening of Industry Network. Toronto, November 1995.

Weterings, R., and J. Opschoor (1992), *The Ecocapacity as Challenge to Technology Development.* Rijzwijk: RMNO.

Workshop (1996), "Toward Sustainable Clothes Washing: Technology, Services and Culture in the Future." Technical University of Delft Sustainable Washing Project Workshop Briefing Paper. The Hague, September 1996.

Chapter 9

Avery, D.T. (1995), *Saving the Planet with Pesticides and Plastic.* Indianapolis, Indiana: Hudson Institute.

Benbrook, C. (1996), *Pest Management at the Crossroads.* Yonkers, N.Y.: Consumers Union.

Berry, W. (1981), "Solving for Pattern." In *The Gift of Good Land: further essays cultural and agricultural.* New York: North Point Press.

Beus, C.E., and R.E. Dunpal (1991), "Measuring adherence to alternative vs. conventional agricultural paradigms: a proposed scale." *Rural Sociology* 56(3):432–460.

Bromley, D.W. (1994), "The language of loss: or how to paralyze policy to protect the status quo." *Choices,* Third Quarter 1994, p. 31.

Burnside, K., and R. Hoefer (1995). Unpublished paper presented at the conference Privatization of Technology Transfer in U.S. Agriculture: Research and Policy Implications. University of Wisconsin-Madison, October 25/26, 1995.

Economic Report of the President (1995), transmitted to the Congress February 1995 together with the Annual Report of the Council of Economic Advisers. Washington, D.C.: US Government Printing Office.

Ehrenfeld, D. (1993), *Beginning Again: People and nature in the new millennium.* New York: Oxford University Press.

Fagin, D., M. Lavelle, and the Center for Public Integrity (1997), *Toxic Deception: How the chemical industry manipulates science, bends the law, and endangers your health.* Birch Lane Press.

Farm Journal (1994), "Remington Farms seeks sustainable cropping." *Farm Journal,* March 1994, J-1.

Foster, V., S. Mourato, R. Tinch, E. Özdemiroglu, and D. Pearce (1997), "Incorporating external impacts in pest management choices." In W.T. Vorley and

D.R. Keeney (eds.), *Bugs in the System: redesigning the pesticide industry for sustainable agriculture.* London: Earthscan.

Goodman, D., and M. Redclift (1991), *Refashioning Nature: food, ecology and culture.* London and New York: Routledge.

Groth, E. (1996), "Review of 'Our Children's Toxic Legacy'." *Science* 274:61, 62.

Handy, C. (1994), *The Empty Raincoat: making sense of the future.* London: Hutchinson.

Hawken, P. (1993), *The Ecology of Commerce: a declaration of sustainability.* New York: HarperBusiness.

John, D. (1994), *Civic Environmentalism: Alternatives to regulation in states and communities.* Washington, D.C.: CQ Press.

Johnson, G., and K. Scholes (1993), *Exploring Corporate Strategy,* 3d ed. Prentice Hall.

Koechlin, D., and A. Wittke (1997), "Sustainable business and the pesticide business: a comparison." In W.T. Vorley and D.R. Keeney (eds.), *Bugs in the System: redesigning the pesticide industry for sustainable agriculture.* London: Earthscan.

Lenzer, R., and B. Upbin (1997), "Monsanto v. Malthus." *Forbes,* March 10, 1997, pp. 58–64.

Lewis, C.A. (1996), *Green Nature/Human Nature: the meaning of plants in our lives.* Urbana and Chicago: University of Illinois Press.

Linstone, H.A. (1989), "Multiple perspectives: concept, application and user guidelines." *Systems Practice* 2(3).

Magretta, J. (1997), "Growth through sustainability: an interview with Monsanto's CEO, Robert B. Shapiro." *Harvard Business Review,* January-February 1997, 79–88.

Maitland, A. (1994), "Chemical group puts organic farming on trial." *Financial Times,* July 6.

Mayhew, M., and S. Allessi (1997), "Unravelling the stakeholder dialogue of pest management." In W.T. Vorley and D.R. Keeney (eds.), *Bugs in the System: redesigning the pesticide industry for sustainable agriculture.* London: Earthscan.

Morley, D., and B. Franklin (1997), "Future searching for new opportunities involving the pesticide industry and sustainable agriculture." In W.T. Vorley and D.R. Keeney (eds.), *Bugs in the System: redesigning the pesticide industry for sustainable agriculture.* London: Earthscan.

Norgaard, R.B. (1992), "Sustainability: the paradigmatic challenge to agricultural economists." In G.H. Peters and B.F. Stanton (eds.), *Sustainable Agricultural Development: the role of international cooperation,* pp. 92–101. Proceedings of the 21st International Conference of Agricultural

Economists, Tokyo, Japan, 22–29 August 1991. Brookfield, Vermont: Dartmouth.

Orr, D.W. (1992), *Ecological Literacy: education and the transition to a postmodern world.* Albany: State University of New York Press.

Pearce, D., and R. Tinch (1997), "The true price of pesticides." In W.T. Vorley and D.R. Keeney (eds.), *Bugs in the System: redesigning the pesticide industry for sustainable agriculture.* London: Earthscan.

Popoff, F., and D.T. Buzzelli (1993), "Full-cost accounting." *Chemical and Engineering News,* January 11, 1993, pp. 8–10.

Porter, B., and J. Fahey (1952), "Residues on Fruits and Vegetables." *United States Department of Agriculture Yearbook of Agriculture.* Washington, D.C.: US Government Printing Office.

Porterfield, J., et al. (1995), *Trends in Pesticide Use in US Agriculture.* Park Ridge, Illinois: American Farm Bureau Public Policy Division.

Pretty, J.N. (1995), *Regenerating Agriculture: Policies and Practice for Sustainability and Self-Reliance.* Earthscan Publications Ltd., London, and National Academy Press, Washington, D.C.

Pretty, J.N., W.T. Vorley, and D.R. Keeney (1997), "Pesticides in world agriculture: causes, consequences and alternative courses." In W.T. Vorley and D.R. Keeney (eds.), *Bugs in the System: redesigning the pesticide industry for sustainable agriculture.* London: Earthscan.

Röling, N. (1993), "Agricultural knowledge and environmental regulation in the Netherlands: a case study of the Crop Protection Plan." *Sociologia Ruralis* 33(2):261–280.

Schmidheiny, S., with the Business Council for Sustainable Development (1992), *Changing Course: a global perspective on development and the environment.* Cambridge: MIT Press.

Senge, P.M. (1990), *The Fifth Discipline: the art and practice of the learning organization.* New York: Currency Doubleday.

Tenner, E. (1996), *Why Things Bite Back: technology and the revenge of unintended consequences.* New York: Alfred A. Knopf.

Tombs, S. (1993), "The chemical industry and environmental issues." In D. Smith (ed.), *Business and the Environment: implications of the new environmentalism.* London: Paul Chapman, pp. 131–149.

US Agricultural Retailers Association (1996), *Food for Thought* calendar. ARA, 11701 Borman Drive, Suite 110, St. Louis, MO 63146, USA.

Walley, N., and B. Whitehead (1994), "It's not easy being green." *Harvard Business Review* May-June 1994, 46–51.

Weisbord, M., and S. Janoff (1995), *Future Search: an action guide to finding common ground in organizations and communities.* San Francisco: Berrett-Koehler.

Wessel, J. (1983), *Trading the Future: farm exports and the concentration of economic power in our food economy.* Institute for Food and Development Policy, 1885 Mission St., San Francisco, CA 94103.

Wolcott, R.M. (1993), "Producing environmental quality: an emerging market for agriculture in America." Paper presented at workshop Reinventing Agriculture, December 8–9, 1993, Chicago.

Wolf, S. (1995), "Cropping systems and conservation policy: the roles of agrichemical dealers and independent crop consultants." *Journal of Soil and Water Conservation* May-June 1995, pp. 263–270.

Chapter 10

BSI (1992), *Specification for Environmental Management Systems.* British Standards Institution BS 7750: 1992. Milton Keynes: BSI Standards.

DI (1997), *Private Owners Do Not Have the Capacity to Manage Environmental Certification.* Stockholm: Dagens Industri, July.

FAO (1995a), "Report of the Committee on Forestry." UN Food and Agriculture Organization, 12th session. Rome: COFO-95/REP.

——— (1995b), "1945–1993 . . . 2010 Forestry—Statistics Today for Tomorrow." UN Food and Agriculture Organization.

FSC (1997a, draft), "Swedish FSC Standard for Forest Certification." Forest Stewardship Council, The Swedish Working Group: Secretariat June 18.

——— (1997b), "Forest Certification—a Major Step Toward Sustainable Forestry." Forest Stewardship Council. Worldwide Web: http://www.forestry.se/fsc/

Greenpeace (1997a), "Greenpeace Leaves the Forest Certification Process." Stockholm: Press release 970618.

——— (1997b), "Forest Certification on its Way to Success, Greenpeace believes." Stockholm: Press release 970415.

ISO (1996), "Environmental Management Systems. Specification with Guidance for Use." ISO 14001:1996. Geneva: ISO.

IUCN (1980), *World Conservation Strategy: Living Resource Conservation for Sustainable Development.* Gland: International Union for Conservation of Nature and Natural Resources.

Kiuchi, T. (1997), "What I Learnt in the Rainforest." *Sustainable Business Network Journal,* September. Worldwide Web: http://www.envirolink.org/sbn/

Moxen, J., and P. Strachan (1995), "The Formulation of Standards for Environmental Management Systems: Structural and Cultural Issues." *Greener Management International* 12:32–48.

Nordic Forest Certification (1996a), Report no. 1. Stockholm: *Nordic Forest Certification,* February.

——— (1996b), Report no. 2. Stockholm: *Nordic Forest Certification,* October.

Swedish Forest Industries Association (1997a), *The Forest Industry, the Ecocycle and the Environment—a Summary.* Stockholm: Swedish Forest Industries Association.

———— (1997b), *From Frog to Prince.* Stockholm: Swedish Forest Industries Association.

UNCED (1992), Report of the United Nations Conference on Environment and Development. Chapter 11 Agenda 21: Combating Deforestation. UN: A/CONF.151/26 (Vol. II).

UNCED (1992), Report of the United Nations Conference on Environment and Development. Annex III: Non-legally Binding Authoritative Statement of Principles for a Global Consensus on the Management, Conservation and sustainable Development of all Types of Forests. UN: A/CONF.151/26 (Vol. III).

WCED (1987), *Our Common Future.* World Commission on Environment and Development. Oxford: Oxford University Press.

Chapter 11

Abramowitz, M. (1995), "The origins of the postwar catch-up and convergence boom." In Fagerberg, Verspagen, and Von Tunzelmann (eds.), *The Dynamics of Technology, Trade and Growth.* Edward Elgar.

Commission of the European Communities (1994), "Economic Growth and the Environment: Some Implications for Policy Making." COM (94) 465, 3 November 1994.

Ekins, P. (1995), "The Kuznets Curve for the Environment and Economic Growth: Examining the Evidence." Mimeo, Birkbeck College, University of London, March 1995.

Janicke, M., M. Binder, and H. Monch (1994), "Green Industrial Policy and the Future of 'Dirty Industries'." Paper presented at the Third International Conference of the Greening of Industry Network, Copenhagen, 13–15 November 1994.

Kozul-Wright, Z. (1995), "The role of the firm in the innovation process." UN Conference on Trade and Development. Discussion Paper 98, UNCTAD, Geneva.

Munasinghe and Munasinghe (1993), "Barriers to and opportunities for technological change in developing countries to reduce global warming." Paper presented at meeting of IPCC/WGIII, Montreal, May 1993.

OECD (1994), *Development Cooperation: Efforts and Policies of the Members of the Development Assistance Committee.* Paris: OECD.

United Nations Industrial Development Organization (1991), "Industry Initiatives in Achieving Ecologically Sustainable Development." Working Paper No.

3 for the Conference on Ecologically Sustainable Development, Copenhagen, 14–18 October 1991.

Wallace, D. (1995), *Environmental Policy and Industrial Innovation: Strategies in Europe, the US and Japan.* London: The Royal Institute of International Affairs/Earthscan: Chapters 11 and 13.

Womack, J.P., D.T. Jones, and D. Roos (1990), *The Machine That Changed the World.* New York: Macmillan, pp. 28–42.

Chapter 12

Angel, D., and J. Huber (1996), "Building sustainable industries for sustainable societies." *Business Strategy and the Environment* 5:127–136.

Ausubel, J., and H. Longford (1997), *Technology Trajectories and the Human Environment.* Washington, D.C.: National Academy Press.

Billatis, S., and N. Basaly (1997), *Green Technology and Design for the Environment.* Washington, D.C.: Taylor.

Clarke, S. (1995), "What is sustainable technology management?" Paper presented at the Fourth Greening of Industry Conference, Toronto, Canada.

Florida, R. (1996), "Lean and Green: the move to environmentally conscious manufacturing." *California Management Review* 39:80–105.

Graedel, T., and B. Allenby (1995), *Industrial Ecology.* Englewood Cliffs, NJ.: Prentice Hall.

Groenewegen, P., K. Fischer, E. Jenkins, and J. Schot (1995), *The Greening of Industry Resource Guide and Bibliography.* Washington, D.C.: Island Press.

Heaton, G. (1992), *Transforming Technology: an agenda for environmentally sustainable growth in the 21st century.* Washington, D.C.: World Resources Institute.

Heaton, G., R.D. Banks, and D. Ditz (1994), *Missing Links: technology and environmental improvements in the industrializing world.* Washington, D.C.: World Resources Institute.

International Energy Agency (1996), *International Technology Collaboration: Benefits and Achievements.* Paris: OECD.

Moore, C., and A. Miller (1994), *Green Gold: Japan, Germany and the United States and the Race for Environmental Technology.* Boston: Beacon Press.

Nelson, R., ed. (1993), *National Innovation Systems: a comparative study.* New York: Oxford University Press.

OECD, Committee on Energy Research and Technology (1994), *Scoping Study on Energy and Environmental Technologies to Respond to Global Climate Change Concerns.* Paris: OECD.

Romm, J., and C. Curtis (1996), "Mideast oil forever?" *Atlantic Monthly* 277:57–75.

Skolnikoff, E. (1993), *The Elusive Transformation.* Princeton: Princeton University Press.

Townsend, M. (1993), "The International Transfer of Environmental Technology." *Environmental and Planning Law Journal,* June, pp. 164–169.

US Congress, Office of Technology Assessment (1992), *Green Products by Design.* Washington, D.C.: US Government Printing Office.

———— (1995a), *International Partnerships in Large Science Projects.* Washington, D.C.: US Government Printing Office.

———— (1995b), *Environmental Technology: Analysis of Selected Federal R&D Programs.* Washington, D.C.: US Government Printing Office.

US Environmental Protection Agency (1994a), *Environmental Technology Innovation Strategy of the United States.* Washington, D.C.: US Government Printing Office.

US Environmental Protection Agency (1994b), *Environmental Technology Initiative, FY 1994 Program Plan.* Washington, D.C.: US Government Printing Office.

About the Contributors

DAVID P. ANGEL is currently associate provost and dean of Graduate Studies and Research at Clark University. His background and training are in economic geography, focusing on issues of industrial restructuring and technology change. Previous work has addressed issues of high-technology industrialization in Japan and the United States. His current research focuses on public and private policy approaches toward green technology development and a "clean" industrial revolution in Asia.

FRANK BELZ is lecturer in environmental management at the University of St. Gallen as well as senior researcher and consultant at the Institute for Economy and the Environment at the University of St. Gallen (IEE-HSG). His main research interests are environmental marketing, ecology, and the competitiveness of companies. He has published numerous articles and books, including *Ecology and Competitiveness in the Swiss Food Industry, Ecology and Competitiveness of Companies* (with T. Dyllick and U. Schneidewind), and *International Business Environmental Barometer 1997* (with L. Stranegard).

SARAH F. CLARKE is a doctoral student at the Schulich School of Business, York University, Ontario. An engineer by profession, her research focuses on sustainable technology management within the context of corporate change toward more sustainable business practices. She has published several articles in leading journals on technology management, the environment, and organizational change. She earned her MBA in 1992, from Manchester Business School, UK, and has bachelor's and master's degrees in electronic engineering from Bath University, UK (1986 and 1987).

JOHN R. EHRENFELD is senior research associate in the MIT Center for Technology, Policy, and Industrial Development. At MIT since 1985, he directs the MIT Program on Technology, Business, and Environment, an interdisciplinary educational, research, and policy program. He serves as a core faculty member in the MIT Technology and Policy Program. He directs ongoing research examining the way businesses manage environmental concerns, seeking organizational and technological changes to improve their practices.

THOMAS N. GLADWIN is professor and director of the Global Environment Program at the Stern School of Business at New York University. He teaches courses on environmental management and sustainable development. He is the author of over 150 articles, books, and cases on international and environmental management. He has served as a consultant to numerous corporations and governmental bodies on issues of sustainability. He serves on the boards of Franklin Research and Development Corporation, The Greening of Industry Network, and Sustainability Ltd. He is the chair-elect of the Organizations and the Environment Interest Group of The Academy of Management.

ANDREW J. HOFFMAN is an assistant professor of organizational behavior at Boston University's School of Management. His research focuses on the organizational and cultural aspects of corporate environmentalism. He is the author of *From Heresy to Dogma: An Institutional History of Corporate Environmentalism* (1997), the editor of *Global Climate Change: A Senior Level Dialogue* (1997), and has published articles in leading journals. He earned his doctoral (1995) and master's (1991) degrees from MIT and his bachelor's degree (1983) from the University of Massachusetts.

JOHANNES HUMMEL is presently working in the strategic planning department of the Bertelsmann Group. His Ph.D. studies examined strategic ecocontrol using the case of the textile chain. His main research work while at the Institute for Economy and the Environment at the University of St. Gallen (IEE-HSG) between 1994 and 1997 covered environmental control and strategic environmental management. Besides his thesis, *Strategic Environmental Controlling,* he has published numerous articles about ecology and the textile chain and environmental management.

DAVID RAYMOND JONES is a lecturer in organizational behavior and a member of the Research Unit for Organizational Learning and Change at Bristol Business School. He has recently earned a Ph.D. at the Center for Corporate Environmental Management, Huddersfield University, examining corporate cultural development strategies for sustainable development. He previously worked as an aeronautical engineer for several international companies both in the United Kingdom and in Japan and has an M.Sc. in technology management.

SUSANNE ÖSTLUND is a Ph.D. candidate in the Department of Marketing, Distribution, and Industry Dynamics at Stockholm School of Economics. Her research and teaching has focused on industry adaptation to ecological demands. Her dissertation is a study of the change processes undertaken by the refrigeration, flexible foam, and electronics industry as a response to a ban on the use of chlorofluorocarbons (CFCs). Her study focuses on the limits and possibilities the technological, organizational, and institutional structures put on the change processes toward a sustainable industry. She has also studied coordinated industrial action toward sustainability in the food supply chain as well as processes of building and introducing new recycling systems in a food retail chain. Currently, she is participating in setting up a multidisciplinary project on "the sustainable city" in a joint project at the Science Center (jointly owned by the four universities in Stockholm).

NIGEL J. ROOME holds the chair in environmental management in the Faculty of Economics and Business Administration at Tilburg University, The Netherlands. He was previously Erivan K. Haub chair in business and the environment at York University, Canada. In addition to his extensive record as an academic and consultant in the field of environmental management and sustainable development for business organizations, he has initiated many new approaches to education and research for environmental management and sustainable development. These include the development of an MBA curriculum related to environmental management and sustainable development. He was the architect of the recently established Center for Globalization and Sustainable Development at Tilburg University.

UWE SCHNEIDEWIND is lecturer in environmental management at the University of St. Gallen and senior researcher at the Institute for Economy and the Environment at the University of St. Gallen (IEE-HSG). His main research interests cover substance chain management in the chemical and textile industries as well as the political role of companies. His publications include numerous articles and books, such as *Ecology and Competitiveness in the Chemical Industry, Ecology and Competitiveness of Companies* (with T. Dyllick and F. Belz), and *Ecological Innovation Strategies* (with J. Minsch, A. Eberle, and B. Meier).

ANDREA SPENCER-COOKE is a freelance strategic environmental consultant and writer based in Edinburgh, Scotland. She is managing editor of *Tomorrow* on the Worldwide Web, a leading business/environment Internet publication. Formerly, Andrea was head of sustainable management and reporting at Sustain-Ability Ltd., where she was a consultant in charge of two major research programs. Before that she worked with the International Labor Organization (ILO) in Geneva on labor standards and equal opportunities. Andrea holds master's degrees in environmental management and social anthropology. Her key areas of interest are corporate governance, stakeholder accountability, environmental management and reporting, and financial markets. She has published several articles and reports and is currently writing a book on Costa Rica.

MARJAN VAN DER WEL studied philosophy. After lecturing in history of technology and technology and gender studies she joined the Technology Assessment Unit of the Delft University of Technology, where she is engaged in consumer aspects of technological developments. She participated in the Sustainable Washing project and investigated consumers attitudes toward future washing scenarios. Her Ph.D. thesis focuses on the history of hygiene, especially the relation between cultural shifts within the field of hygiene and technological developments.

PHILIP VERGRAGT earned a Ph.D. in physical chemistry and then became interested in social and political aspects of science and technology. He taught "Science and Society" at Groningen University, where he started the Chemistry Shop and researched innovative processes in large chemical companies as well as the environmental aspects of materials. From 1991 he has worked for the Dutch Ministry of the Environment—since 1993 as deputy director of the newly founded Interministerial Programme "Sustainable Technological Development," which he helped to develop. In 1991 he was also appointed professor of technology assessment at the Technical University of Delft. Current research projects include sustainable production; sustainable households and endogenous technology (in a third world context); and EC SEER project on the "Social Management of Technical Change," which is about self-organized citizen approaches to technology and environmental problems. Professor Vergragt has published extensively on these subjects and is often asked for seminars and speeches.

WILLIAM T. VORLEY has a doctorate in applied ecology and field research experience in England, Japan, Malaysia, and Indonesia. After nine years working with Ciba-Geigy in Asia and at their Swiss headquarters, he resigned to take up the position of visiting scientist at the Leopold Center for Sustainable Agriculture. His commercial experience covered both new pesticide development and extension. He was responsible for the successful "Farmer Support" campaign, which sought business opportunities built on small farmers' skills in safety and integrated pest management. This program put Ciba-Geigy at the forefront of service-oriented agrochemical business in developing countries. William is currently director of the Environment and Agriculture Program at the Institute for Agriculture and Trade Policy (IATP) in Minneapolis.

DAVID WALLACE is currently at the International Energy Agency, Paris, where he coordinates member country research on fossil fuel technologies. A physicist and oceanographer by training, his career in the UK government covered marine pollution research, international technology policy, and energy policy. From 1993 to 1996 he was a visiting research fellow on the Energy and Environmental Programme at the Royal Institute of International Affairs, London, where he researched and wrote *Environmental Policy and Industrial Innovation: Strategies in Europe, the US and Japan* and *Sustainable Industrialization*.

RICHARD WELFORD is professor of corporate environmental management at the Huddersfield University Business School and director of the Center for Corporate Environmental Management. He is also visiting professor of sustainable management at the Norwegian School of Management in Oslo. He is editor of the journal *Business Strategy and the Environment* and author or editor of seven books about corporate environmental management and sustainable development.

WILLIAM YOUNG is a research assistant at the Center for Corporate Environmental Management, Huddersfield University. He has recently completed his Ph.D. on environmental performance measurement in companies.

BJARNE YTTERHUS is an Industrial Professor in the Institute of Economics and Finance at the Norwegian School of Management in Oslo. He is author of a number of papers on corporate environmental management and author of a number of books on economics.

Index

The Greening of Industry Network Coordinators

Americas:
Kurt Fischer
The George Perkins Marsh Institute
Clark University
950 Main Street
Worcester, Massachusetts 01610-1477 USA
Telephone: 508-751-4607
Fax: 508-751-4600
E-mail: kfischer@clarku.edu

Asia:
Somporn Kamolsiripichaiporn
Environmental Research Institute
Chulalongkorn University
Phyathai Road
Bangkok 10330, Thailand
Telephone: 662-218-8111
Fax: 662-218-8124
E-mail: GIN-Asia@chula.ac.th

Europe:
Ellis Brand, Theo de Bruijn, Johan Schot
Center for Clean Technology and Environmental Policy CSTM
The University of Twente
P.O. Box 217
7500 AE Enschede, The Netherlands
Telephone: 31 53 489 3203
Fax: 31 53 489 4850
E-mail: e.m.l.brand@cstm.utwente.nl